Praise for The Shape of a Hundred Hips . . .

"Frank and fascinating: these words apply to Patricia Cumbie's new book, a memoir. Her bravery is second to none. Raped as a teenager, living with family who settled for little, Cumbie fought for independence, and an understanding of herself consistent with her dreams and abilities. In short, she is amazing, and so is The Shape of a Hundred Hips. Descriptions and explanations of belly dancing—which she studied—are informative and enlightening, revealing how she grew into a maturity from which we can all take guidance. You will want to read this book now and quickly because it is exciting, useful, and memorable!" — Kelly Cherry, author of *Girl in a Library: On Women Writers and the Writing Life* and *Quartet for J. Robert Oppenheimer*

"With courage, empathy and clarity, Cumbie depicts her working class family and roots, the difficulties and triumph of her marriage, and her struggles to tell the truths of her life and to confront the trauma of rape. That the art of belly dancing comes to be one of the ways in which she heals helps makes this a singular and intriguing work. The result is a fascinating narrative whose emotional weight keeps gathering power and will move readers in unexpected and subtle ways." — David Mura, author of *Turning Japanese: Memoirs of a Sansei*

"The reader will shimmy with Patricia, tip and roll their shoulders, and release in time with her as she shares her love and heartbreak on the page. Her words move on the page much like a belly dancer undulating on the dance floor." — Elizabeth DiGrazia, author of *House of Fire*

"In her memoir, Patricia Cumbie brings us 'the news,' illuminating the rigorous, complex and mysterious art of belly dancing. She writes from the perspective of a seeker, a woman aware of what she terms 'body isolation,' of not living fully in body and soul years after surviving rape. Cumbie has found language for the sensation of the body in motion: in joy and exertion, as expression, and ultimately as a "passageway" to living both fully and free. The body's memory—a source of torment after a sexual assault—become ~~~~~~~~~~ ~ wonder. As she trains, strains, performs, and dances alon[_____]bie transforms her life, her marriag[_____]i a gratitude that is contagious. —[_____]*elling: A Memoir of Rape and Recov*

"*The Shape of a Hundred Hips* is as inspiring as it is engaging, chronicling the author's journey from conflict to confidence in her (newly shimmying) body. This testimony to the power of movement, community and self-acceptance through belly dance resonates like the tinkling of a well-tuned pair of finger cymbals!" — Anne Thomas Soffee, author of *Snake Hips*

"Insightful, reflective, inquisitive . . . *The Shape of a Hundred Hips* is a book of journeys illustrated by vignettes of Patricia Cumbie's life stories. She shares how the belly dance ignited her passion, taught her many life lessons, guided her into empowered womanhood and friendship and love, after years of feeling unheard and unseen, healed her after sexual trauma, and acknowledged the beauty of her body and her being." — Paulette Rees-Denis, author of *Tribal Vision: A Celebration of Life Through Tribal Belly Dance,* Transformational Lifestyle Coach, and Global Dance Instructor, and innovator of Gypsy Caravan Tribal Bellydance

"This book chronicles a young woman's life in unflinching, poetic prose. Beautifully crafted, it is vivid, honest and astute. We see how the healing powers of dance are instrumental in the author's courageous and relentless path towards self-healing." — Elizabeth Artemis Mourat, MA, MSW, LCSW-C

THE SHAPE OF A HUNDRED HIPS

THE SHAPE OF A
HUNDRED HIPS

PATRICIA CUMBIE

Bink Books
Bedazzled Ink Publishing Company • Fairfield, California

978-1-945805-64-6 paperback

Cover Design
by

DESIGNS

Portions of this manuscript previously appeared in *Emrys
Journal, The Leap Years: Women Reflect on Change, Loss, and
Love, Stories from Inside the Mirror, A Belly Dance Anthology,
Dust and Fire*, and the *Star Tribune*.

Bink Books
a division of
Bedazzled Ink Publishing Company
Fairfield, California
http://www.bedazzledink.com

Acknowledgements

This book represents to me the confluence of many worlds coming together. I am most especially grateful to the Twin Cities writing and dance communities that have supported me. I am also sustained by many people who I know and don't know, who advocate for me and others in recovery from sexual assault.

Dance, and belly dance, changed my life's path, and along the way I've been in awe of the amazing people who have shared with me their creative energy and buoyant dancer spirits.

Brenda Anderson and Lisa Preston are both biological sisters and soul-sisters at the core of my first dance troupe, Banat Anashat. We had so much fun! Thanks be to the fabulous singer Natasha Atlas!

Minnesota's first tribal belly dance group Totally Northern Tribal introduced me to the power of improvisation and group dancing. I am thrilled to have had the opportunity to dance with Melissa Hansen, Sherry Ripplinger, Barb Tate-Lunde, Roberta Webb, Sarah Bell, Debra Brazil, Angie Bezek, Valerie Vigdahl, Anne Farrington, Cindy Kissee, and Sue Lindgren. The troupe's band, Felahi, comprised of Charlie Obert, Keith Spears and Avni Pandya rocked the house.

I am also proud to count myself as a former member of Dans Askina, a Turkish belly dance and folk-dance group. I have had the pleasure of sharing the stage with Amina Beres, the director, and Allie Abela, Marilyn Christianson, Jennifer Cole, Wendy Famodu, Nancy Holden, Robin Kaehler, Alexandra Howes, Susan Knutson, Kathryn Inoferio, Amy Snyder, Carl Posz, Benjamin Lamb and Carlotta Posz.

I have also benefit from some of the most amazing Egyptian and Turkish belly dance and Romani dance teachers in the world. I have had the opportunity to take workshops with Nadia Hamdi, Nesma Al-Andalus, Ansuya, Lebanese Simon, June Seaney, Reyhan Tuzsuz, Serkan Tutar, Artemis Mourat, Laurel Victoria Gray, and Karim Nagy. Their invaluable instruction on dance, music and culture have enriched my understanding and awareness of different dance traditions.

Closer to home in Minneapolis, the incomparable Cassandra Shore of the Jawaahir Dance Company and the Cassandra School, has been a bedrock for dance technique and performance excellence.

From Cassandra I have learned poise, presence and posture, and I very much appreciate that she has embraced me as a worthy student. Her dedication and passion for Arabic music, dance and culture has indelibly impressed me and shaped the dance scene in the Twin Cities and beyond. It is my great good fortune to have had the opportunity to study with this legendary teacher and dancer.

Every Monday morning at the Cassandra School, instructor Jenny Piper gets me, and my classmates, energized with her positive energy and creative spark. It is an artistic touchstone I've come to rely upon.

When I first started taking belly dance classes, fate stepped in to bring me a mentor. Amina Beres taught at the Pratt School Community Education Program, and her impact on my life goes beyond what words can say. With Amina's encouragement, resourcefulness and fabulous sense of humor, I was able to feel true joy and release in dance. She ignited in me a passion to do more and to confront my fears. I am thankful Amina helped me find "Katze's" natural expression. Her guidance has led me to many stages where I speak with my body and my voice—an incomparable gift.

I would be nowhere without my writing group. Marcia Peck, Carla Hagen, Julia Klatt Singer, Carol Dines and Alison Morse have been there through everything, and our two-decades long association continues to enrich my life with deep friendship and writerly support.

I am also grateful for Carol Inderieden, Milissa Link, Lori Stee, Karen Hering and Martha Bordwell for their feedback on early drafts of the manuscript. I am honored to have the dynamic authors Beth Dooley and Atina Diffley in my corner. Fiona McCrae generously shared with me her advice and insight. Her contributions to my development as a writer have made all the difference.

I also continue to be indebted to the Loft Literary Center for continuing to provide me opportunities as a writer and to learn from their excellent instructors including Rachel Gabriel, Laura Flynn, Jude Nutter and David Mura.

I am thrilled to be published by Bedazzled Ink and am thankful for senior editor C.A. Casey and publisher Claudia Wilde for taking a chance on the manuscript, and for their acceptance of belly dance as a feminist art form.

There are many people who have been instrumental in my rape recovery, none more so than my wizard therapist Betsy Sansby, who inspired me to grow in ways I could not have imagined.

I am so pleased that my family accepted my writing about our shared history. No small thing when you write a memoir. My sisters Peggy Cumbie and Elizabeth LaForge are funny, fierce and beautiful women I am proud to hold fast in my heart. My brother and fellow writer Jimmie Cumbie is generous with his talents, and his devotion for his sisters makes our family unit even closer. My mother Nanette Cumbie bestowed on me the storytelling gene, one that she cultivated by making up bedtime stories for me and my siblings when we were kids. I am grateful for her graciousness in being a part of this memoir.

My husband Sean Doyle makes everything possible. His zest for life, his vision for a better world, and his unequivocal love for me and support for my writing, gives me faith, hope, and strength.

Dance when you're broken open.
Dance if you've torn the bandage off.
Dance in the middle of fighting.
Dance in your blood.
Dance when you're perfectly free.
—Rumi

I

BODY ISOLATIONS

1

MIDWINTER AFTERNOON SUNLIGHT coursed in from three sides of the dance studio onto a smooth and well-worn wooden floor. The floorboards, clean and understated, exuded a tanned and healthy glow, pampered by dancers who didn't want them afflicted by the cold or salt or sand tracked in on most Minnesota floors in winter. I took off my boots and left them in the pile by the door. The footwear ran the gamut, from beefy Sorrels to sensible shoes and a smattering of heeled sandals. Later I learned the sandal-wearing gals were particularly noteworthy, donning floral socks and patterned pants after class. Around their necks were amulets in the shape of hands or crescent moons. This was the late 1990s, before mainstream fashion embraced tribal prints and music festival vogue.

The floor was soon packed with women in black yoga pants and tank tops angling for a place to stretch out. Some had scarves wrapped around their hips that sparkled from the beads and coins on them. Hips of all shapes and sizes. Belly dancers!

I was dressed in a baggy t-shirt and long hippie skirt, my tenuous heart shrinking by the second.

The teacher pointed to a battered box of scarves and veils and said I could borrow one. I put both hands into the fabric scrum. Different perfumes rose up to my nose, floral and musky, and a whole new world emerged through my fingertips. There were veils in a layer of pastels, some stiff and see-through, pink and lavender, a few were wrinkled castoffs, and others were smooth pools of silk-essence that even I could recognize had been held, pawed, fluttered and flung in the air, hundreds if not thousands of times. I heard the sound of metal and beads clacking together as I swished my hands through the box, drawn toward a waterfall. In a corner near the box I saw a dozen canes wrapped in silver and gold ribbon. There was also a clear plastic makeup kit that had been repurposed to hold extra finger cymbals. I aimed to pull all of these fabrics and scarves out of storage and look at each one, and to decipher what all those shiny things were for.

The instructor cued the warm-up music. I heard muted drums and something that sounded like a flute. It sounded like something out of a movie, Middle Eastern-y. The repetition was like a heartbeat. Women ceased their conversations and found their places on the dance floor. It was time.

I picked a well-worn lime green scarf with coins on it and tied it around my waist the way I saw others doing it. The knot rested on my right hip.

MY THERAPIST HAD recommended "movement" for me as a way to expend angst. I had gone to her initially because I told her I aspired to live a more artistic life. I was thirty-five years old, married, and childless, and even though I'd had a few short stories published, I worried that I'd reached the end of my creative capacity.

Betsy had just ditched the social service agency she had worked for to open a private practice coaching people. I found her advertisement in the local literary center's newsletter. She and her husband were drummers and singers and her office was in her home. In session, her husband's drumming was the rhythmic undercurrent to our conversations. This might have bothered someone who wanted a quiet office setting to bawl their eyes out and hear "there, there, dear." To me it was perfect. Betsy was working out of her house, taking clients she preferred, and pursuing music—the artistic life.

One session I told Betsy about Habib.

Habib had emerged from the back of City Billiards in Minneapolis at a private party, an orange silk veil held above her head levitating behind her. Her movements were languid and deliberate. Her costume, a two-piece purple velvet belly dance outfit trimmed with rows of coins, flashed. She moved into the light and full view of the crowd. Habib wore jewels in her jet black hair and leveled her gaze at the crowd and executed a surprising and impetuous full turn. She looked exactly like a flame: purple velvet, orange silk, shiny coins blazing.

People like Habib are stationed in the universe to polish our haphazard lives. We need something to wish upon, after all. The first constellation I could recognize was the Big Dipper. Did you know all those stars have names? Megrez, Mizar, Merak, and so on. Little oaths. No matter what time of year, the dipper stays constant in the night sky, but it is most prominent in spring. I could feel the gentle lamp of those star lights warming my shoulders the night Habib danced.

"That's it!" Betsy said. "That's your physical movement."

There was no way prancing around like that was going to be a good idea. I'd look and be ridiculous.

Then the day had come when a doctor gave me a prescription for Elavil. The doctor had been a full hour and a half late to my appointment. While I waited for him I felt resigned and sad, moving my fingers in figure-eights over the white paper on top of the examining table. Anger and helplessness streaked through my veins. My body stored up lactic acid and doled out cramps as a punishment. I was hunched over and breathing hard. Anxiety. I needed more than just Betsy's meditations.

When he finally arrived, he touched pressure points on my shoulders, knees, and hipbones with unabashed apathy. I tried to look into his eyes when he told me I should take antidepressants. Resentment surged through my limbs and lingered in the pit of my stomach. That's when the Big Dipper's carefully arranged bucket tipped over.

When I got home, I called the Cassandra School of Middle Eastern Dance and ran the prescription with the doctor's indecipherable handwriting through my shredder.

THE DAY OF my first belly dance class, the tall blonde instructor wore pink leg warmers and a ballet neck top over a blue leotard. She looked to me like a refugee from *Flashdance*. I felt disappointment stiffen my neck. I needed a sultry Habib-type to show me how to transfix people. I took off my white tube socks and stuffed them into my purse.

The instructor moved gazelle-like—her long hair swung behind her straight back whenever she turned away from the mirror. I was pretty certain she'd never been diagnosed with "borderline" scoliosis as a kid, like I was. Our warm-up included a simple step and touch with our feet, and the teacher's hips gently swayed as she lead us through the drill.

"Touch right, touch left," she said.

Her hands were out to the sides, fingertips pointed away from her body. I touched one foot then the other, barefoot, lightly toeing the floor. Me in a lime green hip scarf!

What drew me to Betsy was not trauma, but the idea that I should be more accomplished. But I had difficulties being sexual, that were causing big fights with my husband. I couldn't get pregnant. I was uncertain about my place in the world. I wasn't tough at all. But I assumed all I really needed to do was to find out the formula for success.

I come from a long line of shotgun weddings. My maternal grandma fell for my delinquent and scrappy grandpa and found herself, at the top of her high school class, pregnant, suddenly married, and on a train heading to the west coast where she would live with him before he shipped off to Japan in World War II. Ma was a waitress in California when dad ordered a cup of coffee. Soon, she too had a bun in the oven, me, her senior year. Teenage pregnancies afflicted my aunties, too, each one, right after the other. A fortune teller once told me that "a woman in my family" was a thwarted artist channeling herself through me. It could have been any one of them.

I also come from men who were restless seekers. My paternal grandpa was in his prime a handsome man and a mercurial alcoholic. Throughout his whole life he dragged the family place to place, first sharecropping, and in later years, working odd jobs on farms and shipyards. He loved Louis L'Amour westerns and liked to talk about them when he got sauced. He was attracted to frontiers, tough guys, and vigilante justice. By the time I came along, nobody could remember his good qualities. Dad spent his childhood pulling him out of bars to keep the weekly paycheck from disappearing completely.

Dad was as deeply kind and understanding as he was impatient. People naturally relied on him, and he did his best to be reliable. He worked hard all his life, too hard, but never doing anything that made money or made him happy. Dad had a quiet magnetism that he used to save souls after he turned everything over to Jesus. Cirrhosis killed my grandpa, but long hours and too many cigarettes did my dad in.

My family's history is textbook. The opposite of art. My dad's two brothers drowned in a Florida swamp when he was ten. My cousin was shot six times by a deranged neighbor who was obsessed with her. Another cousin died in a car wreck with her best friend, fleeing her violent, drunk-ass husband. My youngest sister's bipolar husband died popping wheelies on his motorcycle. My brother is in recovery. Many of my aunties had abusive husbands. I was looking for an escape hatch, and instead of the freedom I thought I'd find in college, I got raped trying to pass through it.

I grew up with people with certain struggles, who needed therapy, but couldn't afford it. Therefore, therapy was something fluffy, indulgent people did. You would never admit to anyone you were so fucked up you needed a shrink. So the problems piled up like unpaid bills until, bang, someone flipped out, smacked someone, hit rock-bottom, or was court-ordered to go.

When I finally admitted to Betsy I was one of those people with big problems, sans court order, I was certain she would gasp with the admission. It was news that she took as if I'd placed an order in a drive-thru window.

I was the same person as always, who just happened to be sitting in a therapist's office.

I imagined the woman I really wanted to be was outside making a wide circle around the block while she waited for me, idling in my getaway car.

Betsy gave me a tape she made of a meditation, and I listened to it every day, prone on my bedroom floor after work. Her voice on tape was verdant, soothing. A singer's voice. While the tape talked, "Imagine you are a balloon. Orange. Full with air. Breathe in. Breathe out. You are floating in a clear, blue sky," I knew this was definitely something fluffy, indulgent people did. They rested after working all day. They listened to a soothing female voice. They filled their bodies with breath instead of cigarettes or drink.

IN THAT FIRST belly dance class, we did more calisthenics. Raising our arms, stretching our sides, doing crunches, raising our legs while lying on the floor. I was stiff and sore, but I speculated: when would we quit with all this boring stretching and dance? Soon enough, after touching our toes, we were standing. I stood up and looked ahead. A new world of women looked at me from the mirror. Women who might have had dance classes as children. Who knew what to expect. I wished I hadn't worn the crazy skirt. I stood out as a raw recruit.

The teacher told us we were going to learn basic undulations. The movement Habib used in her entrance. I held my breath.

First she demonstrated. Her body was serpentine as she controlled the forward and back rocking of her body, undulating from the top of her chest to the bottom of her tailbone. It was as if she was shaking out a rug with her body in slow-mo. She looked sinuous and strong. A Nordic belly dance goddess. Now she wanted us to get into position and try it.

"Turn your right side to the mirror," she said.

We turned our sides to face the mirror. My chin jutted forward, my shoulders slumped. My front facing view of myself was better, but the side view was truer.

"Ok, put your right foot out in front of your left, about hip bone distance apart," the teacher said.

I did that.

"Lift your chest." She demonstrated by lifting her own. Her breasts seemed to pop forward of their own accord. How did she do that?

"Think about reaching your chest up to the place where the ceiling meets the wall." She told us to use our abs to hold ourselves up. "Relax your shoulders. Get them down and away from your ears." She walked around the room, checking to see that everyone's chest was lifted and shoulders were down. When she got to me her cool hands touched my shoulders. "Relax them," she said in a voice that sounded like a cross between a massage therapist and math teacher.

I made an effort to drop them, but they inched up again when she turned away from me.

"Do not be intimidated by your own breasts," she told the class.

Everyone tittered. What woman does not have a conflicted relationship with her breasts?

"Be proud," she said.

The teacher exhorted us to keep breathing. I held my breath.

I started with simply aligning my feet and raising my chest.

I remembered snowflakes swirling to rest in a snow globe. The pile of grandpa's beer cans. Grandma's hunchback.

Our teacher encouraged us to use stomach and back muscles I didn't know I had. I pulled my chest up and straightened my shoulders again.

While I was still in college, I worked for a social research professor who also ran the Program to Prevent Woman Abuse at a local mental health clinic. Every day I talked to women with abusive partners, dutifully recording their experiences on a scale of violence that would allow the professor to draw conclusions about the nature of domestic abuse. We learned that men who tried techniques for managing their emotions did much better in changing behavior than those that only did talk therapy for their problems. Despite that experience, it was a long time before I internalized the idea that change happens when people take steps to change rather than lashing out and dwelling on past hurts.

I organized and collected data for the professor's study with greater efficiency and zeal than he did. I remembered all the women, all the things done to them, and kept their stories alive in my caved-in chest.

Those women were my secret compatriots. They inspired me and horrified me. I'd referred scores of them to the Rape Crisis Center, but I never contacted the center myself. I was the victim of a lack of good judgment, among other things. The story I needed to bear witness to was my own, but I didn't have the wherewithal to do so. One in four women is sexually assaulted at some point in their lives, but even now, women rarely talk about the violence that happens to them. I was raised to be nice and think of other people's comfort first. Rape is not considered well-mannered conversation.

"Let the movement flow from the top of the sternum through to the pelvis," the teacher said.

How many women in that dance studio had experienced the same thing, and also held a complicit silence?

Will I ever forget the way he jammed himself into me?

I took a deep breath and lifted my chest, pulled in my stomach and then released it. I felt the warmth of the midwinter sun through the window of the dance studio on my body. It looked rough, but I did a real undulation from top to bottom. As I did it I heard a determined jingle from the light metallic coins draping my hip scarf.

NOW, NEARLY TWENTY years later, the doorbell rings, and I know exactly what I will find. I hit pause on the music player and head downstairs. I've been rehearsing the finale to my dance troupe's show, and I'm breathing hard. It's the pop tune "Op" by the Turkish singer Tarkan. The song is infectious, high energy, insidious. The choreography is fast and demanding—I need to undulate, do forward and back hip hits with a shimmy, and then do a pivot turn in something like ten seconds. Someday I will be much too old for this. Different parts are close to broken down. But not yet. Not yet.

I should tell you the beat is danceable, seductive, but the video is sexist as hell. Tarkan going through his day, sleeping with and assessing every woman he meets, hanging out at fashion shoots, going to parties, being relentlessly pursued by the paparazzi.

Why do belly dancers love him? Why does anyone? Google him.

Op op op op dyamadim.

For the average contemporary woman belly dance represents a paradox—a lot of them—Tarkan for example. I have been studying the dance form for almost two decades now, and there's lots about it that is fascinating and empowering, and some things that give a feminist pause. Belly dance can be all that—sexy, thrilling, exotic—and none of that too.

The longer you study it, the more you notice incongruities piling up.

Most people think belly dance equals titillation. But it takes years to achieve mastery of it. The movements you see—shimmies, undulations, sinuous arms—require serious training and practice to make them transition effortlessly through the body. The music alone requires a great deal of study and is suffused with an encyclopedia of formal rhythms. To dance to it well requires understanding this. And there's the language—how many dance students know classical Arabic or Turkish?

Then again there are dancers who do things on stage that make you wonder what they are doing, and why they seem to be making a caricature of the art form. I believe performing and borrowing movement from another culture requires respect and nuance, but that doesn't stop some people from feeling entitled to whatever they want to borrow or mimic.

Others perceive belly dance as an import from terrorist lands, not places steeped in history, musical folklore, and dance customs. Yet some dancers are prone to disregard this tradition too, either on purpose or through ignorance, all in the name of self-expression.

In some Middle Eastern countries, being a belly dancer is synonymous with prostitution, because a lot of times that's what it is. It makes it hard to gain respect virtually anywhere because a dancer's commitment as a serious artist is always in question. Her excellent dancing can support a ten-piece orchestra (all men) playing original musical compositions, and there will always be idiots out there who believe she is for sale. Then again, she may be "contracted" out by a brother, father, or husband who controls her dance income. Non-Egyptians are banned from performing belly dance in Egypt because it is a national art form to be preserved by Egyptians, but according to a dancer who performed there, most dancers are subject to rampant sexism and treated like crap. And there are exceptions granted to the non-Egyptian performer rule anyway. It can be hard to suss out the truth.

The American Bellydance Superstars are wildly popular all over the world, bringing belly dance to the mainstream. Tickets to their shows cost as much as popular rock bands, but thus far no belly dancer has ever been adequately respected by the wider dance community either. Flamenco, ballet, ballroom . . . but not belly dance.

Nobody can pinpoint the exact moment belly dance arose as a dance form. Around 4,000 BC, Earth-based religions flourished and people worshipped a mother figure. Women of Assyria were purported to perform a dance that celebrated the cycles of the seasons, variously known as the birth dance and the welcome dance. The purported beginnings of belly dance.

American impresario Sol Bloom featured belly dance in his Algerian Village exhibit at the 1893 world's fair Chicago Columbian Exhibit. *Danse du ventre* (so named "dance of the belly" earlier by French travelers to the Ottoman courts) was considered "unsuitable" for ladies, especially the ones doing it, which worked to draw a large audience of both genders. Later, Egyptian cinema gave it glitz and sparkle, and Hollywood amped up the sex appeal.

Tarkan's contemporary videos feature parts of Istanbul that are flashy, chic, limo-driven, Hollywood-set-like. I've studied dance there, and I can tell you the regular Istanbul has crumbling streets, runaway graffiti, and so-so flushing toilets. The women in the chic *Nisantasi* neighborhood wear designer headscarves and no woman is flaunting anything, much less a suggestive bare back. Tarkan's video world is a macho fantasy. And yet we dance to his undulant Turkish, and find Tarkan's rhythms in our bodies.

Don't even get me started on stage costuming. Or that people like my parents think belly dance is a sin, or that my grandma thought I was stripping. It can make your head spin.

Despite the epoch, belly dance has always been at the cutting edge of female sensuality and expression. A subject of fascination and disdain. A source of female identity.

Why do I love it? After class or rehearsal, I feel the way I do after a thunderstorm on a hot day. The circulation inside my head calms. The wind and rain have pounded the earth, and possibility slants through the trees.

HERE IN THE twelve degree, minus two below wind chill of a Midwestern afternoon, Tarkan and I have something in common. I am also being relentlessly pursued.

There are two women standing outside my front door, eternal hope in their hearts and a checklist under their bibles.

As long as I have lived in my house, twenty years now, the Jehovah women have been coming over. Generally on a quarterly basis. They are prone to show up on really bad days, windy rainy icy. Today's temps have cracked twelve above, and there's a westerly wind. The women are not wearing hats. I believe they do this so I'll feel sorry for them and bring them inside.

I live in Minneapolis, the coldest of America's hip little cities. Dead center is the Seward neighborhood, named for William Henry Seward, President Lincoln's secretary of state and right-hand man. It's where you'll find an assortment of white lefty peaceniks, college professors, East African immigrants, and people who profess to walk the talk, and bike in all weather.

If you were on a Seward safari, you'd see things like this: Grown men of all ages carrying novels. Artfully mismatched Hanna Andersson-attired families in Subarus. An array of all-gendered individuals. Women swathed head to toe in colorful shawls who repeat the idiomatic "have a good one" in husky new English.

The neighborhood has a Poetry Post, wherein passersby can leave a poem, or read a poem, for sustenance and outdoor meditation. In the summer, the Pedal Pub goes by our house at least twice a night, an exuberant party on wheels replete with shrieking.

Scratch the surface of anyone around here, and you'll find a songwriter, designer, or fiddle player. My neighbor is a flamenco dancer. I am a belly dancer. When it's nice enough outside to have the windows open, you'll hear the hammer tap of Andrea's flamenco shoes as she rehearses, or the rise and fall of Arab music as I cook dinner.

I live in a rehabbed four-square Victorian with my tenacious, practical-idealist husband Sean who I love fiercely and with domestic abandon. I cook because I want to. My house has no kids. No pets. Too much dust. Books by people I know. This particular world of mine is the Austin, Texas, the Portlandia, of the upper Midwest. Depending on your point of view, this is where you want to park your unicorn. Or it is Sodom and Gomorrah, the downfall of moral society, the ruination of all that's American.

I open the door and say hello. All these years I am consistently nice but I have never let them in.

The two women before me. The differences are not apparent if you arranged us side by side. We are all white, widening, have laugh lines, willful gray hairs, and need reading glasses to see words on a page.

Marie is the one who always comes, she brings a variety of other people, but with her today is one of the white regulars. The repeater. Over the years Marie has shown up with African women and Asian women, but the repeater is her regular sidekick.

"Hi, Patricia." Marie speaks in a suggestive whisper with a slight lisp. I bend my head toward her voice.

The repeater nods her head toward me. "Good day, Patricia."

Marie fishes her purse for her glasses, but the page she wants is already bookmarked. "We'd like to share some good news with you. About love. A verse." She scans the page with her index finger. "But besides all these things, clothe yourselves with love, for it is a perfect bond of union."

The breeze is rippling the fringe of my hip scarf. I cross my arms. It's chilly with the door open. I close the door a tad.

I've known of Marie a long time. When I was working at the food co-op, she often came to my line to buy sugar-free treats for her kids on Saturdays after their service. She was married to a handicapped man who drove his wheelchair at a pretty fast clip through the neighborhood streets. She rode on the back of his wheelchair, standing tall, letting the wind tease her hair. She was thinner then, sexy, majestic. I admired her pluck. Not many people would let themselves be so literally carried away.

Here's what these two know about me: I love being read to. I find their fervor familiar.

What they don't know: I have a nostalgic rapport with the bible. My parents were Pentecostals in one of their religious incarnations, and they warned me about the seductiveness of a Jehovah visit. I toy with temptation.

"Colossians 3:14." The repeater nods, pulls her coat up around her throat.

I feel a physical empathy course through my chest and torso, through my pelvis.

Years of this. I troll my memory bank. Colossians? Who were they? Ah. The agnostics.

When I was confirmation age, I went out with my ma on a few proselytizing runs. This was in my parent's Lutheran era, but the object was the same, to get people to come to our church. We'd knock on doors and see people inside, pointedly ignoring us, or else feel the surprising jolt of nerves when someone did answer the door. Ma would lay on the charm. "Hi, we're here from Holy Cross. We'd like to introduce ourselves. I'm Nan and this is my daughter Patty." Ma would smile her lovely smile and I'd stand there wholesome-looking in a dress holding a Bible. Ma had a tract. "Services are at nine and Sunday School at ten-thirty. We'd love to see you there. If you have a moment, we'd like to share some good news with you about our personal savior, Jesus Christ."

I had wished we were out there hawking Girl Scout cookies at their doors rather than the savior. I still loved god and Jesus with all my heart, but adolescence was skulking its way through my limbs. The slinking devil was scrambling for my soul, inching toward me day by day. I read *Are You There God, It's Me Margaret* on the sly and thought that Margaret's basic question—am I normal—was compelling. Normal to me meant having private conversations with god, like Margaret did, not hiking around the neighborhood with your ma selling people on Jesus. As I stood there at the doorways of the unbelievers looking every inch the church girl, I could feel hypocrisy slithering up my back.

Most of the time we were rejected, which ma found hard to take. When we got home she'd cry to dad about how hard it was, how she hated that our lord was so scorned. My dad would hold her and tell her that she didn't have to do it. Door-knocking took a special gift. The lord was just as happy if she decided to do something else.

Marie asks me, "Have you ever thought about what is the perfect relationship?" That's how they get things rolling, by asking "do you know" or "have you ever thought" sorts of questions. Hand it to the Jehovah's. They've got great opening lines.

I know who and what they're getting at. God. I think about all that's behind me and above me. A pile of Sean's worn shoes to the left of the front door. My hot pink walking coat in the closet. Post-coital Sunday naps, digesting the lunch I'd made. The urns for my kitties' ashes. A bag of finger cymbals and dance shoes. Poems written by friends. Bookmarks I can never find when I need one.

I think about my grandparents who lived in a trailer home, hemmed in by packed red dirt ground. Grandpa's beer can pile.

Getting up from a dorm room bed after that shifty shadow had slipped out the door.

I feel the meteor smack behind my eyes. Some of those memories sting.

Not god. Hell no. Not god.

Marie looks at me with what I think is compassion. These people have been working hard at my door for a long time. I feel sorry for her. I am a test of faith.

"The perfect union is the one we have living in god's love," she smiles and looks misty, doped up.

"God is love, Patricia," the repeater says.

God had erected a brick wall between me and my parents.

Marie has something for me. My gift is a little magazine that has an older man pictured in a white flowing shirt with a long brown scarf (not too many guys dressed like that around here in flannel-wearing Minnesota) and a brunette woman in a cobalt blue dress on the cover. They are sitting on the ground and beds of blooming flowers surround them. Usually the topics of their booklets are timely. I got a lot of war stuff from Marie when we were invading Iraq. The Jehovah's are big on having so-called logical explanations for the problems of the world.

The cover says Grow in Love. Valentine's Day is coming.

Sean and I rarely give each other gifts. There is little commemoration of our relationship in things. Our wedding rings cost the same as a week's worth of groceries. It makes it hard to remember to give presents to others when they expect them for all the usual reasons, Christmas and birthdays, and I consider that a personal character flaw. What we give each other is an emotional pulley system to get through the days and weeks, time to read the morning paper, a good night's sleep. I've got enough sexy lingerie to last me the rest of my life.

"Will you read this?" Marie asks.

"Sure." It's always the same. Some earthly kingdom will be established after Armageddon, and based on the illustrations in the booklet, we'll live in multi-racial harmony in a place that looks a lot . like a Community Supported Agriculture farm.

Once Marie asked me what I knew of religion. I told her that I supposed they were all interesting and worthy of study but most organized religions tended to have an intolerant strain that repelled me. I said the kind of spirituality represented by the bible bore little resemblance to life as I was living it. Did she really think someone like me would ever join her religion? It didn't stop her from coming over and it still doesn't stop me from opening the door. I don't turn away the proselytizers and Sean can't turn away the political canvassers. We both know what it feels like to stand at the door and knock.

I look past Marie into a crusty blackened snowbank. A perfect union of earth and water.

Then there is a different kind of amalgamation. On smooth wooden floors that seem to be a thousand years old, where I sweep my hair up to the music, and lure my hips from place to place.

Here I am in an orange hip scarf, the Tarkan choreography in my head, at the door of my four-square smack in the middle of Minneapolis. Marie in her black boots, heavy purse, and the repeater, standing solid and grave while I heat the outside, unable to reject their good intentions.

Marie reads again. "For ye shall go out with joy, and be led forth with peace: the mountains and the hills shall break forth before you into singing, and all the trees of the field shall clap their hands." In belly dance, the signature move, the shimmy, connects me to something ancient and ecstatic.

The repeater clasps her gloved hands.

"Isaiah 55:12," Marie whispers in her attractive lisp.

Isaiah is by far my favorite prophet. Marie looks at me as if it would be good if I said something but I can't. There are things that rush out without a sound, that leave me still unhinged.

I say goodbye to Marie and the repeater and finally close the door. Head upstairs to rehearse some more. My hips feel coagulated. A cloud-filled sky.

2

WHEN I BEGAN to belly dance in 1998, I felt called to it in the same way my parents felt called to Jesus. I had a feeling akin to faith. The beginning was defined by an overpowering sense that I'd found a thing that connected me to something significant. I didn't know it was something I was searching for, but when I'd discovered it, I knew. Belly dance was worthy of my devotion to it.

I incorporated dance moves into everyday life: practicing shimmies while walking between rooms, palpitating finger cymbal patterns on the steering wheel of the car while stuck in traffic, pressing out belly rolls while soaking in the bathtub. All of these things made me feel privately emboldened. These new movements were things I could do with my body that weren't a reaction to anxiety. When I started learning belly dance, the usual dread that enveloped my branches and boughs were infiltrated by an unfamiliar energy. What started on an impulse, a decision informed by fascination and fear, quickly became something important. Caprice evolved into constancy.

I found that I had begun to unravel, not in the falling apart way, but how you untangle a knotted skein of yarn to allow it to flow smoothly from your fingers to a waiting needle. I didn't understand it intellectually or instantly. I became like other women I met who found themselves obsessed by the rhythms and movement. I believe what compelled us is that we moved our bodies in ways that felt rediscovered, ancient, and wholly female. For me it had also quickly gone deep, instinctual, though I didn't immediately recognize it. I was putting real, actual muscle into understanding and unwinding my past.

ALL MY STUFF for college had fit into the back of my parent's station wagon. We navigated around the trailers bearing stereos, TVs, recliners, carpets, refrigerators, pretty comforters, students with straight teeth, and inattentive parents. Ma and dad helped me take my stuff to my dorm room in one trip. I'd had two suitcases of clothes, a box of assorted things, and a bag of toiletries. In the box was a flip alarm clock radio that my uncle had given me, with numbers that overturned on the minute, and an identifying inscription on top: *U.S. Army Private David Hansen.* There was also a clothes iron, a hard-bound *Moby Dick,* and a dictionary. The clock had been the height of technology when Uncle Dave first got it as a soldier in the Vietnam War. It was reliable and loud. My brother's friend Tommy gave me the *Moby Dick* as a goodbye present. It was his way of saying he thought I was smart enough to read it.

Dad sat on one bare mattress, poured himself a cup of coffee from the thermos, and scanned the room. That's one of the first things we all did whenever we moved somewhere new. Check for signs of bugs or vermin. All of us felt palpable apprehension. Dad held his head to fight off a headache. Ma's hands fluttered around her bare neck. My feet were numb and weighted to the dorm room floor.

It was 1981. I was seventeen years old and definitely the youngest person in my freshman class. That's because I started kindergarten when I was four years old. I was born on the last day in November and the cutoff for enrollment back then was December 1.

My parents and I were intimidated by the things we saw and heard, but the school I was going to wasn't even fancy. It was skewed toward white middle-class Midwestern kids trying to get a step ahead by going to their business school. I desired to climb the ladder too. But I didn't belong there. I knew it before I got there.

Ma had come with me to orientation a few weeks earlier, but she was taken aback by the parents who had so many questions about curriculum, student-teacher ratios, and career employment rates by department. Ma was just glad to hear that I'd get three square meals based on my Pell-Grant-funded meal plan. It had not occurred to her that she should find out anything more about the school or should even be part of the decision. I was paying my own way with savings from a part-time job and babysitting money, with the help of financial aid. Ma and dad felt my education was up to me.

It had also not occurred to me to look into the school's curriculum either. When I'd asked my high school counselor about college, she handed me applications to schools she said would be good. They were all state schools in Wisconsin. I got accepted into every one, so I picked Whitewater because it had the nicest welcome brochure. From my parents to my teachers to my school's counselor, I encountered tepid encouragement and downright apathy. Everyone in the system was overwhelmed, and nobody expected too much of my inner-city high school class as graduates. It was enough that we got a diploma and didn't drop out of school. It wasn't an auspicious start. My own reasons for going to college were nebulous, too. I'd extrapolated it was a ticket to a better life. But what kind of life? I had no idea.

I was raised in Racine, Wisconsin, an even smaller city on the rust belt of Lake Michigan. One of its most current claims to fame is that it has one of America's best truck stops. If you are ever in need of a hot shower and a classic heart-attack breakfast you will be in good hands. Somehow the fact that there are miles upon miles of Great Lakes coastline seems to go unnoticed there. The remnants of a once-booming manufacturing age are everywhere near the lakefront. Parking lots with weeds growing through the cracks, slumped chain link fences, empty brick factories, too many people without jobs. The biggest event of the year is the Salmon-A-Rama, the fishing contest on Lake Michigan. Professional work is still hard to get and hard won. Going back there and seeing the strip malls ascend the crumbled core, I feel like I'm watching an economic family feud.

In the early 1980s, Racine had changed from a racially-divided factory town to a bona fide dive when all the factories closed. Anyone with aspirations had to leave or else stay among the forsaken hulks of industry.

At that same college orientation, an exuberant resident assistant assured me that college life was exciting and fun. There were football games and clubs and groups galore. I craved an intellectual life, one of books and philosophy, a place where conversations focused on ideas, not cars or work or shit talk. Her response to that was, "There's an all-girls dorm." What I didn't understand during orientation was that Whitewater was for most students a one-way ticket to being a corporate accountant, and the school was where you kicked up your heels before you had to settle down. What nobody talked about was what the welcome brochure's crafty fiction covered up. The school had a reputation as a suitcase college and was a haven for flagrant drinking and drugs. This summed up higher education in Wisconsin back in 1981, when the drinking age was still eighteen and in a lot of towns and cities around the state, the bars opened at seven a.m. and stayed open until one a.m.

At orientation, most parents and students wore sporty shirts and sweaters in the mainstream fashion of the day: tossed over their shoulders with the arms cuffed in front, resting on their chests. Stuck ups.

I was wearing cutoffs, cheap flip flops, and a Rush band t-shirt, my eyes enveloped in black eyeliner, and ma was in her church clothes, a calf-length skirt with low heels. I didn't look like a promising student whatsoever, and as it turned out, I wasn't. Ma looked exactly like a woman tired of trying to understand her temperamental teenage daughter. Her neck suffered the strain of holding up my compressed teenaged psyche, while my feet swelled over the backs of my flip flops from walking everywhere. I believe we both left orientation with a sense of bodily dislocation. It gave me second thoughts about college, but I was going no matter what.

The day parents dropped me off at my dorm, ma said, "You'll see. Time will go fast."

She handed me a brown bag with a peanut butter and jelly sandwich and an apple. She knew I didn't want to be there, but if my goal was to do something different with my life, this school was the opportunity before me. Did any of us have any better choices? Then I watched the old brown station wagon pull away in the parking lot, headed back to the routine of morning eggs, lunchtime soap operas, and hamburger dinners. In fifteen minutes they had unloaded me and all I owned to a place none of us knew anything about. It was only ninety miles away from home, but it seemed really far. I was the first person in my whole family, both sides, to go away to college. My belief in myself was about the size of an Easter Seals stamp.

THE MODERN DANCE choreographer Twyla Tharp said that she believes dance comes down to three essential movements: down, out, and up. Tharp said, "It has nothing to do with dance steps, but it has to do with a bigger purpose for dance, which is movement in the world."

Movement in the world. That was what I was learning in dance class. Whatever insights I was about to learn on the dance floor or beyond, I would have to earn them. A mélange of naivety and hubris fueled my early enthusiasm. I was a true beginner, and god help me, I always learn things the hard way.

Those early days of belly dance I was alternately drawn to and intimidated by down, outward, and upward movements. Down I assumed I could understand, although a "down" movement in dance is about being grounded, earthy. Intentional expression of out and up movements often originate in a downward push-pull of the body's energy. It gives you impetus to release up and out. For example, there are down shimmies, where the emphasis is on the hips pulling down toward the ground, and shimmies with a hip lift up. The same with chest movements.

In the early years, I studied with a Minneapolis dancer named Amina Beres. I was drawn to her classes because she was so "up." Her passion and energy were a buoy I held on to. No matter how crappy her day at work (or mine) she'd always set up our class to contain elements of challenge and fun. From her I learned important basics. Common finger cymbal patterns. How to hold a veil. To find the beat in the music. Let myself "follow the bouncing hip scarf," as she called it, to practice and refine movements based on her repertoire. She taught us to do figure eights with our chest, a movement that includes elevating the rib cage and moving it through four different stations: up to the right and around, center, then up and around to the back left, come back to center and repeat to the right.

When she did it, it looked smooth, vigorous. Her hips were "quiet" and the only thing moving was her chest. She would call out "right, center, back, left" in a chant-like intonation, and I would feel my heart vibrating in my chest while undeniable sensual feelings fluttered through me. Women weren't supposed to push their boobs up and out! I was sure I looked grotesque.

Those early days are easily remarkable for the herky-jerky ways in which I moved and the crazy self-talk about what I felt like I was "supposed" to do with my body. I was pushing my reflexive hunch away to stand up straighter. I was constantly starting and stopping, trying to apprehend what Amina had mastered. "Keep going," was her mantra. I was liberated by the idea, and fearful in practice, regarding the control I could have over my torso.

"Reach around, pull back," Amina repeated. I tried not to strain and grit my teeth. I held my hips in a clench.

This doesn't sound much like a dance love story does it? As awkward as some of those movements felt initially, it was the repetition and the way Amina held her body in space that spurred me to strive to inhabit these movements. Once I could do them, they felt so good to do. Each session was a mini catharsis of practice and repetition, timing, and control. Clearly, the body is meant to move down, out, and up. A woman *should* be able to freely move her chest in a figure-eight, the mirror image of the infinite.

THOSE FIRST DAYS in my new college home I walked the streets. The town of Whitewater was smack-dab in the Kettle Moraine of Wisconsin over a hundred years ago. It was once a quaint place that supported a respectable teacher's college. Until Johnson's Great Society. An influx of state money expanded the school into a cheap post-Frank Lloyd Wright monstrosity. Architects did things like place buildings in the land's unique geology, but left out the windows that would have elevated them above the plainly institutional.

On my walk through town I passed the bars full of returning students. I had hoped I would be invited in by students who would congregate in hushed groups to discuss philosophy. Instead, every moment away from "parental units" seemed to be a celebration at Whitewater, consisting of camaraderie and ten cent tappers. I couldn't join them because I was still underage. Back home I'd sneak into biker bars with my best friend Nia. We'd encourage the men to buy us brandy old-fashioned drinks and get us high. We prayed we wouldn't get our asses kicked by jealous girlfriends, and that Nia wouldn't get pulled over for drunk driving on the way home.

In Whitewater, people my age were ruthlessly carded by muscled bouncers at the door. So I bought a forbidden electric hot pot cooker and a few boxes of macaroni and cheese.

I walked listening to my own breathing.

I did not understand the difference between loneliness and solitude. That day I'd felt both the lack of friendship in a strange place, and the exhilaration of not having to account for myself to anyone. The timetable of my day was completely my own. I liked that, but I was ill-equipped to make the most of it. I fretted instead. But it was an anxiety that went beyond the need to make friends and what to do with my time. What I didn't want to admit was I'd felt abandoned. How was I going to create this new and incredible life when I had no understanding of how to go about it? I had no words. It was a lump in my throat. I didn't have the right to feel deserted because I'd made the choice to go to college in the first place.

I think my parents might have understood how conflicted I felt, but I was too proud to tell them. I would be admitting I was already a failure, living out a predicted forecast that I wouldn't be able to hack college. I was getting what I wanted, dammit. So be it. I'd swallow that lump in my throat until it killed me.

By nine o'clock that night I still hadn't met my roommate yet, so I decided to go to bed early. I wasn't really tired so I cracked open *Moby Dick*. I didn't know what else to do. I got as far as chapter four, and quit after Queequeg "harpooned" his cheeks in the morning. Too many "salty dogs" in that book. I was grossed out by the descriptions of the ablutions of men at sea. That's still as far as I've ever gotten in reading *Moby Dick*.

The hallway light illuminated the space under the door. From that little space I could tell who was still moving in, meeting people, and getting together, who was pissed at her parents, who had the best stereo, who had drugs for sale.

I didn't want to know all this from my bed. I'd rather have been beyond that door, in the full blaring light, but I didn't know how to get to know people when they weren't hanging out on front porches or cruising in cars. Conversation with the neighborhood kids went like this:

"Did you see that mother-fucker? Dude's driving a Firebird. *A fucking Firebird.*"

"Your sister likes his sorry ass. She's getting with him right now. Oh! Oh! Oh!"

"No that's your mama in the front seat, sucking his dick dry."

"Shutup, asshole."

A punch followed up by the comment, "Yeah, and you've got nothing but a raggedy, limp, pencil-thin pecker."

"Well your ass is flat and your tits look like a boy's."

"Fuck you."

We could talk trash for hours.

I had been limited to a finite inner circle, kids who had run together in packs on the streets and alleyways, and we all just coexisted with the adults in our lives. Grownups could never be our friends. We'd spent too much time defying them and their house rules. I had the skills to make friends, but freshman year in college I didn't get the concept of polite socializing for its own sake, even though it was something I aspired to. Mingling and making courteous conversation wasn't something the people I knew did much. You demonstrated your interest in someone by picking on them, gossiping, or talking shit.

I stayed pinned to my dorm room bed like my things packed neatly away in the fixed furniture. The underwear was folded up, resting in solid drawers, the shirts ironed and hung up in the closet, pencils, pen, and paper sat silent in the dark. I pondered what school would be like.

THEY CALLED HER Sure-Lay. My roommate Chrissy. She was conventionally pretty, funny—curly blonde hair, lots of makeup, giggly, and she wore the kind of perfume that shrieked at you, Avon stuff, and that's what our dorm room smelled like. It was Love, it was Emeraude, it was Siren. It was cloying and shrill. She spritzed herself with it every time she came and went. Everything she did was meant to attract notice. Chrissy loved to talk. Hopped easily from one unrelated subject to the next. Living with her was like surviving an issue of *Cosmopolitan* magazine. How to attract a mate. Skin care tips for the stressed. Take this quiz and find out if you're compatible. Her favorite topic, hopes and dreams, included lots of fun and money. Whenever she looked at me her one lazy eye lolled to the side. She had big blue eyes that she accentuated with heavy blue eye shadow. Her eyes were a wide open sky without a cloud for miles.

"Patty, look at this," she said, her fingers splayed. She'd painted them with some kind of red-brown nail polish. "Dramatic Drachmas." Who comes up with these names? Colors like "Chicago Sky" and "Beets Me." I needed a job like that.

"What's a drachma?"

"Some kind of coin. In Israel I think," Chrissy said. Turns out it was Greek.

She said she lost weight, but still tended to wear fat-girl clothes even though they didn't fit or flatter her figure. Chrissy wore baggy jeans, thick cowl neck sweaters. Boring bras and panties, like mine, even though she talked like she wore something wild underneath. Tube socks and track shoes she never ran in. Sweatshirts in school colors. She was a typical Wisconsin country girl—big boned, broad hipped, full breasted and lipped—completely milk and corn fed from Tomah. No fashion sense. She said she "came to college to get away from that identity." From what I could tell she was full of shit.

We all were. Most of us on my dorm floor didn't know how to become women we wanted to be, which was authentically confident, smart, and sexy. At the time, a popular perfume commercial capitalized on our collective female identity crisis and offered a solution—doing it all. The Enjoli woman was an object of ridicule (her pans would never be crusty and greasy like the ones I had to deal with at home) but she also captivated us with her beauty, morphing from mom to business woman to vixen. The sexy blond sang, "I can bring home the bacon, Enjoli. Fry it up in a pan, Enjoli, and never let you forget you're a man. I'm a woman. Enjoli." The male voiceover said, "The eight-hour perfume for the twenty-four-hour woman."

We were riveted. Likewise we relied on fashion magazines for advice on how to be alluring and expected come-ons from men to feel desirable. Madison Avenue's view of womanhood was to be lovely and talented and non-emasculating. We bought into it, despite the recycled Victorian virtues wrapped in slick advertising because we wanted to imagine it was possible. We believed it was essential to our happiness to have the opportunities our mothers did not. But you had to be sexy doing it, and it required letting a guy have his way.

What Chrissy really wanted was to meet a cutie (her word) who could take her to a more glamorous locale, like a suburb of Chicago. I'd heard jokes about girls going to school for an MRS degree. The problem was she had abysmal luck. Setting her sights on gorgeous professors, the football team quarterback, or the Gucci males, she came up empty every time. She wasn't even a sure lay because from what I could tell, she never got laid.

IN COUNTLESS STORIES there is an initiation. Like every committed initiate I sought enlightenment, mastery. Before that could occur I'd have to understand the secret ways and means of the new world that I'd stepped into so I could demonstrate my aptitude and proficiency. In the late 1990s, that meant learning a new vocabulary for the body. Hip hits. Figure eights. Snake arms. Hip toss. Head slide. Belly roll. The seemingly endless variations of hip circles: Umi, Moroccan hip circle, and "around the world." There is an online belly dance thesaurus of hundreds of words, and no standard terminology among teachers. I heard the many words, saw them demonstrated, and I did them. Or attempted to. Thousands upon thousands of times I have done these things with my hips, arms, neck, shoulders, and stomach.

Raks sharki, known primarily as the female solo in Egyptian dance and translated as Dance of the East, seemed to me a whole new paradigm for bellies, curves, and womanly bodies. Dancers accent their body movements with their arms and hands in addition to signature hip motions, inviting the audience to look. *I am someone womanly and commanding.* It was very revitalizing to view and do. I would watch with appreciation as accomplished dancers seemed to push back centuries of human grief and invite in ritual delight.

My initiation to belly dance included an immersion in music and food, too. I'd discovered "mezze" and was soon introduced to platters of kibbe, hummus, and stuffed grape leaves at the Mediterranean restaurants featuring belly dancers. In addition to dance, I took cooking classes so I could learn how to make those things because I loved the way the food tasted—fresh, flavorful, and satisfying—and, like the dance, part of a long culinary tradition. Soon enough my music collection would include music from Egypt, Lebanon, Turkey, Morocco, and I'd learn not only belly dance, but the folk dances of those countries. I sought out new friends and teachers in an effort to deepen my understanding of what I was learning.

My collegiate initiation, on the other hand, was remarkable for its implied consent. A voucher to a pre-ordained place as a wife and mother. An unexceptional career. I don't remember a special vocabulary. Most of the time I didn't say anything. I was afraid of my professors and intimidated by people in the dorm. I wished to be stylish and cultured but all I did was hold myself back. I did my laundry religiously every week as I had been taught, ironed my shirts, and curled my hair.

Twyla Tharp said that for her, "time moves in one direction only . . . and that would be forward." Tharp said memory screwed up her internal clock because dance is always a process in forward motion. That might be its attraction for her, but for me, dance also discloses a physical history, a place in time.

IN HIGH SCHOOL and college, my pelvis kindled frustration. I had periods that laid me flat, and I tried to appease the cramps with a heating pad and downing too many Pamprin. Ma, who bought generic everything, thought the extra money she spent on a name brand would help. It was a family luxury, bestowed to me with tenderness, ignorance, hesitation.

I took many long naps and stared at the ceiling for hours. I was doing my best to hide my rawness and lack of sophistication. I didn't want to be ordinary, and I didn't want to be part of the collegiate mainstream. I waited for someone to notice me. When someone did I was grateful, disordered, and confused.

When I walked to and from classes I held myself as if my spine was immobile and my hip joints had fused. The very picture of a tightass.

The foundational movement for the shimmy is the hip hit. Push your hip up on the right. Push your hip up on the left. Repeat. Remember. Repeat. Remember.

When a hip hit picks up velocity it is finally a shimmy. It creates a vibrating momentum that moves through the flesh of my thighs and ass. All of the energy is contained in the lower body, relaxed and loose, with feet flat on the floor. A release.

In Amina's class I had to repeat, repeat, repeat. Push my hips up and down. Circle back. And did I ever: *Reach around, pull back.* Recollect.

THE FIRST WEEKEND after school started, I got invited to Rita's wapatui party. She was the one in the dorm room next door, the one with the hippie-looking mother. I wanted to be liked by her. She had a round open face, long, Pia Zadora hair, and a way with people. When she bent over, you could see the dimple in the small of her back centering the top of her girlish hips. Bob Marley's reggae music had everyone jammin' at her party. I'd never heard of his music until Rita. Rita was from Brookfield, a new money suburb of Milwaukee. She was well-traveled and sophisticated, but not loaded. She was a very entertaining, enthusiastic girl. I really wanted to be like her too, cool, pretty, and popular. Rita drew a crowd when she talked. She was talking about her grandpa, how he found her stash.

"My mom's cool, you know? She smokes too. So she told him it's a special cooking herb I found. So you know what he said? He said," and Rita imitated him, "I'm glad the granddaughter is finally learning to cook."

Everyone cracked up. Of course someone as cool as Rita did not cook.

I intended to be Rita's friend, but I knew she invited me to her party because I lived next door and it would be rude not to invite me. Nonetheless, I was both afraid and thrilled to be there. My heart thumped underneath my freshly ironed shirt, and my freshly curled and spritzed hair signified florid yearning. I came with Chrissy, and we put a green liqueur she had in the wap, which was in a plastic lined garbage can, and turned it purplish-green. Everyone stood around looking at the wap, and us, stunned, before diving in and drinking. Someone had brought a bottle of some clear alcohol, poured that in, and declared it "dangerous." Decades hence I concur. It was.

Rita had a bunch of people visiting for the weekend. Friends from Brookfield. Rita was tripping on acid that night with some of those friends.

One guy kept touching her hair. "It's so shiny," he said devotionally.

Rita laughed ravenously, teeth forward, cup of wap and cigarette in one hand, twirl of her own hair in the other.

I'd never had wapatui, or even knew that it was a stew of whatever kind of hard booze thrown together. A college concoction. Nobody ever made that at bonfires on the beach in Racine. The drinks were relegated to one thing, local beer. Pabst, Miller, Old Milwaukee. You drank that until you pissed it all out or threw up. Rita's party was the first and last time I've had wap.

Bringing the cup of wap to my lips, I smelled the vacant smell of an entirely alcoholic drink. Is this what it took to fit in here? As far as I could tell, the stuff was made with mostly grain alcohol and Kool-Aid. I held that grenade in my hand, felt its plug, and pulled. I drank it down in gulps with my eyes closed. My whole mouth burned to the back of my throat, causing my eyes to water. But that gave way to a refreshed and relaxed feeling. I could party, behave like I should around people, and flake off the isolation of my dorm room.

I was flirting with a guy who looked like Tom Petty, wiry, blonde hair to his shoulders, but with a more translucent skin tone. He was a compact model, packed into snug blue jeans. Sexy. He said he was majoring in Economics. I couldn't believe a guy who looked like a rocker would do something so dull. I was majoring in English and on the sly wanted to become a writer. I had a notion college would show me how to become one. I'd written a few short stories that I'd shared with my dad and my sister, and was writing a poem every day. I'd heard that's what Emily Dickinson did, so I assumed that's what I should be doing. I'd written a poem about a crow once, and that had been published in Racine's daily paper with my picture alongside it. This triggered creeps who called the house wanting to know if the foxy poet was available. That kind of attention freaked me out, but I kept writing.

The rocker said his name was "Whitey" and lived above me on the fourth floor. I was touching the ends of my hair with one hand too, holding my plastic cup with the other. Nobody was worshipping my hair, but Whitey seemed charmed enough to offer to get me another cup of wap. I was flattered by the attention.

I ended up finding out that his nickname was not due to the translucent hue of his skin, but his cocaine use.

I sipped it, feeling experienced. The corn clamoring in the field outside the dorm didn't scare me anymore. The third glass had no flavor. When a keg of beer arrived, someone got the idea to play Quarters, a game where you land a quarter in a pitcher of beer to make somebody drink, and if you miss, you drink. I was always good at Tiddly Winks so I kept landing the quarter with precision every turn I got. People were cheering me on. People were smiling at me, having a good time. Drinking like this was gaining me entrée into a place I sought to belong.

It speaks to my incredible lack of sophistication that a wap party seemed like the height of urbanity. Years later, when I watched *National Lampoon's Animal House* for something like the fifth or sixth time I realized that offensive comedic domain was actually the world I'd been plunked into. Despite the movie's portrayal of the scuzzy heroes as challenging outdated and oppressive fraternity systems, it was a truism that in the 1980s to fit into college life you had to drink. And drink some more.

The guy sitting next to me held out his hand and introduced himself. The third finger on the hand I was holding bore a serious ring. Was I holding hands with a married man? His name was Kevin, and he lived off campus, but still kept in touch with "the fourth floor guys" of my dorm. He seemed nice, down to earth, the eye in the center of a hurricane. He good-naturedly swigged his beer. His smile was sweet, white, even, and sincere. He smelled laundered and fresh. He was wearing a blue polo shirt and top siders on his feet. Like so many of the people I saw at orientation. Not my type. But I was not sure. I'd never known a guy who didn't wear a t-shirt and flannel. I felt an instant attraction to this open-faced, brown-haired, brown-eyed guy, and I caught him looking at me a few seconds too long. I liked this Kevin, and when it was my turn to sink the quarter I made him drink.

Kevin told me that it was his senior year, and after he finished he was going for his MBA.

"A what?"

"Masters of Business Administration."

"Hey, watch out for this guy. He's straight A all the way." A dude named Dogger winked. Dogger had spent the summer hiking the Sierra Nevada Mountains, and it looked as if part of him was still gone. He and Kevin were good friends. They were both from Oconomowoc.

I flirted and danced with Kevin and Whitey, getting drunker by the hour, getting the two of them, and others, confused. Was I blindfolded and playing Pin the Tail on the Donkey? Who was who? Everything blurry. One smelled freshly showered, and the other smelled like a day at the beach—suntan lotion, ale wives, hot sand. Another one smelled like donuts or a night on the Midway at the county fair. One of them held my hand. One of them kissed me. I was held up against the cinderblock wall of Rita's dorm room. Was I okay? Who asked that? The small dorm room expanded and contracted on the waves of my inebriation.

The ones on acid suddenly felt like they needed to get in touch with the trees, saying they needed to experience the universal "go-go." Me and a handful of the just stupidly drunk gave each other high fives and left to crash in our own rooms.

WHEN I PUT the key in my lock to my dorm room, someone from the party appeared and helped me stand upright. He put his hand over mine and turned the key and came in the door behind me. Weak light from the parking lot leaked in through the edges of the school-issued drapes. My ears were ringing from the party's loud music and too much to drink. The lock clicked in the tumbler from the inside. Chrissy was out with the stoners. We both crashed down on my bed in the dark.

"I love pretty girls. Especially you." He stroked my hair. "Especially you." He walked his fingers around my neck and it tickled. I had lolled my head down on my pillow and curled up on the bed. I felt like throwing up. He rolled me on my back and straightened my legs and pulled my feet down the length of the bed. Oh, it felt so good to be prone and let the world spin.

Had I felt any sense that something was amiss? I still ask myself.

I asked him to get me the garbage can from under my desk.

"Shit man, are you gonna barf?" Irritation scratched at his throat.

Even when I wasn't drunk it seemed like the velocity of vertigo I'd felt since arriving at college had increased exponentially. I didn't belong at this school, but where did I belong? I had no idea how I could find my place; I didn't want to go home and be a waitress or a wife. I yearned to be a writer. Known as a smart person.

"Who are you?" I asked. Was I asking him or myself?

"You don't remember?" I had a recollection of someone at Rita's party.

He pulled off my tennis shoes without untying them. I heard them plop, one, two, to the floor. It felt good to be attended to. I wanted to be cradled and warmed. I wanted my stomach soothed. I reached for him.

He rolled his body on top of mine, and his weight took the breath out of me.

"Hey," I groaned.

I tried to see his face in the dark. Was this the guy who wore a green baseball cap that shaded his eyes? Because he loved the Green Bay Packers? Did he bring me another cup of wap? Close up his body smelled. Cigarette smoke, hamburger grease, cologne.

I'd been in this situation before, sharing slobbery kisses with a guy I'd met at a party or a bar. I'd make it home to pass out. Technically I was not a virgin, but I'd not gone all the way to climax. My first serious boyfriend had penetrated me, but it hurt too much, and I pushed him away. We tried a few more times before we broke up. I never had sex I enjoyed.

"Ugh," I said. "You're too heavy."

I struggled to move his hands away from my waist and get his body off mine. He rolled over and undid his fly and grabbed my wrist and made me hold his penis. I twisted my wrist to get out of his grip and to remove my hand from his engorged dick.

"You're such a prick-tease. You know that?" I felt the threat in his breath as he yanked on a handful of my hair. He let me go after a second yank. My neck felt like whiplash.

"College girls." Exasperation and dismissal hissed through his throat, as if we were in an argument about the different types of terrible women out there. Nobody had ever called me a college girl before and I did not think of myself as one.

He started to unbuckle my belt with his other hand and began tugging at my zipper.

"Wait." Don't do that.

He slapped my free hand away and yanked at my jeans, pulled my pants down. He shoved my legs apart when he got my jeans down far enough.

"What are you doing?" The tinny warning I'd been too drunk to confirm before was now in my own heartbeat and ragged breath.

"Don't do that," I said and strained to push him away.

"*Don't!*" he mimicked me. "*What are you doing?*"

I couldn't see it, but I felt his hard penis between my legs.

"You know what? You're a stupid little bitch."

I tried rolling over to get away from him, but he grabbed my wrists and held my hands over my head. I bucked and kicked. He kneed me between my legs and it felt like the time I accidentally fell on the top bar of a boy's bicycle. A bright bolt of light. Misery and agony behind the eyes and in the groin. After I fell on the boy bike's bar, I'd hopped around and danced, my hands between my legs, waiting for the pain to abate. It hurt like hell.

He found the opening he wanted and thrust in. I felt the force of him thump through my body.

I believe when someone says something like stupid bitch to you, especially when he is on top of you, in you, you completely absorb his assessment. I was a stupid little bitch. I felt this all the way through my fingernails as true. I believed it. I had as much compassion for my innocent self as he did. Nor had I understood the defenseless position I was in. Not just as a drunk young woman, but as a person trying to figure out all by herself how to ascend the underclass. I didn't know that rape was about control, not unchecked horniness, and that idea, among others, held me back. I believed it made me susceptible to bad luck because that was the only kind of luck that seemed real.

He began to saw away, his cock so hard, I was rubbed raw. With his one arm over my arms and the other over my mouth, he worked at me. I struggled to breathe. He was reaching. Panting. A sound of laughter. A car door slamming. It was how long since he began? He stopped. Listened for noise. Started again. I tried to bite him, but all I could do was tongue his palm. He tasted salty and stale. Holding his hand over my mouth seemed to invigorate him. He came with a groan and laid his whole weight on top of me. I felt my spine crack.

"You wouldn't be a bad girlfriend. Nice and tight." His sour breath weighted his words.

He pushed me into the mattress again and heaved himself off me. I felt skinned and sticky. I kept still and willed him to go away. I heard him zip his jeans and felt the disturbance in the air as he moved. He made his way to the door, and I heard the lock disengage. It clicked again. Afterward I contemplated the creaking wooden house where my parents were certainly asleep, the many nights I'd turned the key in that antique lock, swaying from drink, but safe at home. My rapist disappeared into an orange sliver of hallway light before the room went quiet and dark.

3

WITH EVERY NEW and complete undulation I unwound a tiny bit of dread or guilt. I redeemed loss by tossing the coins on my hips. I realized I had only just begun.

The basis of all the moves in belly dance is the center. The core. Good arms flow from an uplifted chest and strong abs. A beautiful shimmy is the result of pelvic strength, which starts with good posture all the way down to the ankles. A full-body undulation isn't possible without a strong center and body awareness. It's an organized religion of movements designed for a woman's body.

My posture has always been iffy. It's better than my cotton-picking grandma's was, but from the edges of my crooked teeth to my borderline spine, I needed more core control. The repetitive drills and practice of belly dance technique—the shimmies, undulations, and isolations—make the core stronger. With each practice I felt like my hips were marking time, setting things in order.

I used to live as if my body was an apartment I could drive up to and look through its windows. This is the past I saw:

When I was in junior high I joined the Lutheran church choir with my ma and sang my off-key tone-deaf heart out. I especially loved singing the dirges of Maundy Thursday, the night of the Last Supper. We sang melancholy incoherent songs in a candle-lit church on a chilly school night. We sounded like a pack of monks on Quaaludes, and to me that sounded downright sensual. It was as spooky as Halloween, the eve of Jesus' betrayal. The centuries-old church music fit my dark, erratic teenage moods perfectly. As I sang, I demanded from god a boyfriend sent down from heaven. But god knew I was sheltered and naïve and completely unprepared to have one, so he didn't follow through.

Before we got to sing Handel's *Messiah* replete with a trumpet player on Easter Sunday, ma and I had the first of many fights that befit a girl in spiritual and hormonal transition. I had bought a pair of shoes to go with my Easter dress.

"You are not wearing those," ma said.

They were blond espadrilles with a sweet t-strap. Four-inch heels. My dress was a white tube top with shoulder ties and skirt. I'd shaved my under arms and legs for the occasion, bought a curling iron, mascara, and eye shadow to complete the ensemble. It was my first and last major makeover.

"You look like a hooker," she said. I looked like one of the girls I idolized on *American Bandstand*, that's what.

"Those shoes attract the wrong kind of attention," she emphasized. What she meant was that my shoes would be a come-on to the wrong kind of man. One who might be bad at shepherding a young woman's tender soul. The kind of man I wanted, and eventually got (without a high-heeled come-on), wasn't going to be a Bible thumper.

Despite my parents' best efforts to raise me to be an obedient daughter, and I was, mostly, I resisted the idea that men were chosen to lead women. This was something my parents both believed was a god-given truth. Dad didn't like loud or opinionated women and demonstrated a preference for soft-spoken self-effacing women. He didn't like "harsh" women who wore bright clothing that called attention to their bodies, or were bold enough to tell people off. Ma wasn't a pushover, she had her abrasive side, but she let dad make the decisions about family life. It was part of the reason we moved so often—dad wanted to—speaking up didn't necessarily lead to anything different. Every year or two she'd dutifully pack our boxes and scrupulously clean the home we were leaving just to unpack and scrub out the flawed new one.

Every time we did this, I'd be forced to leave something behind. Once it was a bike, or a nice household amenity, but most of the time friends. Each time we moved I learned to harden my heart against the losses. By the time I'd softened back up in the new place, we'd be moving again. Whenever other families fell apart, my parents said it was because the man of the house wasn't properly in charge. Yet I accepted as normal that our family was always on the brink. You would think that because of my parent's belief in the power of men in charge, I would have blamed my dad, our ordained family leader, for our instability. I didn't.

I'd grudgingly acknowledged my father's command of the situation because he was a benevolent dictator. He was loving and rarely unkind, and liked to get his points across through stories that had a moral, versus handing out edicts. I'd also understood that my father was bowed by forces out of his power to control. He couldn't change the economy or the weather. Most of the jobs he held were shitty. He couldn't will God into dropping much-needed hundred dollar bills into our living room. I received the pressures on our family to feed and house ourselves as god-given trials to be overcome, as my parents did.

But I still felt acutely the unfairness. A man's opinion should be the final ruling on any issue. God chose men to lead women.

At the Lutheran church we went to, only men were allowed to step foot on the sacred altar and read the sacred Gospel, and only boys could be acolytes. Until I saw women dusting the sacred altar after church.

At the next confirmation meeting I raised my hand.

"You say that women can't go up on the altar, only men and boys, but I saw Steve Monal's mom vacuuming it after church. So how come she can clean it all she wants but not be allowed to step foot on it on Sunday?"

Steve whipped his neck around, wondering what his mom had to do with anything. He'd been skipping youth group to hang out with his school friends, purposely ignoring us "church" girls.

The other girls in confirmation spoke up. "Yeah, why can't we be acolytes, too?"

Pastor looked up at the ceiling panels straight through to Jesus before giving our class an answer.

Looking attentive during sermons, lighting candles, and holding a tin of communion wafers lost its appeal pretty quickly after we became "equal." The boys dropped out like flies, happy to be free of the burden of their gender, and us girls got stuck with the whole job. There I was up there at the altar playing the role of dutiful child of god while fuming inside. To be considered a good girl. I definitely wanted to be sexy. I wanted to be equal. This trifecta of wants crashed down with unfeasibility. My parents worried about my good character, while the boys thought I was too goody-goody. I adopted what I believed was a pleasing persona, but I had a lot of zits on my face and a pack of arguments I held inside my mind. Be nice? Pretty? *and* equal? Did it really have to be so much work? Was it worth it? What about that Roger guy who wanted to pull my pants down so he could *see the real thing*? With each candle I lit or communion cup

I held, tottering at the altar on my four-inch heels, an innermost fire threatened to burn me up.

That was 1977, and "women's lib" was causing tumult in every major institution from churches and schools to families. The reverberations of the movement were felt everywhere by young women like me. I remember watching a report on so-called bra burning on TV with ma and her saying "those girls are going to want those back when their boobs start to hang down to their waists." Which you have to admit is very funny. At thirteen years old, I was too young to fully understand what was at stake, but I was attracted to the fire and verve of women speaking out, sagging tits notwithstanding.

My parents always believed that a woman's highest calling was motherhood, and if I spent my life waiting tables while raising a family, I would be fulfilling my destiny. Nobody we knew ever turned a hobby into a career, took vacations, or went off somewhere to try to make their dreams come true. You stayed home, responsible to the people in your life. If that meant getting by, pushing a broom, or a baby carriage, so be it.

THE DRUM IS the heartbeat of mother earth. The drum is the heart of the world. *Doum-doum-takatek-doum-doum-tek* (hold)— is the ancient rhythm of the *chiftetelli*. *Chiftetelli* is a Turkish drum rhythm played in 8/4 time, and it can be played both fast and upbeat or more hypnotic or slow. The fast version is found in folkdance where couples or groups dance together. In American cabaret belly dance, the *chiftetelli* is usually played slowly for sensuous effect. In the slow *chiftetelli*, there is the place in the rhythm where you hold, skip a beat as the *tek* rests on the tongue like salt, the tart accent that brings out the sweet. This hold is a necessary rest, giving the *chiftetelli* rhythm its classic soul-stirring quality.

I come back to it time and again. The break in the beat of the drum, the hold, is filled with questions nobody can ever answer— why is there war, cruelty, hatred, bad luck? Are people essentially good if given the chance? I have a religion and it is the unlocked beat. I believe in it with all my soul. I believe in its power to sweeten life. Its pauses give me something to come back to again and again as the hold that gives the whole rhythm meaning. To me, it is a force as great as any god.

A belly dance *taqsim* is an invitation to glimpse this inner life of a body, to give an emotional charge to performance. The word *taqsim* means "division" in Arabic, and in the music means that a specific instrument will play an improvised solo. In belly dance, the meaning is similar. A dance *taqsim* is an improvised response to a melody instrument in the musical *taqsim*, and often involves undulating movements. A dancer can shimmy the live-long day, its exuberance and ecstatic expression carries many a choreography. It's stimulating and fun. But the true artist has absorbed the *taqsim*—the slow sensual movements of circling the hips, the fluid arms, the flick of an eyelid that reveals something more—allowing the music to flow directly into and out of her body. *Taqsim* rhythms move a dancer to interpret the music emotionally by adding different textures to the performance with slow and fast and big or small movement. A moment of stillness.

I have never stood before people, not counting charades, and used only my body to emote. Is that, then, what could make me stronger, more resilient?

THE NIGHT I'D been raped, I imagined I'd been asleep in some imaginary ship off land where neither god nor my father, nor anyone else, was going to save me. My arms were white and exposed as the underbelly of a pan fish. My veins were regal blue warnings pulsing under my skin, frigid waters splashing first my ankles, then knees, then over the crest of my waist. I could not swim or squirm. I had roots like the bottom of the lake has plants, rocks, and sand. I was held down, and I heard waves: slurp, slurry, slip.

He'd put himself into me with pistons that made me burn up and dry all the way to the tips of my fingers. Then he emptied himself. He was so sure of everything.

When I woke up I observed myself from the top of the ceiling. My whole body was in an s-shaped cringe.

Chrissy had just come out of the bathroom, turban-headed in her towel and robe. The clock read 7:32 a.m. She carried a big pink pail, like the ones kids use at the beach. That's what we used for carrying shampoo and soap to the dorm floor's bathroom.

She was annoyed. Disrupted. Chrissy explained she had to go find someone to let her crash at their place last night.

"So. Who were you with last night little missy? Some cutie? Musta' been wild, huh?" she nasaled.

Had she wanted to come in and stopped because she heard something, thinking I was having fun? How many guys had I led on that night, playing with both their dicks and their feelings? I didn't even know the guy's name or where he was from. Cute? I really couldn't say. I was grateful to be conscious, considering I'd lost count of the plastic cups filled with wap.

I was embarrassed. My behavior was rotten. Stupid. I needed emotional guidance and spiritual cleansing, but I was sure I had gone too far for anything like that to be of any help. Silence slammed into my chest.

I considered myself smart. Sassy even. If I was so smart, why would I try to justify a stranger coming into my room and my bed uninvited and taking what was left of my virginity? I felt like the best thing to do was forget about it. Rape on college campuses wasn't acknowledged or considered the outrage then that it should be, and in many cases, still isn't. There was no way my seventeen-year-old self was going to step out for justice.

Chrissy's face softened in response to my muteness. "Girl, you look wrecked. Let me go get you a Coke or something." She shook some change in her robe pocket. "I'll be right back."

She had set down her pink pail. The beach pail reminded me I had not puked after all. I wished I had.

I HAD A friend at Whitewater who'd gone to the same high school in Racine. Meg lived with two other women in a rickety house off campus. I'd met Meg in our sophomore year in a sociology class and we had bonded over our mutual dislike of a cheerleader who was in our class. We had no real reason to hate her, she was actually a nice person, but her status in our school meant that she was better than us, and we were smug in our nobody role. We might be dogs, but we would never grovel before anyone on the sidelines of some dumb football game.

Meg had grown up the child of a single mom on welfare, and like me, was consumed with getting out of Racine. Meg had a head start. She had older brothers and sisters, and had been influenced by their hippy lifestyles, and her older sister was a lesson in transformation. Jane was the first lesbian I'd ever met. It was in the kitchen of the duplex Meg lived in with her ma and brothers. Jane had long, straight, ginger hair, a firm handshake, and I learned from Meg afterward, a sharp, assessing personality. She had judged me a "femme," and wondered how Meg and I came to be friends. I deemed Jane reasonably pretty and strange, and meeting her stunned me. Here was someone who upended her whole life to be a social reject for the sake of another girl. Why?

Soon enough I would see Jane hold her girlfriend's hand (whoa!), and hear her condemn the patriarchy (the first I'd heard of it, Meg had to explain it to me). Jane said it so casually there at the kitchen table. "Well, Mom, that's what you get from the patriarchy." They had been discussing how the cops were condescending to Meg's mother when her car got broke into. I found out Jane went to political demonstrations, had rejected makeup and shaving her legs, and only read books by women. I listened and saw these things and swallowed hard.

Meg adored her sister, and I was in silent awe and dread. A bona fide radical! To be an out dyke in 1979 in Racine took a special constitution. Nobody hid their disdain of homosexuality. My friend Nia thought it was "nasty" and my mother reminded me of the destruction of Sodom and Gomorrah and warned me about getting too close to people like that. I reasoned it was weird. Get with a girl? No way. All it took to "flaunt" your "lesbian lifestyle" back then was to wear baggy jeans and Birkenstocks.

I'd asked Meg if she'd like to be Whitewater roommates, and she said there was no way in hell she was going to live on campus. Never mind that freshman and sophomores were required to live in the dorms. She got a special dispensation to live off campus, but maybe she didn't, and that was that. I wish I had followed suit. While Meg was cultivating her fiercely independent intellectual traits, I was discovering another world of drinking, drugs, and men.

I ran into her the day after Rita's party in the school bookstore. I was beyond hungover and sore. I was downing Coca Cola after Coca Cola to wake up, to feel normal. I was strung out on caffeine, and my head was pounding from repellent thoughts and insistent questions. Who was that guy who had followed me and then fucked me? How much of a slut was I? Could I be pregnant? I understood pregnancy would alter the course of my life, and not for the better. I should have been writing my first English class paper, not wandering around that bookstore suppressing a cry.

After we greeted, Meg got right down to business. I had not seen her since the beginning of summer after we graduated from high school. It was like no time had passed.

"Are you ok?"

"Oh yeah. Fine." I knew Meg was a very perceptive person. What did she see? I had already begun coating myself in a resilient film of denial.

"No you are not." Shit, man, I wasn't.

"I hate this school." I picked at some invisible lint on my sweatshirt.

"Me too," she said. Meg looked me hard in the eye. "You're not buying that are you?"

I was holding a cardboard-backed movie poster of *Gone with the Wind*. Something to decorate my dorm room. It was the image of Rhett Butler carrying Scarlett in his arms, the scene where he takes her upstairs to his bedroom. The bottom of the poster was an image from both the start of the civil war and Scarlett's escape from burning Atlanta.

Meg pointed to Clark Gable. "That image really disturbs me. You couldn't pay me to buy that. I mean, he's, it's about his power over her. The movie glosses over that. And don't get me started about Hattie McDaniel."

"Who?"

"Mammy. It was a debasing portrayal of a smart black woman."

I looked at the poster again. I'd always thought Rhett was overpowered by his feelings for Scarlett. He couldn't help but take her to his bedroom. She fought him because she didn't know how good he was for her. And I loved mammy. She was so feisty and funny.

The poster had a palette of red, black and white. Bold colors. There was civil war, flames and danger, a great escape. An epic story. I had to be similarly transported. To bewitch someone like Scarlett had Rhett. It had not occurred to me, and wouldn't for a long time, that the poster glorified marital rape as well as nostalgia for a society that profited from slavery. I'd read the book over and over in those years, perhaps a dozen times, swept up in Scarlett's scheming and passionate character. She demonstrated that's how women got ahead—they used their sex appeal on gullible men and conned everyone else, Miss Melanie and hellfire be damned.

Not long ago I'd gone to visit the Margaret Mitchell house in Atlanta and came away struck by how small she was as a person. The curators had laid out this tiny dress on a little antique bed, what used to be considered a double.

Mitchell was quoted as saying about writing *Gone with the Wind*, "In a weak moment I have written a book," which felt ironic in the Anne Taintor way, the woman who writes things for refrigerator magnets like "hopes and dreams would only distract me from making awesome casseroles." I left amazed by how this little author who lived in a tiny house wrote this larger than life and still-enduring character who could still conjure up a whole pile of mixed feelings.

"I think it's romantic," I said to Meg.

She rolled her eyes. "That's nuts."

I rolled my eyes back at her. "I need something for my room."

"Ok, well, why don't you come over? It would be good to see you. Call me." She gave me her phone and address and went on to purchase her high-falutin poetry books. I bought the poster.

FIVE YEARS INTO my dance studies, I believe learning *taqsim* will make me a better person, in the same way that doing improv comedy or learning to throw knives will. I can't do much more to make it worse; I can only get better.

Cassandra is a master of *taqsim*. The first time I watched Cassandra Shore perform one on stage I was sure she was capable of carrying the world on her smooth-moving hips.

During the class Cassandra played pieces of music and explained different *taqsim* rhythms, like *chiftitelli*, that start slow and pick up speed, and the dramatic Arabic masmoudi *dum dum te-ke tek dum te-ke tek te-ke* that seemed to go straight into my chest. She then demonstrated how she responds to them with dance movement.

Cassandra was dressed simply in black leggings and an Oasis Dance Camp t-shirt. She pulled her hair up with a jaunty clip of her barrette, re-knotted her hip scarf, and performed a short *taqsim* to illustrate. Her hands seemed to float over her head, and her hips trolled earth and sky by dipping and releasing. She wanted us to try our own *taqsim* by looking into the mirror and playing with movements. "Imagine you are sharing an emotion like sadness or contemplation," she said.

This is not what most people think of when they think of belly dance. They imagine dancers in two-piece costumes, women doing movements they think of as sexy or titillating. They'd be surprised to know that Cassandra was encouraging us to find our sensual side, one that is not about how we look, but rooted in how we move and what we think about, going deep within ourselves to consider, hold, and express an emotion physically. It goes against nearly everything I'd been raised to do and be as a young woman.

It is at that point in my dance studies that I understand the ability to do a passable *taqsim* requires the ability to live in the body. Most of the time I'm sitting at a desk, macerating my wrists and shoulders with bad posture. I sit like that for hours, out of my body, all in my head. My mind is one of the Great Lakes, my body the tiny rowboat.

Living in the body is not just about releasing myself from too much seat time, though. What I learn from Cassandra is that it's about being physically liberated. Giving your body the means to speak in its own inimitable way, and allowing it to, before the mind and its attendant social strictures shut you down. That's the story I want to tell in my *taqsim*.

A WEEK AFTER the assault a campus health clinic doctor was looking between my legs and in the bright hot light I knew what she saw.

"Oh, I see you've got a lot of redness," the doctor said.

We both listened to the buzz of the fluorescent lights overhead.

Ever since that last weekend everything about myself seemed dirty, smelly, and gross. I lay on the crinkly paper on the exam table, bare assed, and waited for the doctor to proceed.

I ruminated obsessively about pregnancy and was certain that I was because I felt so waterlogged. I was sure the itching that drove me to call a doctor was a pre-symptom. I'd spent the week in an underwater daze. I kept my class schedule to stay moored to a normal routine, but I couldn't and didn't study. After class I'd stare at the cornstalks outside my dorm room window and imagine there was a well-worn secret path. That there was a girl in there who couldn't find her way out. What an obvious metaphor that was, my way of coping, but thinking about some other, imaginary girl in trouble gave me a way to dissociate from my own thoughts and fears. It was better to care about someone else, this abstract lost woman, instead of myself.

"You have itching?" I nodded down at her.

"You've probably got what looks like a trichomonas yeast infection, but we'll do a lab test to make sure."

She gently pulled apart my labia and then my anus. The warmth from the light shining on me made me feel itchier. Her touch was confident and light. She told me she was going to proceed with the exam to get lab results and would go ahead and do a pap as well since I hadn't ever had one.

She pulled a metal speculum out of a drawer and ran it under warm water. "Sometimes these things can feel really cold," she apologized. It looked like a duck bill contraption, and I couldn't believe that thing would fit inside me or any woman.

The doctor slid the speculum in and it did feel cold, and I drew in a sharp intake of breath. "Keep breathing," she said. It felt like she stabbed my cervix and then when she opened the speculum I felt every bit of it. It was hanging out of me as she grabbed specimen slides and started poking my insides with the swabs. Once again I felt a stab on my cervix. She grabbed a can of hairspray, and fixed the slides before pulling the speculum out. It went out with warm relief.

"I wanted to get that out of the way. At a glance, Patricia, your skin and tissues look unusually chafed, even for trich. Have you been having a lot of sexual intercourse?" she asked. The smell in the air was partly me, partly medicinal, partly beauty parlor.

I nodded my assent to the ceiling.

"Trichomoniasis, or trich, as we call it, is usually sexually transmitted. Have you been having sex with multiple partners?"

"No." My armpits were sweating, and I could feel a line of water trickle down my side. I was not promiscuous or slutty, and my sins were not out of the ordinary, but it appeared that way. It would have been impossible to explain to her or anyone. I felt the disgrace of it all. And I had this trick thing.

"Do you have a boyfriend?"

I could hear her clear her throat, but it could have been a groan from the stool she was sitting on.

"Do you have a boyfriend?" she asked again.

"Yes."

Was it a true crime? He hadn't jumped me or scared me like rapists I'd read about in the papers. I liked the attention I got when he was helping me with the door, with my shoes. I hadn't invited him in, but I didn't tell him to leave. I liked the feeling of his body before he got out his cock. I'd been with guys, blitzed out of my mind like that. Before.

"He doesn't go to school here, though." I was playing that game. The one where you tell your questioner whether or not they are "hot" or "cold." Nowadays practitioners are supposed to have rape kits and training to handle patients like myself. Even though I assume medical professionals are better informed, I know what has not changed. A woman still needs to be willing to put herself on trial before the world in order to talk.

I couldn't handle what would happen if I told her. A guy I didn't know fucked me in my dorm room while I was too drunk to defend myself.

I was seventeen years old. Not able to drink legally. Not above the age of consent, either. I'd heard the campus cops were on a tear to stop and punish underage drinking. Rita, and everyone in my dorm who was at the party, would be busted for providing. Rita might have known the guy who followed me into my room, but there was no way I was going to ask her, or anyone, about it. The whole entire residence hall would hate me for bringing scrutiny to our dorm. All in all I blamed myself and covered my shame with a corrosive hair shirt of guilt.

"Are you two using birth control? Lubrication?"

I was worried about pregnancy, and that maybe I'd contracted some kind of venereal disease too, but I kept clammed up about those concerns. Was what I had in the same league as gonorrhea or syphilis? I'd heard there was some women's clinic that did abortions in Madison or Milwaukee. I planned for these things as if it was rational, and I told myself I was prepared, an adult, even though I was far from it.

"Patricia, every woman needs to be adequately protected and lubricated to enjoy sexual intercourse."

The doctor turned off the vagina light and stood up. She looked at me on the examination table for a minute as if she were weighing her options. She told me she'd like to examine my breasts and do a pelvic. Again she apologized for having cold hands. I opened the hospital gown front when she asked me to and she felt up one breast and then the other. It felt strange to be touched there by a woman, but no guy had ever felt my chest without my bra on. Even the man who came into my dorm room didn't seem too interested in my breasts. I assumed they were too flat. I didn't understand that sexual attraction wasn't what led men to assault women.

"Have you been doing self-breast exams?"

If you could call soaping your boobs in the shower an exam. I nodded my head.

"We've been encouraging all our patients to be more aware," she said. Then she turned toward the sink in the room again. "I'll need to do the pelvic exam now." She put on gloves again and gobbed her first and index fingers with lube. The doctor explained that she'd put one finger in my vagina and another in my anus and press down to feel my uterus and ovaries. I felt her fingers inside as she pressed down outside. Whoa. Sweat broke out on my forehead. That hurt. He'd pushed down on my body, too. I shivered when she was done.

"Is everything alright, Patricia?" Her question was strung between the table I was on and the door.

She smiled a frozen smile. Things weren't adding up, but I was not talking. She finally left me to check on the results.

When she came back she had a prescription for metronizadole and two brochures. One was for Planned Parenthood for more information about contraceptives, and the other brochure was for me to hang on my closet door. It was a graphic of a woman with one arm up over her head and another showing her fingertips on her breast. Clockwise arrows surrounded the drawing's nipple to demonstrate how to check yourself for lumps in ever widening circles. I looked at it as a map to nowhere.

CASSANDRA PUT ON a CD of Natasha Atlas. The singer we all adore. The one who has launched at least a thousand belly dancers, who has inspired many a taqsim around the world.

I heard the familiar strains of the song "Kidda" and Natasha's drawn out "Oh, oh," and the Transglobal Underground band backing her. Natasha sings as if she's a woman on the verge. It's the song we all practice slow moves to in my regular classes. The one I think of as the orgasm song because of the strength of the ohs.

I noticed all of the other students' eyes roaming around the room and into the mirror, as we checked out each other's moves. Two minutes is an eternity in a *taqsim*! What do you do with yourself for that long? I had put my arms up in supplication toward the ceiling, hoping for inspiration. Anything. A small insincere prayer: Dear God, in whom I don't believe, send me a snake arm. A figure eight. Extend my emotional openness, help me to stretch as I stretch.

Inside the mirror my hands and wrists were working to achieve a relaxed, elegant look. A bit of a floreo.

The translation of the title "Kidda" is "like that." Natasha was singing *why are you like that when I love you so?*

I remembered being scared and alone in the dorm room the night dad dropped me off at school after Christmas break. I had paged through my college roommate's neglected calculus book. The smell of coated textbook paper and Chrissy's lingering crappy perfume rose high into my nose, the words and numbers meant nothing to me.

I was turning pages, turning pages, thinking I should drop out of college.

I spent that night with the lights on, looking at the ceiling, as I am looking at it now. My stomach nattered because I'd had no supper. I tried levitation, being still, staring, sitting up. I had no way to say anything through my arms, hips or fingertips. I'd separated myself from my body because it was the source of heartache not solace.

Why am I like that?

DAD DROVE THROUGH a snowstorm to take me back to school at the start of second semester in 1982. All the buses were canceled. I told him he didn't have to. I didn't want to go back.

He'd go through anything to help me get ahead, he was trying to show me, as he chain smoked cigarettes and steered the aqua blue station wagon through the swirl, taking me back to Whitewater. When I applied to go there, I had no idea what I was getting into, what collegiate life might be like. My idea about students grouped in logo sweaters talking in hushed tones about philosophy was laughable.

Us coeds were holed up in prefabbed '60s era dorms, towels stuck into doorjambs to hold back the smell of marijuana smoke, the jar of "Black Cadillac's" passed around like jelly beans, girls too, flattered and suddenly popular—sleeping with boys we barely knew.

Dad didn't know a thing about college life either. How could he? He was lucky to graduate from high school. I could not admit to him the amount of trouble I'd got myself into in a few short months. How a man I didn't know forced his penis into me, his hand over my mouth while he did it, how I got arrested for underage drinking after a night of bar hopping, and that I flunked a number of classes. Just a few weeks and some booze. Boom. Slut city. The free-fall stunned me.

I told my parents over break I didn't want to go back, but was too chicken to say why, even though I scared the wits out of them, or awed them anyway, wearing black eyeliner, ripped jeans, and a rock t-shirt that probably smelled like dope, newly restless. Nonetheless, they were adamant about me finishing school. I'd never quit a single thing before in my life, they pointed out. Some things I'd never had the chance to start. But I'd never quit. The best thing for me was to go back.

I tried to see through the snow. I knew there were ditches, farmhouses, barns, but I couldn't see them. I looked at Dad. His new glasses made him look smart, but aged. A Dad with glasses was not going to see his way clear through that mess.

I could have told him how nobody studied. That everybody had figured out ways to sneak into the bars. We danced and drank, a DJ whipping us into a sweaty frenzy.

Dad's eyes peered above the dash; there was really no seeing anything in that snowstorm. Too much wind. He was concerned. We could hear wind whistling in the crevices of the car doors. It seemed like we were the only two people alive in the world. I expected to get to Whitewater and discover that everyone simply evaporated. Christmas decorations would still be up, and "Jingle Bells" piped in on the streets, but no people.

"You should see the food they serve in the cafeteria."

He'd heard all that before.

"One day they made this Sloppy Joe stuff. Then the next day they added beans to it and called it chili. The day after that they added corn chips and called it Fiesta Surprise." I sort of liked the Fiesta Surprise. The corn chips were salty and mushy, not bad. "But I don't think school cafeterias should do such brazen recycling with leftovers."

I was developing an ironic way of talking. I considered it entertaining. I wanted to have a real conversation with my father but had no idea how to start one without making him feel defensive. I would like to know, how did he survive his nervous breakdown? How did he get through the hard parts of his own childhood? How I wish I could change that now. I held him apart from my heart because my fear of being found out as a bad girl, someone who would disappoint him, was greater than my need for his solace and understanding. I was still a child myself. I imagined I was being clever and discreet.

"Sounds like your mother's cooking," Dad said.

We both laughed. I was the only one from the dorm who trooped into the cafeteria for three square meals. It *did* remind me of home.

Dad lit up yet another cigarette, unconcerned about sudden death in a snowstorm or the prolonged kind by lung cancer.

"So you've got a boyfriend at this school?"

I shook my head. I knew what was coming. Something about being careful, that I just couldn't be too careful.

"A girl's got to be careful."

He said it. I felt like I could predict the future. I was so fucking smart.

"I'm sure you're not a, ah, a—"

Virgin. I didn't think he'd go quite that far. Dad was very genteel in practically all matters. Not only was I not a virgin, but I'd also been—raped. I couldn't say the word out loud. If I did, I felt like I'd have to call the cops, file a report, and call attention to my stupidity.

"I just hope you keep in mind the word 'respect.'"

I reflected on recent nights at the Playpen bar, Aretha crankin', all the girls mouthing r-e-s-p-e-c-t, swiveling their hips.

Dad would cringe to know the stories I made up about him. He was a businessman, very busy, not a person who drove a forklift and unplugged toilets.

We finally saw the edge of town, and it was blurry and pointed as the Seurat painting I saw at the Chicago Art Institute with college friends.

Despite my hopes and fears that we'd have the world to ourselves, we passed through campus, and I saw students bundled up, each with bright backpacks.

The dorm's parking lot had been plowed. Dad followed me into the residence hall. The dorm hallway smell was familiar and funky, and against my better judgment, I breathed it in, inhaled the strange odors of macaroni and cheese cooked illegally in hotpots, bong water poured down drinking fountain drains. Stale mint emanated from the door of the communal bathroom.

Once inside my room, Dad sat on my roommate's bed and poured himself a cup of coffee from his thermos. The ever-present thermos.

I watched him scan the room. It appeared he'd like to bolt for home, too. I wanted to yell I told you so.

"Are you hungry, Dad?"

"Sure, what've you got around here?" I actually thought he wanted mac-n-cheese, but I ate my last box before I'd gone home.

"There's a vending machine. Is that ok?" I would have loved for us to go out and get a cheesy, hot pizza.

The vending machine was practically empty. When I came back, I gave him a pack of cookies, and he ate them, fast and serious, beige crumbs falling on Chrissy's purple bedspread. I expected him to say, you're right, this place gives me the willies, let's get out of here. Instead, he stood to go, told me to remember what he said.

He walked out of the dorm back into the snowstorm, which wasn't quite so bad anymore. I watched him from my room's window. He brushed the snow off the wagon, adjusted his scarf before he got in. The windshield wipers went on. Then the headlights. He backed out in a smooth arc. The car pointed toward the exit, but idled in place. I held my breath and stood still while my father wrestled with either second thoughts or his gloves. Then I watched the car's headlights gently illuminate the snow covered cars in the lot one by one until he was gone.

FINALLY, NATASHA ATLAS stopped. Cassandra explained she wanted us to try moving to a drumbeat, to pick out a part of the music that we resonated with and fix a move to it. The rest of the *taqsim* could be any kind of improvisation, and usually the whole part of it is, but in order to get comfortable doing it she wanted us to find something we could depend on to groove with.

I moved my arms out from my sides and began pulling in and reaching out, pushing away gravity's force and bringing it back. *Dum dum te-ke tek dum te-ke tek te-ke.* All the way through from my shoulders to fingertips. I peeked into my center and found a whirling kaleidoscope of snow. A collage. Parts. I felt the drumbeat, the one that expands and holds, and it dropped me, *doum doum*, into its chrysanthemum waves.

4

WE WERE THE girls of Pierce Woods. A two-acre wooded picnic area with a bathroom, sandbox, and of course, picnic tables. Towering oaks stood guard at the entrances and were rooted in constellations on the grounds.

What the girls of Pierce Woods didn't know was what had the power to uproot them, but until then, iced over puddles, branches released by wind-shaken trees, piles of leaves, the edges of a rolled-up chain-link fence, all those things appeared as a dream from a certain life. A body, a young one, mine, lived in Pierce Woods with all the intensity of a homesteader.

There were three of us. Sixth grade, Racine, Wisconsin, 1974.

My family had moved into the house that is a half block away from Pierce Woods, so I met them: Julie and Nia. Both of them lived across the street. Julie's house was on the corner, bigger than ours, and at night her dad's dump truck was parked in their double driveway. Nia's house had a picture window her mother was always looking out of. Our house had a front door only the paper boy ever knocked on because the side door was more visible from the street. Julie was our leader, Nia the soul, and I was relegated to natural-born follower. Those two girls would both love me fiercely and be willing to throw me to the wolves. Best friends.

Our house was small, but had been built by a carpenter. Every wall was straight, every corner plumb, the wood floors gleamed. The yard was fenced so our dog stayed put. Dad was secure in his job. He worked for Eaton Corporation then, which used to be Yale locks. He started out on the shop floor, but worked his way up to a promising desk job and served as a go-between for assembly men and the college-educated parts designers and engineers. And ma's workload had eased—my youngest sister was in Kindergarten. At that point in time my parents had finally achieved what they wanted. We moved to live near Pierce Woods because things were going to be better. Our better-ness settled on us as a warm comforter and made our life glow with goodness.

For Ma and Dad, as well as Julie and Nia's parents, every day still meant putting food on the table. Bills. Unread books and unused ideas piled up at all our houses and the TV was an incessant backdrop to everything we did.

Us kids came in for meals and decamped to whatever activity called to us—housework, TV, or homework—but for me, Julie, and Nia, we strove to spend as much time as possible with each other. All of our moms expected us to do things at home—dishwashing, vacuuming, laundry. Julie's mom gave her the longest list, which she had written out, and included mopping the kitchen floor and making her brother's beds. Her brother's beds!

Pierce Woods was a strategy to escape the work that our mothers wanted to add to our days. The 1970s were the waning days of regimented housewifery and our resistance portended its doom. We were going to get away, see things, and have things we'd been denied, housecleaning be damned.

When the weather was all but hideously cold, my girlfriends and I lived in Pierce Woods. It was ours.

We divided up the park into quadrants. The northeast side had the merry-go-round and huge sandbox and a cluster of picnic tables near it where adults might hang out, to either watch kids or get drunk. The south section had the bathrooms. The word "Fuck" had been spray painted in bright orange on the building by Julie's oldest brother. By then I knew what the word meant, when penis met vagina, and I also knew it was the worst word you could say. I never said it; taboo weighted my tongue. Soon, though, I would use it with impunity.

The western part of the park had the swings and that was where the boys would hang out, pretending to be outlaws. They would chase us girls away from that patch of land if we came too close, and we pretended to be scared. The southeast side of the park had the entrance that faced Julie's house, and squirrels ran through the grass collecting acorns from the oaks. Dead center was the dip that turned into a pond during the spring freeze-thaw.

On rainy days Nia and I stood perched on the edge of the sandbox (we never sat at the picnic tables, ever—why was that?) Julie stood inside it, sand crusting her wet shoes. We tested our equilibrium against the slick wood time and again, circling the sandbox up on our toes. Nia could pirouette; which she did at every corner. I just pointed my toes and walked pretty. I wanted to leap through time and space and do beautiful turns all the way, just like Nia. I held a handful of oak leaves in each hand, waving them like pompoms. I had aspirations.

Julie would start most rainy-day conversations with this question: "You know who I hate?"

Julie always had some secret hate. Her pronouncements came from someplace far away and important. My feelings were primitive and prehistoric. I could never match her stature, no matter what kind of clothes I cajoled Ma into buying me, or whatever swear words I might use. Julie was some kind of warrior princess, someone whose look could wound my hot heart.

"I hate that kid. The one who wants to be Hank Aaron."

We never questioned Julie.

We understood. Julie really meant that she hated why we were out in a soaking wet park.

Hank Aaron was a baseball player then with the Milwaukee Brewers. Pretty much everyone under twelve idolized him. I didn't know then that his career was marred by racial hatred, and that when he broke Babe Ruth's home run record he had death threats against him.

I shrugged, and Nia pretended to be deaf.

"I mean *really*," Julie goaded. She said really like a grownup.

"He's so stupid," Nia and I said, our voices a sing song of defiance and agreement.

The kid she was talking about sat behind me in class. He'd crossed off his given name on his desk nametag and wrote Hank Aaron. Everyone started calling him Hank, even the teacher. During recess we all watched him leap around, pretending to hit homers and catch fly balls. He danced around the playground, throwing his body into the air, spinning, landing on two feet, a huge smile on his face, completely absorbed in the fantasy of Hank. That kid had big dreams of baseball and greatness. I had unarticulated dreams of grace and beauty that felt as far away as Hank Aaron's immensity.

"Why act like you're Hank Aaron when you're not black?" Julie asked. Whiteness was supposed to be the long-term insurance policy against poverty for us. Tête-à-têtes like the ones at the sandbox reinforced our superiority.

I stopped walking around the sandbox perimeter. My damp toes felt clogged.

At my previous school I had a friend named Rhonda, who wore her hair in multiple ponytails with small white barrettes securing the ends. Her ponytails bounced when she ran. In class I liked to play with her hair, and she liked that too, but I'd have to wipe my hands on my dress after. "Hair grease," she explained. I desired hair like Rhonda's. I wanted my hair to stand out, bouncy, charged. Rubber bands would slide right out of my hair. Even one whole ponytail was too thin and limp.

I threw my pompom leaves away and put the sleeve of my raincoat in my mouth.

I DIDN'T COMPREHEND that my mother, who I thought of as the domestic enforcer, also wanted to stand out, and had her own dreams of grace and beauty. She lost forty pounds after we moved near Pierce Woods. She kept a Weight Watchers food diary in a school-issue three-ring binder, diligently recording all her meals. She ate things we didn't like. Poached fish. Dry toast. Skinless chicken. All her baby weight vanished, and I noticed my mother was suddenly svelte. She had her hair cut and dyed a lighter shade to celebrate; and her bangs fell in her eyes, sexy and sweet.

Ma looked the best she'd ever looked in her life, but everything else was wrong. She complained all the time. The appliances that ruled her life never worked right (vacuum cleaner, washing machine, stove). There was unending laundry, and most especially, she never got to go anywhere. Nobody needed her, she said, except as a housekeeper.

She grumbled she wanted to do something interesting. So she planted marigolds along the side of the house and sorted socks in front of the TV.

What she didn't say was this: Dad was friendly with a beautiful single woman from work. Daria. I knew about her because Dad was getting together with her after work and I'd heard Ma and Dad fight about it. I'd met her once. On Halloween. We had come home to find my father entertaining not one, but two, young women in our living room after Ma had taken me and my brother and sister trick-or-treating; one of them was dressed as a nurse, the other in a bunny costume. Ma had on a bent witch hat and had rubbed green eye shadow under her eyes and on her nose. I was wearing the plastic blonde princess mask my sister wore the year before. It smelled funky and the eyeholes were too small because it was made for someone half my age. Ma had cut down an old crinoline so I could have a ball gown.

I remember feeling guilty and clumsy. I was too old to go trick-or-treating. Nia and Julie didn't go, but I hankered the free candy. I felt like a giant scammer the whole time.

The bunny and the nurse grabbed for each other, hugging one another with hysterical laughter when we walked in. I believe those women saw through my lame mask and dingy skirt straight through to my full bag of candy.

Did we look stupid because of our costumes or circumstance?

Daria the bunny had on a white leotard, floppy ears and on her feet were two fluffy pink fake fur slippers. The nurse had on a skirt skimming her behind and high heeled shoes. You could have used her chest to hold up a shelf of nick-knacks. Daria and her friend were propped against each other on the floor. Dad sat on the couch. Legs folded under him like a hippie. A bottle of some hard liquor on the coffee table.

Dad introduced us. The two women on the floor put their hands up to their mouths simultaneously, muffled giggles behind them.

Then Daria complimented my mom's housekeeping in a tone of voice that said what she really meant: Is this all you do? It's what I had been thinking too, that there was more to life than clean floors and endless laundry. Daria's tone of voice trivialized my mother's hard work, and I had silently agreed. I had taken Daria's side. I remember I lowered my head and kept counting out my trick-or-treat candy haul.

PIERCE WOODS WAS most alluring during the late winter. The freeze-thaw of February created a pond in the middle of the park, and Julie and Nia and I played in it, crushing its thin ice, our ankles submerged in the freezing water.

My boots zipped up the side and water always seeped into them. I started wearing bread bags over my socks to keep my feet dry, which worked some of the time. I wouldn't go home until my feet were chilled and thoroughly numb.

Most days we were pioneers. What should we eat? Something that must be in the water. A fish. Julie declared we needed fishing poles.

We all grabbed the biggest sticks we could find and we waded back into the water casting for the fish we were certain was in there. That's what Dad did. He fished with faith and conviction.

"If I catch something, you're cooking it," Julie told Nia. Julie always made Nia pretend cook.

"No way. Make Patty cook for once. I'm not cooking for you the rest of your life." This must've been something Nia's mom said to her. Nia's mom was known for her cooking, and she was making Nia learn.

Every night Italian. Everything homemade. Everything delicious. Nia and her brother ate well. Julie and I both begged to be invited over for dinner, but were always turned down. Julie's mom warmed up a lot of frozen dinners that her brothers and sisters ate on trays in front of the TV. That sounded pretty great to me too. A lot of nights we had some variation on ground hamburger at my house. Anytime I invited them for dinner, they turned me down.

"You wouldn't want what I would make!" I warned, which is something my own mother said when asked to bring potluck. Both Julie and Nia laughed.

"I feel it!" Nia squealed. She ran out of the water. "It wrapped around my ankle." Julie and I looked down and didn't see anything. Just stirred up mud and drowned grass. It was only a pretend fish.

"You'll never fucking survive out here acting like that," Julie said. The orange F word snapped through my head whenever she said it. Nia slowly waded back in. Mittens her mom knitted drooped from her hands. Wet wool. They didn't fall off entirely because the string that held the pair together wound through her coat's sleeves, even though she was way too old for that. We were between childhood and nascent adolescence, pretending to fish because we were still kids, but acted grouchy about it because that's what adults did.

"I'm cold," Nia said, and her lips were white with her lack of resolve. "Can't we just go to the store in town? Even Laura Ingalls did that."

Julie had the whole boxed set of the *Little House on the Prairie* books. She knew that was true.

The pretend fish had become a domestic monster, and Nia was surely going to be swallowed up.

"Fish." Julie demanded obedience.

We all started casting our sticks-as-rods, the imaginary fishing line hitting the water, coming up empty every time.

As my boots filled with more water, I knew they wouldn't be dry in time to walk to school tomorrow morning. More bread bag crumbs and damp socks. I heard about the kids across town at another park, perfectly warm in a recreational building, willing participants in organized activities. We had heard they had board games and dancing. Backgammon and checkers. Boys and girls learned the Bus Stop and how to Hustle. I'd seen the moves on TV shows and marveled how you could do that, remember all the steps and swing your hips that way, coordinating side-to-side pushes in unison. I had a yearning to do that, to understand counterbalance, to take special steps in sequence. I didn't know then it was called choreography, and the prospect of doing it was quickly bulldozed.

Julie had said about it: how dorky. Everything was dorky except what we were doing in Pierce Woods.

It was getting dark. Time for real supper. "I got one!" I said.

"No you didn't," Julie said.

"I did. Nia saw. Didn't you?" Nia gave Julie a hopeful look. It didn't matter. Julie didn't like it when Nia took my side. The two of them were perfect friends before I came along.

"See?" I dangled my rod over Julie's head, my invisible fish hanging right in front of her face. She needed to see. I was capable of great things.

She snapped the fish off of my line and threw it back into the water. "It's diseased," she said and turned away from it and pretended to puke. That's when I had to accidentally crack my fishing pole over Julie's head.

"What the hell?" Julie's face looked rubber with surprise. Her eyes glittered.

"You're not hurt," I said.

It was exactly what she would say to me.

The hat she was wearing cushioned the blow, and truthfully, that reduced my satisfaction. I would have loved to see her cry. For once.

"It's time for you to take a ride in an airplane," Julie said. "Huh, Nia?"

Nia nodded, solemn.

"We are pioneers," I protested.

"We're done with that."

Before I could say anything more, Nia grabbed me from behind, and Julie pulled my feet toward her. Even though I kicked out at her they both got enough leverage to throw me in the pooled melt water. It lapped up to my chin and splashed my face. My whole back was wet and my boots completely filled. I pushed my mittened hands into the water to get up and the freezing temperatures went through me up to my temple. Both of them laughed as I dripped and sloshed out of the park. When I charged at them they ran home.

MY PARENTS HAD staked out their own territory, finding their own Pierce Woods to hide out in. Dad's friendship with Daria was a sign my parents were pulling apart. As long as regular meals were on the table and clean clothes available, I didn't worry too much about the tensions between Ma and Dad. They generally held their fights until we went to bed, and skulked through chores during the day. Sometimes Dad would throw down a tool and hiss "goddamit" or Ma would slap plates around the table with a half-stated pronouncement like "you kids better not . . ." before dinner. Adults always appeared mercurial to me; it was their natural state of being.

Then Dad was hospitalized for a nervous breakdown, which was both surprising and inevitable. Years later when I found myself in a similarly unstable frame of mind, I understood that among many possible causes, a crushing lack of self-worth and confidence had probably overwhelmed him. He was trapped between the abject poverty of his childhood and reckoning with an alleged American Dream, of being a married man with children who found himself spellbound by a vivacious young woman, he was a man who knew few kind words growing up and tried all his life to make up for it, but didn't know what to do about it all. He crashed.

Relatives and friends came by to care for us and console Ma, telling me and my siblings that Dad had gone to the hospital for a rest. My sister intentionally lost her glasses, our dog dug its way out from under the fence, my brother got in trouble for pushing kids on the playground. At school we all got shots and were checked for lice. Girls my age were checked for scoliosis and I was determined "borderline" so nobody did anything about it.

Dad came home looking pale and shaky. By then frost had demeaned and dried the tomato plant branches and melon vines. While he was gone, I'd eaten one of the tiny melons, breaking it open on a rock to scoop out the cooled flesh with my fingers. It tasted surprisingly good, but when he got back, I withheld from him the satisfaction of knowing it was delicious. I assumed it would push him over the deep end again by admitting I was the melon thief. I kept my questions to myself. Did he quit loving Ma? Did he hate us kids? Did he not want to be our father?

I'd always assumed that crazy was someone ranting in a straightjacket on TV, not your own father sitting in the kitchen quietly chain smoking.

Nia and Julie explained. I was from a peculiar family, strange, not normal. Like aliens.

So I spent even more afternoons after school and weekends huddled with Julie and Nia in Pierce Woods.

The oaks bowed to us. They had to. We grabbed sticks and whipped their bark until we nearly cried—we would never be transcendent beauties or smart enough to conquer the world. I understood that the grace and splendor I aspired to was simply a mirage. We told each other so, our two-faced selves always right. Who would ever understand why we did this?

When I could hold it in no longer, I flat footed it toward the west side of the park without Julie and Nia to be chased by the boys. They called me ugly, ugly, ugly. They tackled me, felt me up, pulled my hair, and sometimes punched me. Everyone wound up in a pile of punches, me at the bottom. We were all feeling pent up, angry, ardent. Other girls were not being pounded on like that. But I believed girls should be scrappy fighters, not tattle-tales.

I enjoyed kicking away at the boys' limbs to defend myself and the whole wide world felt good when I felt soft belly flesh give way to my foot or crooked elbow. It was worth the effort it took to fight them, the soreness afterward. With every motion I was defying them: I was going to own this place and nobody was going to hold me back. I punched away at the things that gnawed at me—my ugliness most of all. Afterward, I shook from exhaustion, feeling winded and triumphant.

I knew who was acting crazy and I hid from the thought.

I DIDN'T CRY when I told Julie and Nia we were moving away but they did. The two of them never expected that the year we spent scheming in Pierce Woods for a different life would actually result in one—for me. We were moving to Alabama to be near my grandparents, for the warmth, fresh air and a new start. I hoped I could disappear entirely into another Pierce Woods.

After our little carpenter-built house was sold, my parents packed up our household and loaded up a trailer. Julie came over to my house and gave me a musical Nutcracker ballet snow globe as a goodbye gift. She whispered in my ear, "For you. From Kresge's." The Dance of the Snowflakes. To remember winter. I didn't say goodbye to Nia.

We left on a dark snow-packed morning. No lights on in any of the houses on the block winked a goodbye.

The seat belt I had on chafed. I held the snow globe so it wouldn't get broken, heavy from patchy solidarity. The ballerina inside had her arms up over her head in a permanent reach. She was getting ready to fly. She lived in mini snowstorms that made me heartsick every time I shook the globe. I remembered the oaks of Pierce Woods and how the leaves at the tippy top of the trees always reached so high, persuading the elements to trace through the leaves and branches all the way down to the roots. If I could, I'd stand on my toes, like the ballerina in the snow globe, in a pose that lifted me up over the treetops.

II

Hip Accents
and Shimmies

5

I WAS JUST not getting it. I needed to master an important basic move: the three-quarter shimmy. Without it, I could not progress to the next level of my new dance studies. Marcie offered to help me.

Marcie opened the door and welcomed me in. She pointed to a big pile of shoes at the door, and I took mine off and entered her living room in stocking feet.

I showed up at Marcie's apartment with a tote bag containing a hip scarf and finger cymbals. I touched hands for bravery before I knocked. I was in the neighborhood everyone moves to post-college. The street was filled with late model cars, bikes locked to anything that didn't move, and porches that held ratty couches and cigarette butt containers. The whole diorama made me shiver. I was thirty-seven years old, long past college. I didn't belong there. Belly dance had taken me so far, but it could not make up for lost years.

I worked with Marcie at the food co-op where we were employed. Marcie and I discovered our mutual love of belly dance when she told me about a performance she did as the featured dancer with a local band.

She always walked as if she was part of a posture commercial, shoulders back and relaxed, her head forward, hips that slid sweetly in their sockets. Marcie moved all day between grocery aisles and customers in a pleasing panther gait. I ran around in a hurry, shoulders hunched, exuding proficient neurosis.

On the wall across from the couch was a mural of a nude woman. She floated in space above the TV, her hair flowing, feet off of the ground.

"Wow," I said about the funky earth goddess image.

"Yeah. My roomie did that." Marcie lived with two other women who were big on female empowerment.

"Inspiring," I said. Only to be nice. Despite all the time I'd put in with various women's groups, locker rooms, saunas, hot springs, and hammams, nudity still unsettled me, my own most of all.

I remembered the battered women's shelter I volunteered at for a time. A portrait of an earth mother had been painted on the living room wall there. She was (thankfully) fully clothed and was surrounded by babies and vegetables. The three couches in the room faced the painting. Kids' toys were all over the floor. It was just like years ago when I used to babysit for women in the neighborhood. Helping women in trouble who had problems with childcare.

I put my coat on the couch while Marcie went to the kitchen. I ignored the nude and her poignant brown nipples and put my hip scarf on my waist, knotted just so on my left hip and tucked up onto my right hip.

Marcie set two glasses of water on the table and motioned me to follow her. She invited me to sit with her on the carpet on the living room floor. We needed to warm up. I lay on the floor next to Marcie and felt the knobs of my back as we breathed together, relaxing the stomach, relaxing the back. We did leg lifts and stood and stretched out each side of our torsos.

"So you're having some difficulties with your shimmy," she said when we were done warming up.

Every time I practiced the shimmy I looked like I had a terrible autoimmune system condition. My body filled with unbidden shakes and tremors I couldn't figure out how to stop or start. When I used to watch *Soul Train* as a girl, I always hoped for that crazy feeling when I danced along to the show. My failed attempts to shimmy left me feeling vetoed, out of place and time. Out of control. A three-quarter shimmy showed you knew what you are doing. A beautiful shimmy looked uncanny and supernatural. If I could do it, I would hold in my possession one of the secrets of the universe: how to be strong and alluring. The three-quarter shimmy was one of the tests. If I passed it, I could begin to call myself a belly dancer.

"I can't," I told her and opened my empty hands toward her. She looked me in the eye, evaluating the job at hand. My problems were way beyond shimmies.

I have also been to group therapy. Sitting there with Marcie felt a lot like it. The expected need to reveal my angst in a room with an image of a liberated woman on the wall. I was always surprised by the things that made me cry in group—the fear of public speaking and being misunderstood by my parents—but everyone who has been to therapy has cried about those things. Talking about rape didn't make me cry. Instead, I felt a hardening inside. A reflex to hold myself still against memories I tried to ignore. My body became inflexible and stiff. Marcie's kind concern about my shimmy could also make me cry. It was hard to accept her generosity.

I really wasn't that good at helping women at the shelter. They liked the talkative take-charge staff members—who wouldn't? I was too scared someone's abuser was going to figure out where the shelter was and blow us all to kingdom come.

Marcie's teeth gleamed with confidence when she said in her trained singer's voice, "Show me what you've been doing." She would have been a good counselor at the shelter.

I took a step forward and pushed my right hip out, and then pushed it the other way and stepped, and oh, it was all wrong. I clenched my fists in frustration. I was trying to master a move where the thighs and hips reverberate softly, creating a captivating shimmy in motion. It is a quintessentially feminine movement. Done well it is smooth, nuanced and enthralling.

My hips were stone tendons.

THAT FIRST SEMESTER in college I had lost my foothold. Quit studying. Spent my days skipping class to go to the library where I would read novels, but not the ones for any of my classes. I signed up for an additional six-week course that everyone claimed was an easy A—the "leadership" class—where all you had to do was show up and follow marching orders (literally) given by students in the Reserve Officer Training Corp. I had told Marcie about that, and she laughed.

Young men in starched blue shirts shouted at student loafers like me, "Order! About face! March! Left, left, left-right." I held the edges of my sweater in my palms and shuffled about in cowboy boots. That wasn't so hard, but as soon as the Rotzie yelled, "Column right" or "Reverse" I would always screw up. Marching is walking, but turning on command turned out to be tricky. I was always the one breaking the line.

I missed two Leadership classes without an excuse, and couldn't follow directions when I was there. Could I turn left or right on command? No. I stood there, totally lost, the army's choreography a complete bust. A noncommissioned officer talked to me after class as if I could understand what he was saying.

So I left. Right, left.

I WALKED STRAIGHT into trouble when I'd met Griffin in the middle of that first semester. Griffin had a corner room on the fourth floor of my dorm and in his window he'd put up a poster with a hand-lettered sign that said Give Peace a Chance. John Lennon had been murdered December 8, 1980, in our senior year of high school, and although Griffin was terminally upset that his musical hero was dead, his grief wasn't the whole reason for the sign.

The sign was a guidepost in the pre-internet pre-cell phone era for kids who wanted to buy drugs. Griffin sold an impressive array of pills, pot, and acid that he kept meticulously stored in his dorm room bolster: jars, envelops, and bags displayed impeccably in retail fashion. He was an incredibly clean and entrepreneurial young man. His room was spotless, he made his bed every day, and he would always be available to make a deal, any time of the day or night.

I would learn what all those things he sold could do, the postage-stamp sized acid blotters, misshapen shrooms, the black uppers, and red downers. I always held off against the acid, and much preferred the pills over pot, although I smoked plenty. I didn't think about mixing those pills and pot with drinking. I wouldn't have called myself suicidal, but being fucked up was both my greatest fear and biggest attraction. In my relationship with Griffin I was placating two monsters.

Griffin took after his father who was a driven executive at a paper company in Green Bay, and his dad had a beautiful and impeccable home on the lake. Griffin was the child of divorce and grew up disassociated from real affection, placated by toys, a new car, motorcycle, television, you name it. Griffin's main task in life, according to his dad, was "not to fuck up." Which Griffin did every day, on the sly, parlaying his allowance to further his drug dealing. His major was accounting, but it seemed like he had no need for Whitewater's curriculum. He was a natural businessman.

Griffin was handsome in a classic Nordic way. He was tall with a full head of blonde hair, striking, kaleidoscopic blue eyes, thin fingers, and an aggressive manner. He wore Izod shirts and rugby jerseys, not the first thing you imagine when you think of drug dealer attire. When I knew him, he drove an orange Mustang sports car, and everything he did was overt and theatrical. I'd known of his existence in the dorm, had seen him speeding around town in his car, prowling the campus sidewalks between classes, but I had never been introduced to him. On a seasonably warm day in early March, Griffin had placed a blanket on the lawn in front of our dorm. He had a few books out there with him, presumably studying, but he'd been obsessively plucking at the lawn. I was just coming back from the Leadership class that I'd been attending half-heartedly, and my backpack dug into my shoulders. It was heavy with books, including one of the Norton anthologies on short stories. I'd just read Hemingway's "The Hills Like White Elephants," and Tillie Olsen's "I Stand Here Ironing." The bitter realities of motherhood in Olsen's story made infinitely more sense to me than a man's story about a woman's inability to communicate her objections to having an abortion. But I should have paid more attention to the connections between the two narratives in my own story.

"Patty, right?" Griffin said as I approached. He patted the blanket. "Come sit." His invitation was strange and irresistible. Disarming. Calculating. I sat down, as if I were a cool girl, like Rita Brooks, the kind of girl who was happy to put down my backpack and hang out with a fellow co-ed. I sat on the blanket, stiff in the prison of my own skin.

"I'm Griffin. Griff." He held something green from the lawn pinched between his thumb and forefinger. I felt equally plucked out and held up to scrutiny. I waited for the verdict. Detection of my fall from grace, recognition of my film of ugliness.

"You are perfectly beautiful," he said, "like this blade of grass." He had perceived my vulnerability and positively identified it with the dexterity of a private investigator. He handed the grass to me. It was green and unremarkable. I held on to the gravity of the moment the way young romantics do. Griffin was unconventional and courtly, didn't swear or stumble on his grammar, and I liked that. I let myself be wooed.

Of course I was a big fat idiot when it came to Griffin. I refused to acknowledge that my boyfriend was a sophisticated brute. Even against my own survival instincts. He'd beg me to sleep over and either screw me with no foreplay, or fall asleep with a limp dick that he'd try poking into me. He dropped acid almost every weekend, and as long as I was his "girlfriend" I was also his babysitter while he was tripping. I prevented him from streaking and talked him down when he said that he was surrounded by retards.

Chrissy told me she thought Griffin was odd. "Not that you shouldn't date him," she qualified. His idiosyncratic nonconformity drew notice, and I felt the heightened awareness of other people's interest. I liked being part of the attention, as if we were the campus Bonnie and Clyde.

We never dated, just met up for meals occasionally in the campus cafeteria or hung out in his room. Griffin had zero appetite because the uppers he liked to take kept him hyper and strung out. Real food was his last priority. He subsisted on cheese puffs and Doritos.

Once I told him I was tired of watching him get high all the time and he grabbed my arm so hard I cried out from pain. "Shut up," he told me. "That's what women do." I was hurt and angry when he did it, but I decided to let it slide. I didn't know that complicity was part of the pattern of abuse.

Sometimes we took rides in the country, the roads like tunnels in the cornfields. He would drift over into the left-hand lane, someone's headlights in the distance waking the night, yelling at me, "Do you want to die? Do you?"

I'd conceded to the same seismic tremors of self-doubt as my father, and could barely discern the invisible wire of want connecting addiction and abuse spiraling through my life. It swelled beneath my skin, and pushed into my blood and bones, where it stayed.

IN MARCIE'S APARTMENT, my eyes were riveted to her buoyant hips.

"Let's start just one-two for now." Marcie snapped her right hip up and then her left. Right and left, right and left. I followed along easily. It was satisfying to be able to physically command each hip. "Now pick up your feet with each hip." I did. She turned around to watch me.

"Real slow, we'll start real slow. Right, left, right, in a Z, and at the same time you're also stepping with your feet. Same foot with the same hip."

Real slow. I remembered why I took belly dance in the first place. To feel exhilaration. To release humiliation. Give my body the permission to feel relief. Consolation.

Why, then, did the three-quarter shimmy have to be so hard? I'd picked a very layered and complex dance, one with ancient origins, to hurl my recalcitrant body into, that's why. There would always be something to master. Belly dance moves are almost always focused on contracting and releasing core muscle groups—it gives the dance its dynamic tension. Likewise my long-dormant physical awareness and suppressed mental acumen would follow the same pattern of opening and closing.

Marcie walked over to the water glasses on the table and handed one to me.

"Let's take a little break."

I drank down the water in gigantic gulps, breathed hard when I set the glass down. Marcie looked at me, concern shaded her features.

She put on some different music. I heard the opening strains to *Leyelet Hob.* "Night of Love." It's one of the classics. "Let's just walk and do hip hits." I followed Marcie around into her dining room, into her living room. I was hitting each hip and walking on the beat. I followed Marcie's hips as if they were the Rosetta stone, and my mimicry was passable.

"The shimmy is a rhythmic vibration from knees, to thighs, to hips. Watch." She pumped her knees right and left and the miniscule bit of flab on her ass jiggled. "It's just a matter of practice. Shimmy as you walk between rooms. Shimmy at the sink when you're doing dishes."

Ma was always at the sink or stove. Or with the vacuum, or in the basement sorting the laundry, or keeping my youngest sister from crawling in the dog's food. The drumbeat she danced to was whiney kids, spare change thrown on a dresser, the clatter of dishes in the drying rack. Could she have ever learned how to shimmy? What if she had the time to indulge in such a practice on Saturday afternoon? How would her life have been different?

Marcie and I spent our days working at the food co-op explaining to people how to cook quinoa and educating them about herbal remedies. Marcie and I inhabited the well-informed underpaid Minneapolis world of peaceniks, artists, food service wage earners, and environmentalists. People who thought all manner of artistic expression was cool. One of our co-op's members was a famous gay performance artist. Another was known for starting the local Kale Revolution by wearing only leafy greens over his dong in the annual Mayday parade. The very people my diligent blue-collar family warned me about getting mixed up with when I left home.

When I told my grandma at Thanksgiving I was taking belly dance she thought I was stripping, and Ma didn't think a woman should shake her "hinder," as she put it, in public. It would have been easier to disregard their opinions if I didn't love them so much. What they believed stayed in my blood and body long after I had rejected it in principle. It caused shimmy problems among other side effects.

"Now. Three quarter." Marcie drew a compressed letter Z in the air in front of my hips. "That's what the hips are doing. The shimmy comes when you do that and let go."

"Show me," I told her. She shimmy walked to the built-in buffet in her dining room and walked back to the living room. Her hips were toned, rhythmic. Beautiful. "Notice how I didn't bob my head or bounce up and down? It's all about being smooth, putting the emphasis on the lower part of your body."

Together we practiced the hip zig zag. Right left right, left right left. My feet started out feeling like blocks and my hips dragged along in time.

I BROKE UP with Griffin at the end of second semester and moved back home. I considered "counseling" but knew therapy was something only other people did. Not me.

Instead, I buried myself in books. I found an essay by F. Scott Fitzgerald who wrote in *The Crack-Up*, "Of course all life is a process of breaking down, but the blows that do the dramatic side of the work— the big sudden blows that come, or seem to come from outside— the ones you remember and blame things on and, in moments of weakness, tell your friends about, don't show their effect all at once. There is another sort of blow that comes from within—that you don't feel until it's too late to do anything about it."

Fitzgerald had me all turned around. Was it too late? Or was it that the realization something can hurt you comes too late? Was it possible to change that? I didn't appreciate that Fitzgerald was talking about maturity, trying not to be self-pitying or morose, but looking at things from the clear, cold pool of recognition. It would take me half a lifetime to understand that impetus myself. To view the past not as something to be defeated or left behind, but as something to acknowledge and understand.

I started to have a recurring dream that was a direct result of my subconscious pushing me to see the danger of my condition.

I had dreams of panthers roaming my bedroom, pacing, pacing, pacing. Nights felt charged and cold like the time when I was five, and I nearly killed myself by sticking my fingers in an electric socket. I still remember how utterly alien that felt, the strange and compelling vibration of pain and pleasure before my ma slapped my hand away.

It wasn't the last time Ma had found me on the brink.

When I moved home, Ma and Dad warned me about corrupting my siblings (too late). My parents knew I smoked pot because someone's kid from church had narced me out. They told me they were concerned about it and they prayed about it too, asking Jesus to guide me. I'm sure they knew things were deeply wrong, but they never asked me what was troubling me. They didn't know about the other drugs I'd done, or that my situation was of the sort that potentially lands a person in rehab. Yet the routine of family life, regular meals, and the re-establishment of the sibling pecking order put me back on an even keel. I veered off the path of budding addict and became a druggie opportunist instead. I would do them if they turned up in social situations, but I didn't seek them out. I tried harder to be the example of goodness my parents wanted me to be.

For weeks after we broke up, I got love letters in the mail from Griffin in stout loopy handwriting with call-me phone messages. When Ma handed me the letters she would look at me with exasperation whitewashing her features. We never talked about Griffin, but she knew Griffin was bad news.

One day out of the blue, he drove his motorcycle two hundred miles from his hometown to tell me how much he loved me, needed me, and wanted me back. He stood at the backdoor while I listened, hesitated. His blond curls trembled and his blue eyes reflected the sky. As I listened to his entreaties I remembered what it felt like to be embraced by him—the firm sinew of his body, the beguiling smell of smoke and laundry soap in his clothes—the vertigo-inducing rides on country roads. He touched my fingers through the door screen. I stood wiggling my toes and flexing my bare feet. I could do it. Just get on the back of his motorcycle and go.

My mother's words spit behind me. As she made her way to the door and pushed me aside, I'm not sure if she was talking to me or him. "You. Get out of here. Now." Ma threatened him with the cops. "Got that?" She was ten feet tall, a she-bear. His protests were surprisingly weak, my backbone mush. Moments later I watched him start up his motorcycle, peevishness pulsing through his leather jacket as he steered his bike out of the alleyway.

"Good riddance," Ma said to me and to the air outside before she headed back into the belly of the house.

I stood there a long time. I looked at the scrappy grass in our yard, browning in the sun's glare, and thought about what had happened.

I still considered making a run for it by the time Dad got home from work, six hours after Griffin's appearance. That evening, I heard the familiar crunch of gravel underneath our family's station wagon as Dad pulled into the driveway. The sun had made its shift to the western part of the sky. The backyard that glowed too hot and bright was cool and shadowed. I sat at the table, looking out the window at my father coming over the grass toward the door. He walked as if every blade hurt his feet.

I was wedged between excitement and the rest of time. I'd taken all the clothes I had in my closet off their hangers and threw them on the floor in a chaotic sort. Gave the college sweatshirt to my sister. Found a feather boa I'd forgotten about. Made a pile for Goodwill. Put on a pair of cowboy boots. Faced with the mounds of wrinkled and spent fabric, I waited for Griffin to get my telepathic message to come back for me. I was lightened, but not liberated.

As Dad opened the back door, Ma stood ready in the kitchen. Words omitted her mouth. She had stopped me. A kettle of water boiled and sang. A cigarette lighter clicked. They both turned to look at me.

Dad tried to show me how to change a car tire once, insisting that I learn so I could take care of myself. I couldn't get a single lug nut to budge. "You have to worry it loose," he told me, showing me how to tap it with a hammer. I remember fighting madly against gravity and too-tight bolts instead, and using my foot to leverage my weight against the tire iron. "Don't do that," he'd said, and in one startling gasp the nut released and my foot slammed so hard to the ground I could have broken it. I knew my father would never stop loving me, but as I hopped around the yard in pain I believed he gave up trying to help me.

I held an empty coffee mug in my hand. In my mind's eye, I was surveying a food scrap bowl and empty beer can pile, appraising a ruined woman, seeing myself spin through the arms of all those boys and men. I was calculating my fortune as my mother's daughter as my tongue pushed hard against my teeth.

I FOLLOWED MARCIE some more, *Layelet Hob* still blasting from her music player. I wanted to know deep in my marrow what I was doing, and why I was so determined to learn despite the contrary evidence related to my dance talent. Why did it matter that one more woman in the world knew how to three-quarter shimmy? What would Dad, Griffin, or even Daria the bunny think of me as I stumbled around Marcie's living room as her clumsy acolyte?

As Marcie marched me back and forth, it occurred to me that it was my lack of faith in myself and others that had been the problem. Caused my mind to spin and my hips to twist off course. That feeling that I was left alone to figure things out simply was not true.

After some time with Marcie, the movements began to feel more normal, driving away the winter air in my bones. I had seconds where the shimmy walk was fluid, sensuous, fun. I got a fleeting understanding of what it meant to walk, sway, and shimmy. Marcie framed my hips with her hands. "Show it off when you got it, sister." The nude on the living room wall officially notarized the motion.

It was what I'd hoped for when I decided to take Marcie up on her offer to give me a lesson.

The shimmy created an opening, a tremulous and small scaffolding. It vibrated through me from the bottom of my feet to the seat of my pelvis.

6

BEDLAH. THAT'S THE word for a belly dancer's beaded bra and belt set. In Arabic, *bedlah* means "suit" and in this case it is used to describe a certain type of costume for dance. It is what most people associate with belly dance, apart from the hip shaking. Even today, most Americans think of the TV show *I Dream of Jeannie* and the actress Barbara Eden when they think of belly dancers. She had become the world's most famous two-thousand-year-old suggestive genie in a two-piece outfit with harem pants—from hedonistic Babylon—wearing what appeared to be modified *bedlah*. She embodied an ongoing fantasy. She was a spicy, sensual woman with wish-granting powers. I fell for Jeannie. I didn't immediately question why she lived with a man she called "master" and decided to ditch her superpowers and be his housewife. And at twelve years old, I especially liked her outfit—the crop top and harem pants. Her body seemed plush and elastic in those clothes, and I speculated if I'd ever be that womanly.

The two-piece cabaret belly dance costume often looks like the lovechild of a showgirl. It's a costume that takes an exuberant liking to beaded fringe, sequins, coins, rhinestones, and all manner of flashy, decorative embroidery. What you want your costume to look like depends on your taste. But also what you want the costume to look like, and do, for your body while dancing.

The classic American *bedlah* is a beaded fringe bra and belt set with a full circle skirt. This is the kind of costume that best shows off the intricacies of a vibrational shimmy or staccato chest or hip drops because the beaded fringe will move with the dancer and reflect the light and the movement. The skirt will also convey its own movement and drama as the dancer turns. You won't see any knees pumping or bending under the full skirt, promoting the illusion that the hips are moving of their own volition. Other costumes, with a sleek body conscious mermaid or straight skirt will enhance slinky movements, like undulations. Some of these costumes have a couture quality and dancers pick them to best show their dancer physique.

Before the advent of the internet and companies that import ready-made costumes, women in the 1960s and '70s sewed their own belly dance costumes. Getting the accoutrements to decorate them required scouring fabric stores and ethnic markets. It took a great deal of patience and sewing skill to create costumes that fit well, held up under the rigors of performance, and didn't look substandard. Often those costumes could not be washed but were sponge-bathed and aired out or smoked with fragrant incense to best preserve the fabrics and decorations.

Respected dancers, most of them from the Middle East who had settled in the U.S. or Canada in the 1950s and '60s, often had local dance apprentices who helped them sew costumes and maintain them in exchange for training. Dance schools and classes in Middle Eastern dance had not been formally established, and those apprentices often got an in-depth first-hand understanding of the music and traditions of the country their virtuosos had come from. It was a short-lived and bygone era of close cultural exchange facilitated by live entertainment at Middle Eastern restaurants. Sometimes those dancers of status would bestow upon their apprentice a costume to show appreciation and recognize that she had finally made it as a dancer. It was an old-fashioned and quaint tradition, one that has largely disappeared over the decades. Today's teachers still mentor students, though, and they feel mutually blessed by the relationship.

To me the *bedlah* has always signified a level of dance mastery, but having my own bra and belt set still feels like an extravagance to me. Do I deserve to wear it? Is my dancing good enough? When I consider *bedlah*, it conjures up a before and after portrait in both its gleaming appearance, and my ability to wear it confidently.

I also consider it a definite marker in time when I got mine— the year 2000. Long before I was emotionally prepared to perform, I bought a beaded *bedlah*, and having it was an outward symbol of change even if I didn't wear it. It made me realize there is certainly a before *bedlah* life, and an after *bedlah* life.

GOVERNOR WALLACE LEERED his segregationist welcome to folks like ourselves on the giant billboard at the Alabama state line. I was twelve and it was 1975. Wallace was notorious for being against pinkos, niggers, anarchists, and hippies. Ma and Dad were apolitical and socially conservative, but they didn't like Wallace's abominable campaigns and racist rhetoric. Ma had hissed her disapproval as we passed the border, and called him a "creep." He sure looked like one. Since his assassination attempt, Wallace was often in a wheelchair, looking every inch like the rapacious Mr. Potter in the movie *It's a Wonderful Life*. I twisted restlessly in the car as we passed through Wilmer, then Semmes, and then down a winding red clay road to Grandma and Grandpa's trailer. If the way to the spirit is through the body, mine was being restrained by my held breath. Down south was where my father's emotional frailties were formed, and it was another place of induction in the art of long-suffering womanhood.

We rode the way down the clay road, spongy and dotted with mysterious dark things, to where my grandparents lived. Their rusting, powder-blue trailer home was stationed between tall, skinny pine trees that showered foot-long needles on the grassless yard, giving it an unnatural lift and bounce. Going south was powerfully stirring and strangely nauseating. As I looked up at the tops of those different pines, puffy and brown against the scrubbed sky, a combination of the sights, smells, and tropical humidity made my head swirl. I left the snow globe that Julie gave me in the car. The vision I'd held for one thousand miles—of sugar plum fairies and dreamy ballet—seemed utterly capricious in that humid rustic habitat.

Grandma was first out to greet us, wending her way between the coffee cans filled with houseplants that decorated the dooryard. Everywhere I looked there were bold red cans bearing the visage of a turbaned man sipping coffee, plants pouring out of his head. Someday I'd go to places where men wore turbans and drank undrinkable strong coffee in tiny cups. The southern relations drank so much coffee, as well as sweetened iced tea, that Grandma always gave me an empty can "to put things in" before we left. That time we were there to stay.

Her hunched form nimbly moved forward to grab one of us around the waist. I'd reached for her slight waist and low bony hips.

She exclaimed with a toothless smile, "Well, how you doin', sugar?"

She was only about four-foot-two and humpbacked from years of picking cotton. She refused to wear her false teeth, an act of rebellion no one could understand then. Ma said the advent of modern dentistry made them wearable and Grandma was too stubborn to change her ways. But they probably were ill-fitting and hurt too much to wear. Because of it, her voice sounded like it came through a pennywhistle, high pitched, melodic, a tad slurred. She looked like a benign leprechaun, and acted like one—at once idiot savant and sharper than the pine knots that people used to start fires with. Grandma's hugs squeezed the breath out of me with hurricane force.

WHEN I HOLD my bra and belt set in my hands I let the beads slide cool and lustrous through my fingers. It's probably the last thing you would imagine a sharecropper's granddaughter would possess, but having it in my hands is tangible proof of my momentum. My grandma wouldn't have approved of my wearing it, but I like to think that the way the costume was made would have pleased her. Nearly everything my grandma did, she did with her hands.

A woman named Gina sewed the costume when she was an aspiring restaurant dancer. Gina grew up in Minnesota, and like me, found herself living in urban Minneapolis, attracted to an art form her family thought was questionable. She didn't have money to buy a premade costume, and by the time she sold it to me, it had been in countless solo performances on the Mediterranean Cruise stage.

It was made with a modified bra, probably from Victoria's Secret, that was covered with iridescent lace and tacked down with binding ribbon so the elastic would not stretch. Rows upon rows of beaded gold fringe and bright gold palettes descend from the top and bottom of the bra and the base of the belt. Each strand is knotted so the ends of the beaded fringe do not come unraveled. Both the bra and belt are trimmed in gold sequins. The palettes are attached in a random pattern and catch and reflect the light. Depending on the stage lights, it can be dazzling if you look at them straightaway.

I doubt Gina ever submerged the costume in water, and I never have. Surprisingly the costume does not stink, and I am certain every time I've ever worn it, I sweated when I danced. I've kept it resting in a cloth-lined box so the fabric won't be stressed being on a hanger. Surely Gina did too. It has the smell of a stuffed futon instead, like the grassy smell of cotton batting with a muslin cover. Go figure.

Gina wore this *bedlah* multiple evenings a week for two years and danced with velvet panels draped from her waist front and back, instead of skirt. She had long blonde hair that plummeted to her waist, and had the most beautiful side-to-side Tunisian-style hip twists I had ever seen. When she wore it in performance, the costume appeared to animate her determination as well as enhance her body's movements. Gina saved up tips, what she called "belly bucks" to upgrade her costume wardrobe, and used the experience to move her performances from the restaurant venue to a theater stage. Not an easy feat. When I bought the well-worn costume from her, I thought of it as a hard-wearing stepping stone on a path I hoped was designated by splendor and action.

When I hold my own bra and belt set next to my skin I can't help but think about all the incongruous things I've tried to release and save. What wearing the costume conjures up: being judged because beads are dripping off my boobs and I am being ridiculous, and the hope of walking through a doorway and seeing myself and the women in my family changed, the striking and extraordinary things about us suddenly seen in a luminous light.

THE WHOLE FIVE months we lived down south in 1975 I felt big and weird. I towered over my grandmother and Southern aunts. My nasal northern accent sounded snotty to my cousins who asked me who was I trying to be. I was trying, on occasion, to be more like them, and hunched my shoulders to be smaller, petite. They wore dresses and skirts every day because they believed shorts and pants were a sin for a woman to wear. They were Seventh Day Adventists, which meant that they took the Bible's stories as the only true source of spiritual belief. I was sophisticated enough then to know that nobody in the Bible commanded women not to wear shorts. I didn't argue, and kept my own shorts on. I was starting to understand that the world was full of contradictions when it came to religious beliefs and secular practice. For instance, you could be a rabid Christian virgin girl and still have a heart full of lust.

One day my older cousin Sarah Ann hauled a *Tiger Beat* magazine out of her purse and called me over to the swing on her porch (she lived in an actual house not a trailer). *Tiger Beat* is a fanzine still published for adolescent girls that had its heyday in the 1970s, featuring teenage boy bands and soft-rock stars like Donny Osmond and David Cassidy.

She said she wanted to fix me up.

"Look here," she kindly advised. I was flattered she deigned to talk to me. I considered her look glamorous. She wore a blue dress that accentuated her small waist. My cousin's blond hair was sprayed and feathered on each side. She wore heavy blue eye shadow (that my aunt didn't approve of) over eyes that looked bright and glassy. Sarah Ann was called boy crazy by everyone. Yet nobody questioned her good-girl status except me.

"You'll never get a boyfriend looking and acting the way you do," she sweetly drawled. My unkempt pixie haircut, forsaken scoliosis, and scabbed knees were definitely outside the realm of the feminine ideal, especially down south where ladylikeness seemed even more rigorous.

Sarah Ann's southern adaptation was to be controlling and composed.

"Now sit down and tell me which one you want."

I searched through black-and-white pages of boys who looked identical: bangs falling over the eyebrows, unbuttoned or no shirts, hairless chests, tight jeans, and maybe holding a guitar. The center of *Tiger Beat* contained a full length color photo. Soft-peddled male sexuality for innocent girls. It was irresistible. I licked my lips and rolled my tongue behind my unevenly spaced teeth. I felt wary assessing boys' bodies this way, yet speculated what those smooth chests felt like. I didn't know where to place my longing for it, either. I curled into myself on the porch swing next to Sarah Ann.

"This one's Eric from the Bay City Rollers. You know them? They sing 'Keep on Dancing.' Isn't he a hunk? I'm putting him up by my bed tonight."

"Are Seventh Day Adventists allowed to do that?" Sarah Ann looked thrown, uneasy.

I was graceless and clumsy. Of course not. She was sharing her contraband with me.

"Oh," I said. We were two unworldly girls aching for excitement, but too naïve to understand how eager the world we lived in wanted to corrupt us first. Our girlish boredom was expected and channeled by powerful forces outside ourselves, and its intensity was conducted by the sensual currents in *Tiger Beat*, stirring our inevitable restlessness.

I looked at the boy. He had long hair that covered his eyes. No shirt, but he had a tartan scarf draped over his chest like a beauty queen. Eric Faulkner. "Keep on Dancing." It went something like this: *shake it shake it shake it shake it. Show me how you work.* The fearful flutter and anxiety those words set in motion would eventually change into eagerness when I did learn how to properly shimmy. But a whole way of life I couldn't understand was pressed into that boy's scarf.

"I think he's a fucking gay wad," I said. It felt cool to say it, like something Julie would say in Pierce Woods.

Sarah Ann snapped the *Tiger Beat* closed, rolled it up, and smacked my arm with it. "I think he's sensitive. That's more than I can say about you."

I ALWAYS THINK about the words to the Bay City Rollers song "Keep on Dancing." *Shake it, shake it, shake it. Show me how you work* when I wear *bedlah.* The anxiety I felt as a teen about looking at young men's bodies amuses me now, because that apprehension was quickly replaced by worry about my own body.

I had never understood why my body insisted on its own desire while I continually rejected it. I considered my body an unfortunate reality. Because of the fact of it, I singled it out as something to hide away. I was very thin as a child—maybe too skinny—and that contributed to a driftless feeling. I had no weight in my body and therefore no heft to my thoughts. When confronted with the erotic feelings conjured up by my burgeoning sexuality and the young men in *Tiger Beat*, I felt the duality of attraction and fear that made sexual sensations feel wrong. The idea that a girl would want sex seemed dangerous and contradictory. Sex in most circumstances was a sin. I disassociated from my body's desires.

The crazy thing about it is that in so many ways in our society women are reduced to being merely bodies. I rebelled against having one. Women are taught to keep physical expression and anxieties to ourselves as dirty secrets. After I was assaulted, my body's response was unprocessed. I gave in to the pressure to be silent. My fears were too primitive.

Even though it took me a long time to feel like I'd achieved a level of serious accomplishment with belly dance, I bought my bra and belt set during my third year taking lessons. When I first saw it, I had to have it. As Amina held it before me in her outstretched arm on a hanger (Gina was her friend), it appeared full of verve and sass. Just the thing to bolster my courage. I'm also sure that Amina wanted to give me an emotional push, she wasn't giving me a costume like virtuosos did in the old days, but she was expressing her confidence in my ability. For some dancers, earning your rank in a beautiful costume is powerfully motivating. I was moved by its tactile symbolism. As the beads sparkled of their own accord, it was a huge temptation and a want and a need. It wasn't that expensive, but I couldn't afford to buy it outright. In a no-turning-back breath, I bought it. I paid for it in installments. My girlish boredom was long gone, my grandma long deceased, but the sensual currents stirred by the Bay City Rollers lived on. Could *bedlah* expedite my body's creative spirit? I had to find out. Genesis itself swished through those animated beads.

THE BISCUIT RITUAL was always the same. Grandma would reach for her large, plastic, speckled bowl and flour sifter. She'd set the flour sifter in the bowl and fill it with Pillsbury All-Purpose flour straight from the bag. The loose skin on her arm waved freely as she sifted flour into a mound in the bowl. Next, Grandma would grab the can of Clabber Girl baking powder and put some in the palm of her hand until just so and released it into the bowl. She threw in a bit of salt. She put a hand in the flour mound and swirled it around in the bowl. Grandma made decadent biscuits with gravy, smooth like rich chocolate, beans, and okra that satisfied, corn-breaded salmon patties that glowed pink with translucent onions. And sweet iced tea in tall jars that floated more than three ice cubes.

Stuff we never had up north.

"Look here. This isn't hard, sugar," she said, holding court over the bowl, determined that someone pay attention to her making biscuits.

Grandma called everyone sugar.

"Your momma can do this too." She glanced at Ma who was sitting hot and anxious in a metal chair—the kind with legs that pressed little circles into the ancient linoleum floor. Ma shifted her smooth white legs. Legs that were out of place in a rusting, roach-infested trailer. Legs like the kind I really wanted even though I acted like I didn't. I sat quiet. I lacked a presentable grandma with pearls around her neck, wearing a clean frilly apron. Mine was bent crooked like a field hand in a cramped, dim and greasy kitchen. She didn't even use a spoon to stir with. No one up north would believe it.

Grandma took a butter knife and scooped out a blob of Crisco and dropped it into the center of the bowl. I felt something stick in my throat when she asked me to mix the grease and flour with my hands. It used to be my favorite part of every visit, but now I was growing up.

"No, Grandma. I don't think so."

Her shoulders hunched more. She didn't meet my eye.

"That's ok, sugar. You don't need to get all that fat on your hands, anyway." Over cheerful. That's how she sounded.

She began the cutting-in of the shortening and flour in the bowl with her bare hands, squeezing the fat and flour through her fingers. She could have squeezed my neck that way. Once the flour and shortening resembled coarse crumbs, she made a well of the mixture in the bowl and poured in buttermilk.

I was stuck between love and lady hood. That meant spoons not hands. Between standing up straight or hunching. My words "no grandma" replayed in a silent groove.

In dance, your head should rest calmly between the shoulders, expressing grace and courage. From my grandmother, I was learning the gestures of acquiescence.

I loved my grandmother like nobody else in this world. For almost as long as I could write cursive, we sent each other letters monthly, and her letters to me were often barely decipherable as she was nearly illiterate. She bought lined tablets for the sole purpose of letter writing. Her handwriting was large in a wobbly old-fashioned script, round and twisted. She always told me in her letters that Jesus loved me, that I should be a good girl and listen to my parents, and that she also thought I was "perty" and smart. I would send her drawings of horses, goats, princesses, and chickens accompanied by blow-by-blow accounts of my day in school. Word volume was a feature of a letter's quality. Who wouldn't want a big fat letter? When one came for me from her, I loved to read it curled up on the couch, letting Grandma's love and her idiosyncratic syntax encompass me.

Those letters were a sincere source of joy to both of us. That those letters have crumbled to dust in termite infested southern attics and were beset by mold from storage in damp northern basements is a source of real heartache. What I wouldn't give to have another glimpse into her mind and heart—and mine. Of course there would be things I would understand differently, things I couldn't appreciate as a child. Would the abjectness of her life come through in her letters, or not at all? What would be revealed of my discontent? Were there any portents of the future? And why were we such loyal correspondents? I'm certain she loved me even when I was being a brat.

Grandma plunged her hands once again into the bowl and maneuvered the flour and milk together by swirling her fingers into the milk and flour along the edges of the bowl. She continued gently patting the flour and milk mixture until a doughy full moon appeared in the speckled bowl. This biscuit orb was put on the table dusted with flour and pressed flat with her hands. She used a Welch's grape jelly glass as a biscuit cutter.

She finished quickly—expertly—not saying anything. Just once she muttered, "Lordy" to herself, and I was not sure if it was from the heat, the work, or her cold Yankee grandchild. The doughy circles were efficiently placed on the cookie sheet waiting to be popped into the oven.

As Grandma wiped up the table, various pots with dinner boiled on the stove, making the kitchen close with the smell of beans and pork. It was unbearably hot and steamy in the trailer. I noticed Grandma's favorite picture, "Jesus Knocking on the Door to Our Hearts," had faded just a little more since we arrived to live down south. Grandma explained that because there was no doorknob on the outside of the door, only you could let Jesus in. He hung above the small TV, his holy presence was in competition with the rabbit ear antennae of the TV set. He looked like a lost traveler to me, stranded in the trailer with us, white and glowing from the heat.

THE FIRST TIME I wore my beaded *bedlah* it was for a piece my dance class was putting on for the local community center. As the recorded music gurgled out of the speakers, the beaded fringe on my hip belt whipped into a golden froth as I turned. The unfamiliar feeling of something heavy and animate on my hips made me doubt centrifugal force. I forgot whole phrases of the choreography and did what my teacher said to do when you fuck up: do a basic hip movement until you remember what you are doing and fall back into line. I was searching for different neural pathways, ones I hoped would make me more at ease in my own skin. Instead I was messing up a lot, the fringe continually tickling my skin.

The Whirling Dervishes, as the Sufi spinners are known, can whirl for an hour or more to bestow blessings on the Earth. They are lightning rods, taking divine energy and disbursing it. Turkish Sufis from centuries ago practiced whirling by using an upright nail pounded in the floorboards to secure their spot on the floor between the first and second toe. That gave them stability and guidance as they learned, meditated, and turned. What they do isn't considered a performance, even if people buy tickets to watch it, but a religious meditation and an honoring of the spirit.

I remember so many beginners had danced in that exact spot at the community center where I had been and tried to make their mark. I had succumbed to some of the repressed spirits—I couldn't stop them; they will find their kin—cluttering my head with all the ways I could fail. My shoulders hurt, and I hunched. My lips trembled involuntarily. People around me were a blur. The meaning and promise of wearing shimmering *bedlah* had slipped under the bed and hid. My body was shivering in its twinkling costume.

I wasn't ready. What I was doing was not a performance, nor was it a meditation.

MA STARED OUT the screen door of the trailer while we waited for Dad and Grandpa to get in for dinner. All the while we lived down south, it seemed Ma and Dad lived in separate spheres. It seemed Dad was always gone helping my grandpa do something or other, and the gap it created between Ma and Dad extended a prickly tightness between them. Ma was trying to tamp down resentment. Dad was trying to please everyone, but his wife and children were the collateral in an unspoken deal that was unraveling.

We watched my thin and handsome father walk with Grandpa, keeping him from stumbling and falling, leading him toward the trailer path that wound around the coffee cans of potted plants. I had heard Grandpa was considered the "black sheep" of his family. I assumed that had to do with his sharp-eyed look and full head of hair. That year I understood it was the result of his alcoholism. He walked with the exaggerated genteel gait of a drunk. From a distance, he looked good.

Up close, his shoulders were sloped in and his hands were knobbed and hard. He had turned his mind against himself, and it made him mean. He always seemed to be squinting into bright light. Dad said all those years of sharecropping and having stubborn pride did it to him, but that it wasn't no excuse. But I knew Grandpa could be nice if he wanted to be.

"You sure love horses, don't you, girl? Let's go look at some real perty ones," he drawled into the open air one day, his thumbs resting in his belt loops.

He took me in the car to a farm he said he used to work at to let me pet the horses there. As I lavished love on the friendly spotted one, inhaling the musky salt of her mane, the farm owner came and asked Grandpa what kind of son-of-a-bitch would dare to come back after what he'd done. I felt ashamed, like I was taking something that didn't belong to me. I also felt my fear go warm. Grandpa was willing to get in trouble on my account.

Most of the time the only thing Grandpa liked to do was read Louis L'Amour Western stories and chew tobacco. Grandpa also liked to drink whiskey and Budweiser. Behind the trailer my brother and I found a mound of empty beer cans about four feet tall. We were looking for pine cones to collect in a stand of trees we hadn't ventured into yet. We found a heap of weathered and fresh beer cans, silent and undisturbed, and a small glittering pile with emptied clear glass bottles. So that was what he did with them all! Just left them out there. We poked around in the pile and started lobbing cans at each other, calling it beer can tag.

Eventually I hit my brother with one. Squarely in the forehead. "You're it," I said.

He pushed me with both hands. "No I'm not—you are."

I held my balance, skimming the edge of the pile. Cans clanked at my ankles. I menaced, "Fucker what's your problem?" I was moving with majestic comportment, queen of the beer cans.

My brother looked up. Surprised.

Ma circled the stack of cans, careful not to step on any as she accosted us, examining the pile of rusted, faded and new cans. "You kids want to get lockjaw? Just stay out of this mess."

She pulled her hair off her sunburned face, brows high, eyes wide in confirmation of the worst. The pile was a metallic red, white, and blue blur in the Alabama heat.

I HAVE A small hump. It's not nearly the size of the humpback my Grandma had. She was completely bent over from being a farm hand her whole life. If you look at my shoulders closely you'll see the little mound back there. Is it possible for a hump like that to be inherited through the generations by birth, or has it simply been cultivated in me? A protuberance of insecurity. Now an inheritance. I wish I could sand it off and start anew. If I had a daughter, that would be the first order of business.

Long after I learned how to enter a room or be on a dance floor without automatically slouching, dance teachers still encourage me to stand up straight. It's the hump. They gently tap it between my shoulder blades or silently push their chests out toward me as a reminder to quit stooping. Once a teacher did a postural alignment with me and in the mirror and showed me that the natural way I held my stomach and tilted my pelvis contributed to the rounded shoulder. It wasn't just about one thing.

She told me that we learn to walk and stand the way we learn a lot of things, through mimicry. The people in my life had to hunker down to work and duck away from trouble. I'm sure there are some people for whom this dynamic is obvious, but her insight was magical. Her discerning analysis went beyond dance technique and made me want to weep into her arms. She understood this aspect of physical ancestry, how self-defeat perpetuates at the most granular level.

WE ALWAYS PRAYED before eating with the southern relations, everyone holding hands. Grandpa mumbled something about being blessed by the company and having yet another meal. Grandpa was in a "state." That was Grandma's word. She looked wounded and tired as she stood at the stove ready to serve dinner. The table groaned with the additional weight of dish after dish she placed before us. Fried chicken wings and drumsticks stood at attention in the center of the table. Black-eyed peas glistened with steam and fat from the slabs of salt pork Grandma threw in while they boiled on the stove. Anticipation coiled through the vapors at the table. A plate of cornbread, cut squares the bright yellow of sunflowers, nestled near my plate. I ate everything with equal gusto to spite my guilt; from the tender beans that rolled from the fork, to the mucus slide of okra slipping backward off the tongue, down the hatch.

But biscuits were what everyone was waiting for. They came from the oven like the perfect gift: expected but extravagant, something you've always wanted. Grandma picked the hot biscuits off the cookie sheet onto a plate the way I imagine she used to pick cotton. With the tips of her fingers she snatched one hot biscuit after another and in one, two, three time stacked them on a plate. Grandpa slurred something about wanting the biscuits on the table sooner. "After all these years, you ought to goddam know I like my biscuits with my peas, not after."

Grandma's deeply scored face pressed into a mask of servility. She smiled at the rest of us sitting quiet, Dad's head bowed—reminded he'd forgotten something about his own dad he should have remembered.

"You all know Papa likes to tease me," she nearly whistled, her drawl high pitched, strung.

Everyone stopped eating. I looked at the sheen of sweat that formed above Grandma's upper lip. I was never going to let a sorry man walk all over me. Never.

Dad cleared his throat. "Daddy. Mama. It's a good a time as ever to let you both know that Nan and I decided that we're going to move back north." I still couldn't get over how Dad called Grandpa his daddy. It sounded so childlike to me.

No one spoke.

"Come ahwn now, I bought my northern grandchildren butter for their biscuits. Papa likes his dipped in gravy," she hastily explained, as if we had been discussing that all along. Grandma's denial—that Grandpa was a sick man, that we were leaving—was also part of the silent contract. If she had ever felt any desire to change the situation, it had quickly dissolved in the heat of the day. Among all the factors weighted against her possible freedom, no prospects for employment, poor health, no education, was the fact that she didn't even know how to drive. When she sat in the car, her head barely cleared the dashboard because she was so small.

It was just better to pretend. I imagined a bright circle in front of each of my eyes. I wanted to let them sparkle and demand something better, but I closed them, and let worry consume my inner vision. That was one way to survive. This kind of "strength" is what is commonly allocated to women and was certainly handed down to me. Cause no friction. Or be like Grandpa and drink yourself into oblivion.

Grandma proudly presented a stick of butter from the icebox, and unwrapped the cold pale stick while we sat still.

Moving. Again. Right after I rejected Grandma's hand-stirring ways. I felt like I caused it. I hadn't proved I was southern enough. I suppressed my insurgent scorn.

She reached for the topmost biscuit on the plate still steaming from the oven. Grandma expertly sliced it open with a butter knife, slid the knife over the top of the butter, and popped the curled shaved butter into the biscuit. She clapped the biscuit closed and handed it to me.

"Now, sugar," she said solemnly, looking me in the eye, her blue eyes shiny. "Let this set awhile. Then when you open it up the butter will be all melted inside."

When I opened it later and took a bite of that biscuit, I felt like I had opened the door to Jesus.

TERRY TEMPEST WILLIAMS wrote about being bequeathed her mother's journals—all of them blank—in her memoir *When Women Were Birds*. The whole book is an examination of female silence and love and power. She said it best and most elegantly about what it means to be the bearer of a certain female legacy and trying to overcome the past and understand the present.

> *I am my mother, but I'm not.*
> *I am my grandmother, but I'm not.*
> *I am my great-grandmother, but I'm not.*

I could say it as a chant.

As long as I dance, I feel a need to reconcile the effervescence of *bedlah* with my grandma's ugly hump. You want your *bedlah* to be tight, dig into your skin if need be, to hold you in. You want to feel its uncomfortable embrace always.

7

I CONSIDER *AMERICAN Bandstand* and *Soul Train* my earliest dance "training." Both shows were on Saturdays. *American Bandstand* before noon, and *Soul Train* at four. Between the shows I was expected to change sheets, vacuum, scrub the tub; whatever Ma wanted me to do.

I liked the Rate-a-Record part of the show where Dick Clark asked a couple dancers whether a new song would be a hit or not. The first time I heard "Heaven on the 7th Floor" I knew it would be a hit and it was. I also saw John Cougar (ne John Mellencamp) sing "Ain't Even Done With the Night" about sexual frustration and more. Yes. He knew how it felt.

Nothing worked out in Alabama. There was no good job or dream house. Money ran out. I gave the snow globe to Sarah Ann. She liked watching the snow flutter in it. To her, it was romantic.

I remember I had looked out the car window the whole way back to Wisconsin, watching the soil change from red to black, feeling the hills flatten out into the Illinois grassland that made me feel adrift.

For that hour every Saturday I'd be somewhere great, like California, Burbank Studios, a cute boy and me in the Spotlight Dance. I danced along to the songs in the living room, an imaginary disco ball sparkling above me. I held a hairbrush and sang along to songs I knew. I loved the bump and hustle. I gyrated. I bobbed my head in time to the music. I flung my arms around. I wiggled my shoulders and high stepped all over the room. Turned this way and that. Feeling out what I was growing into.

I moved unconsciously to a rhythm that I held way down deep most of the time, but I was a girl in love with the beat. I liked to get loose and sweaty, feeling the pulse of music propelling the very blood through my veins, through my body. For those hours I felt like I'd evaded the whole dog pack of my insecurities.

WE MOVED INTO a rental outside Racine in Sturtevant in 1976 that nobody had ever lived in before. One whole block of new blue, grey, and tan side-by-side townhouses with the same mirror-image layouts inside. Our block retained a crew of social and economic misfits, not the young white families the developers might have envisioned. Our nearest neighbors were a biker, his "old lady," and their kid; a Mexican family with boys my age; and the tool and die maker in the unit next door who drank on weekends, had a wife with severe saddlebags for thighs, and a toddler they both called "hey you." A black couple moved in across the street shortly after we did. We were interracial, but I wouldn't say integrated. We coexisted. We were all in-between something; me, my family, my neighborhood.

The transition from town to country occurred right on our block. Where our street ended was a rutted service road and a pastured horse. A pond across from the horse's barn on "our side" revealed layers of junk when it dried up. We garbage-picked the dirt-blackened treasures. A regulation size football. A broken sled with the rope still attached. Horseshoes. A foot-pedal Singer sewing machine. Each thing was good to go after being hosed off. The horseshoe in the best condition went up above the door between the kitchen and living room. Ma hung it the wrong way, with the luck running out, and everyone who saw it said that was a bad idea. She claimed it looked better that way. She wouldn't change it.

Bordering two sides of our block was the cornfield. Someone had bushwhacked a path through the cornfield to the town's water tower, and it could be accessed at the edge of our street. I'd walk it frequently and alone to go holler up into an open spout at the tower as big around as a softball. I filled my lungs and pushed out my eyeballs, screaming all the fuuuucck youuuuus I had in me. The words tasted like metal and sounded like hell. I would go like that until I couldn't breathe and then I'd find a spot in a corn row to sit and rest my raw throat and tired diaphragm. I contemplated how small my feet were compared to any other part of the body, how much they carried, how much distance I could cover walking on them. I wished my feet had springs in them to feel a bouncy seismic tremor through to my pelvis.

The red lights at the top of the water tower blinked on and off, day and night, a sure sign that it was unperturbed. The tower was impervious to anything anyone would do or say into it.

The neighbors, who lived in a real farmhouse on the corner of our street, were living in a state of perpetual anger and shock that made them hate us.

"Some SOB," according to one of the girls who lived there, "sold out, and your god-forsaken townhouses were built."

Now her family had to deal with a dumbass motorcycle every day and my brother's football games in the street.

"There used to be chickens right over there," she pointed at my shoes and phantom chickens lasered out from her eyes to peck my feet. I wanted to stop the ceaseless whirling earth and feel a new world beneath my feet.

"YOU LOOK LIKE a total spaz." This from my brother's friends as they passed through the house. They were on their way to go outside to play Frisbee or football in the street. "Disco sucks," they assured me. As they bounced over the porch steps, I heard, "Your sister's a dog."

Ma ran the vacuum often as not in front of the TV, and I'd sulk on our plaid couch and wait for her to be done, willing the picture of Jesus over the TV to come alive and do something about everyone's rudeness.

To get away from them, I'd beg a ride from dad and watch *American Bandstand* at Nia's house. Saturday afternoons she had the TV all to herself.

We loved the song "Ring my Bell," and we sang along at top volume "Bell, elllll, eeellll" along with the TV and grooved to the music, flipping our heads around, making our hair go crazy on our heads. I interpreted the song as innuendo for orgasm, even though the lyrics suggested it was merely about getting a phone call. It was the way it was sung that clued me in.

Nia would let her hair fall in her eyes and asked, "How's my hair?" because we both harbored a not-so-secret jealousy of the *American Bandstand* teens. The girls had great hair and outfits, straight white teeth, and were definitely not swishing out household toilets on weekends. Because we were clearly not TV dance studio material like they were, we mocked their looks instead.

"That girl's shag makes her head look like a mop."

"Her boyfriend dances like a dork."

THANKS TO SARAH Ann and *Tiger Beat* among other things, I understood that I had a sexual destiny, and from church that my virginity was supposed to end only with marriage and eventual motherhood. My virginity was something I wasn't supposed to "give away" before that. But from what I could tell of my mother and other women, wedding night virginity was a thing of the past, and I knew acting like it wasn't was hypocrisy.

I also turned thirteen in that year when we moved back north and in that in-between time figured out how to masturbate, and doing so felt subversive and underground. If sex felt as good as masturbation, then it would be hard to hold off, no matter what the rest of society said about it. But I also resisted the idea of marriage and motherhood based on a simple logical equation. At that age I didn't know any women who didn't feel burdened, hurt, or repressed. One of my aunties moved all the way to Maine to get away from my uncle after he threatened her with a shotgun. Another had recently got a black eye and had her arm in a sling. My southern aunties cooked and cleaned and kept their mouths shut. Loss and lust commingled on my fingertips as I touched myself. Could I conjure up a different life through my body's yearnings?

I strained toward those enthralling pulses, either in the privacy of my bunk bed or in the bathroom, and held my legs closed to keep myself from crying out—instead, releasing a big breath and an arching back. The possibility of pleasuring myself made me feel shaky for hours. Afterward, though, I felt estranged from my body and overcome. The edges of that new place—the cornfield, the hostile neighbors, the end of a city road—were obvious signposts. We were unwelcome squatters in previously unmapped territory. So I played with myself to fill the void.

There were no other girls around but the next door meanies and my sister, five years younger. She still played with dolls, not her clit. I missed Julie and Nia who lived seven miles away. I missed the world we had created in Pierce Woods, filled with our own imaginings and a letup from explicit domesticity. My mourning was offset and conjoined with masturbation.

I spent too much time on the toilet seat stroking myself through my underwear and coming out of the bathroom flush with a sense of stupefaction.

I waited for the exasperated orders from Ma. That was what things had come to. She'd stand at the foot of the stairs in her brown polyester stretch pants and t-shirt and call for me. "Patty?"

Make your bed. Vacuum. Sweep. Throw in a load of laundry will ya? Fold this basket there. There's garbage that needs to go out. Here's some Pledge and a rag. Hang up those wet towels. Set the table. Do dishes. I'm sure Ma figured out what I was doing in the bathroom, and that's why she nagged, but what could she say to motivate me?

Ma was equally disoriented. Coming back to Wisconsin wasn't any great homecoming. Bills were piling up, my adolescence was coming on, and it wasn't something she was prepared for, and her own life seemed to be in remission. She believed living up north was better than the heat and lack of opportunity down south. But we were all on edge. Dad was driving a heavy lawnmower around in an old yellow Chevy flatbed to lakeside neighborhoods in Racine where rich people were happy to hire him to slave over every inch of their yards. He'd come home every night sunburned and tired, with cash in his pockets but not nearly enough. Ma chewed her nails to the quick and made cheap meals with lentils or hamburger that always tasted watery and under-salted.

Orgasms and yelling *fuck you* in secret didn't do anything to calm me. During that summer I waited for my period with the same apprehension that I waited for eighth grade to start. How would I handle being the new girl at yet another school? And what could I do that wouldn't make me an outcast before I could even say anything to anyone? I reread the booklet on reproduction and periods, the one I got after watching the movie on it in fifth grade. I studied the instructions that came in Ma's tampon box. I considered the labyrinth of my insides: vaginal walls, ovaries, and uterus seemed as mysterious to me as going to a new school.

I found a used copy of *Our Bodies, Ourselves* at Goodwill. I read every last word, and it went into great detail—menstruating, birthing, lactating—and I found all of it sickening. Blood and milk, contractions and paroxysms of all kinds appeared to be the life of a woman's body.

When I learned the belly wave in dance, it was a surprising and relaxing move, and I discovered it could be done waving up or down the torso. Having that kind of control was a revelation.

For a long time, I believed that the natural woman's body was one big rebellion against tidiness. That was one of my proto-feminist insights: that's why all the moms seemed so bent on making us girls clean house so much. But the pictures of blissed-out hippy women in labor at home, their granny dresses hoisted up to there—I couldn't relate to that either. My teenage dread went unresolved.

SOUL TRAIN WAS different. The show started with a shout out. "Sooooulll Train," and the camera would pan over a dance line of people, black and white. And they danced all out, kind of like I did, except better. It was way sexier than *American Bandstand*. Don Cornelius, a very sharp dressed black man, would come on the TV and talk in this smooth voice. "Love, peace and soul." It was nothing like Dick Clark and his placebo smile. Sometimes I danced along, sometimes I just watched. Some of the music was funk and soul, not all top 40 pop, and the people looked like they were at a party where I wanted to be. Having fun.

At that hour of the day, Ma was often in the kitchen, starting dinner. *Soul Train* helped me avoid her there. The gang of my brother's friends would pass through again, sweaty and punchy from beating each other up all afternoon. "Bunch of jungle bunnies," Roger said, flipping his Nerf football at the TV.

I vowed as soon as I could get out of that f-ing neighborhood filled with dumbasses, I would.

Once *Soul Train* got rolling I smelled something cooking, some kind of meat.

"Can't we change the channel?" my younger sister Peggy asked.

Dad sat in the recliner and smoked and read the paper. He claimed to like *Soul Train* which left my sister to pout on the couch.

I stared at the TV harder. I had a burgeoning understanding that the show was about something. It was about belief in people. Lifeblood. There was no way I was changing the channel.

MY OUTCAST QUESTION was settled when my Aunt Mary showed up at the townhouse with two garbage bags full of her old clothes.

She came over unannounced. I saw her pull them out of the trunk of her car, a cigarette resting in the gap of her front teeth. She came to the door laden with a full garbage bag and ticked her head toward another left on the curb. "Pffatty," she mouthed holding onto her cigarette between her teeth. I went out to grab it.

With the sacks in the house, Mary stood under the horseshoe, luck pouring out overhead, and I yelled for Ma.

She walked to the table and stubbed out her cigarette in one of dad's ashtrays on the kitchen table. She didn't sit down.

Aunt Mary is only a few years older than me, but at that point she already had a baby, her own car, and could smoke and drink coffee right in front of everyone.

Ma came up from the basement with a basket of laundry she set down in the living room in front of the TV. I put two empty cups on the table and poured into them the sludge roasting in the Mr. Coffee. "I'll get that." It was Ma's you-can-leave-now voice.

"I can't stay. I just. I brought some clothes for Patty," Aunt Mary said. Since she had my baby cousin she cut her hair short, but grew the bangs long. The fringe hung over one makeup smudged eye. She looked sexy and wild. There was no way she went into labor looking like someone from *Little House on the Prairie*. I bet she screamed her head off before my cousin came out, too.

She nodded toward the bags. "None of it fits me anymore. None of it. I can't wear this stuff anymore and neither can Boiler." Boiler was Mary's legendary best friend. The one who had the dangerous Mexican boyfriend and had encouraged Mary to skip school, leading to everything else, including her own pregnancy.

Ma stood in the doorway of my room, relieved that one of her immediate problems—how to afford new school clothes—had been so easily resolved. I tried on a pretty white top with tassels that tied at the top, but the shoulder slid down my arm. The jeans slipped over my rear with room to spare, but cinched up with a belt at the waistband would stay put. It would take me all afternoon to try everything on. I swallowed with anticipation and felt my throat down to my shoes.

I put on a light blue top with giant fluttery sleeves. I waved my arms and flitted around the room. I didn't give a shit about fingernail polish, hair accessories, or girlish gossip, but those clothes were a revelation. I sashayed around, pretending to be somewhere, like a cookout at the beach. That was my idea of fun and excitement.

My throat felt suddenly healed. I looked in the mirror. I had cheekbones. Hazel eyes. This is what I would wear when I went on *Soul Train*.

I stood on tip toe and smoothed the top over my naked flat chest and stomach. The top covered my butt and the tops of my thighs.

"I don't know about that shirt, Patty," Ma said. "It's too long."

It was too long.

"It's too see-through."

I moved in to the mirror for a closer look. There they were. Bare little titties underneath.

"I just need a bra, Ma."

"Then you'd see *that* through it."

I picked out some more things. Everything was too big.

"Maybe we should save these clothes for next year. Or give them back."

I was determined that with pins and belts I could get the clothes to stay on. The array of teenage bohemia on my bedroom floor had spoken. I was seduced by the different fabric textures and the range of colors. It gave me hope. I had instantly traded my Woodsy Owl Give a Hoot t-shirt for the oversized contents of the bags. Having those clothes showed me an outward and alluring personality, not a person I knew how to be, but something to shoot for.

Ma was shaking her head, and it was strengthening her resolve. "No, Patty."

"Why?" All the air that filled my lungs seeped out.

It was Mary. She'd defied my grandparents and whatever rules they tried to enforce. She smoked cigarettes *and* pot. Stayed out all night. Hung out with dirty Mexicans instead of doing her homework. Swam naked in Lake Michigan. Had a best friend who lived in the worst neighborhood. Snuck off to Chicago. Shoplifted. Knew gay people. Made pottery in a studio not at school. Slept with an older man. Had a baby out of wedlock. She wasn't even out of high school and she'd done it all. It was as if she'd been to all the places I was curious about when I looked at the globe at school.

If I looked like Mary, I'd end up like Mary.

"No way." I wrapped my arms around the shirt. "I'm keeping it *and* wearing it."

"You're just too small. You look ridiculous." Ma walked to the piles of clothes, picked them up, and put them back in the bags.

Ma believed her role was to protect me from the kind of situations she believed racy clothing led to. Things that Mary did. Moms are righteous guardians against too-short skirts, pierced ears, and makeup, and the enforcers of practical shoes and winter hats. Like mothers everywhere from anytime, mine was trying her best to keep me from growing up too fast. But the night I was sexually assaulted, I was wearing jeans and a striped top that tied at the elbows. What I was wearing was not the problem. If only we had both realized that what I really needed was a healthier self-image.

Mary's generosity wasn't going to redeem her or save me from the taint of her rebellion.

Mary dropped out of school and didn't work. She got welfare. Some people said those things were bad.

"You did the same thing," I lobbed at ma. She'd been pregnant with me before she married my dad. I knew that. She'd fooled around. She might have dressed like a girl was supposed to, but she still wasn't chaste.

"What are you talking about?" She knew exactly what I meant.

"You and Dad. When you had me."

"Your father and I were in love. There's no comparison," she snapped back.

I didn't care. I would never be that dumb, let some guy sweet talk his way into me. I didn't think Ma's situation had anything to do with mine. I knew that people used to believe that a girl "in trouble," meaning pregnant, had to get married. Ma's quip about being in love was her justification for getting married when she had to. That was changing. I stood my ground, but Ma's stance was definitive.

"Your aunt has no idea all the hurt she's caused."

"What about you, Ma?" My mother and father had gone down south and back and didn't ask me one iota how I felt about it. Those hurts had piled up, weighting my chest and shoulders until I felt shrunk and flattened.

Ma grabbed more clothes and stuffed them back into the two garbage bags. In my head hung two words: fuck you.

ONE DAY I found an opening in the corn field with a bed of straw strewn on the ground and a wall of hay bales built in a half circle almost up to the tips of the tassels. The sky was touching down on the bales, a scrim of blue and clouds.

Two boys I've never seen before and my brother's new football friend Roger were sitting in the straw leaning up against the bales.

They had created a maze of paths in the cornfield past the water tower. The roots of the corn were knobby as hell and the space between rows was slim. Those kids really had to bushwhack to knock the corn down flat.

Roger was bigger than my brother but real skinny with long blond hair. All the boys were wearing shorts and a t-shirt.

Where the boys were sitting in the straw was a coffee can filled with cigarette butts and an empty bottle of schnapps. On the ground in front of them was a magazine with pictures of naked women.

The boys squealed when they saw me. Roger rolled up the magazine. The younger boys jumped up. "No girls allowed. This is our fort." They flanked me to make sure I didn't walk any closer. Roger stood up too. Enforcement. I was trapped.

"Hey, hey. Guys, girls are cool," Roger said. Those were just words. There was not a drop of nicety in his voice.

"Jimmie's sister, right?"

One of the boys with brown hair poked his pointer finger into the air in front of me. I felt my chest throb. "No way, man. We don't want her or anyone. She'll tell."

I put my hands on my hips. I was taller than all of them.

"I'm not a narc," I said. The things that troubled me nobody could do anything about. I never told. It was a point of pride.

The boys assessed me while I stood before them. I kept my hands on my hips, slouched. Squinted at them so they looked blurry and weak. No crying allowed. They were trying to determine the level of truth in what I said. They were sizing me up in an age-old ritual of female intimidation.

"Girls always tell," the little brown-haired one repeated.

"We'd like to see the real thing. Show us." Roger tugged at the waistband of my pants. He coiled a finger through my belt loop. "C'mon." I looked down at my dirty feet in flip flops and his in tennis shoes, hate and fascination swelled my tongue. Blood flushed through my groin.

The evidence was stacking up. They probably took their own pants down together.

"You wish," I said and slapped his hand as hard as I could. Then I ran. Knobby roots sunk deep into the soil made me clumsy. Back into the corn my flip flops seemed to slap the back of my head, my ass, my knees. I was out of breath, thirsty.

When I got home, Ma kept asking me what was wrong and I wouldn't tell her.

MY WHOLE LIFE I went to one school dance. It was a '50s themed sock hop. Homecoming for eighth grade. Ma helped me get costumed by drawing a poodle on a piece of white felt and cutting it out for me. I got a skirt and crinoline from Goodwill, to which we pinned the poodle. I couldn't find any saddle shoes, but I had flat white tennis shoes that I wore with ankle socks. Ma had an old chiffon scarf and she tied it around my ponytail. I looked good. Authentic. I didn't know a single dance from the '50s, but I liked the music even if I would never admit it to anyone. It wasn't music that was on the dance shows or on the radio. Oldies. "Blueberry Hill." "Rock Around the Clock." I was eager to dance the night away and ready to roll.

Dad drove me to the junior high to drop me off. We agreed on a time when he would come back, and as I left the car I noticed other kids were coming to the dance together. I walked to the gym alone, my crinoline rustling, announcing all my wishes for a good time. When I got to the gym, crepe paper streamers in school colors drooped from the basketball hoops, and I saw our principal and the office secretary were in charge of spinning records. There were folding chairs set up on both sides of the gym and people sat on them or congregated in groups, boys pushed girls, girls giggled. There was a table with a punch bowl, cookies, and pretzels. "Tutti Frutti" played at full volume.

The dance floor was huge. Empty!

I slumped down on one of the folding chairs. Dad wasn't coming back for another three hours. I picked at my poodle. How long would three hours take?

A girl named Denise from gym class sat down next to me. She had on a pink skirt with a similarly attached felt poodle in black. Another straggler.

"I've got a cigarette," she said. "Let's go to the bathroom."

In the too-bright light of the bathroom we both sat on the edge of the sinks. The female version of a secret fort in the corn. Denise extracted one cigarette from her shoe. "Got a match?"

"No."

"No?" she said. "Then I guess there's nothing to do."

Denise put the cig back in her shoe. We both hopped down off the sinks in the bathroom and went back out to the gym.

Denise ditched me to find someone with matches. She would be better off hanging out with someone else. I felt like the trash that was lobbed into the pond behind our rented townhouse.

I tapped my toes on the floor to the beat, smoothed out my big black skirt, and watched my classmates' posture a good time. I looked at Phil, a boy who copied off my papers in science class, to see if he would cross the divide of the gym floor. I even got up and went to the punch bowl. A big hint. The punch was grape Kool Aid. On another fateful night not too far into the future I'd be staring into a garbage can of booze and Kool Aid, similarly questioning my ability to get along.

Nobody danced.

Finally the principal played a contemporary song. A love song. "Best of My Love" by the Eagles. Boys and girls paired up as if on cue. Girls with their arms around the boys shoulders, the boys with their hands resting on the girls hips. It appeared that girls were expected to rest their head on the boy's chest.

A boy I barely knew, chubby and zitty, asked me to dance. I was chosen by default, the last girl left on a folding chair, but I was eager anyway. We adopted the position. His hands on my hips felt strangely solid. I could hear his breathing, and his breath smelled like the sweet punch from the bowl. I was alarmed and stiff and felt like running away. Would I ever be comfortable in my body's terrain? My ponytail hurt my head. A boy had his hands on me, and I had mine on him. He felt like a durable animal, like touching a big dog.

My hands on his shoulders shook as I lifted my head up and away and looked past his face. Was that love? I did not know. I searched the gym's rafters for an answer. The song ended, and a new one started. The boy wordlessly dropped his hands from my hips and looked at the other dancers, wanting a new partner.

I was starting to feel the inner split between my longing to be visible and the social expectation that I didn't deserve to be. I felt the pressure of this halving from the top of my head to the bottom of my feet. Right then my place was supposed to be the background. I trudged gradually over the gym's wood floor back to my folding chair, but I stepped on the free throw line because it was really a balance beam.

8

"WHAT DOES A women expect of the life?" Nesma Al-Adalus from Spain stood before us, a dance class of about forty Minnesotan women, in a full body leotard with a small triangular scarf on her head that held back her long curly hair. She wore a simple pink hip scarf with fringe, and she was small and a bit plump around the middle.

We all looked at Nesma like a bunch of window display dummies. Was there going to be a warmup session? Music? It was 2010, and I was over a decade into my dance studies. Nobody ever started dance class with a question about what we expected out of life.

Nesma touched her chest and looked skyward before looking all of us in the eye. We were an assortment. Some of us were young, beautiful, lithe. The rest were like me, in various stages of aging gracefully. Or not.

"Is the heart. Respect," she said. "That is the Baladi Woman. I will show you now."

She cued some music and walked toward us and away. Her hip movements were small and contained. Her eyes acknowledged each of us, and she was smiling, and as she added more movements to her dance, she swayed her body, expressing a reserved sensuality. Her hips appeared voluptuous, her arms relaxed. A story unfolded. Wherever her hands and eyes moved, we followed them. Look, they said. A story of a woman in love.

MY LOVE STORY started in the Intellectual History of the United States class discussion section at the University Wisconsin-Madison in 1986. The object of my desire had on a wool driving cap, a flannel shirt, and wore round tortoise-shell glasses. He looked adorable, and most attractive to me was his radiant Midwestern goodness: straight teeth, clear eyes, and translucent skin. Those flannelled arms were meant to hold me. He told the class during introductions he'd just got back from Ireland, but he loved contemporary American history, and his favorite thing to do was to have a pint at the Rathskeller. He said his name. I wrote it down in my notebook. Sean. Spelled the Irish way.

Our teaching assistant Chris had asked us, in a thick East coast accent, to introduce ourselves to the group by saying why we took the class and what we liked to do *ohn hour time off.* Chris volunteered he liked jazz and was happy he found B-Side Records on State Street. He stood in front of us in the classroom, glowing from nerves, needing a haircut, and moving with a noticeable limp. He was from New York, a jazz-loving intellectual Jew, and he seemed singular and exotic in the upper Midwest. Unlike the English majors who were all reserved, reflective, and quiet (me), History majors were overtly political, prone to argue, and much hipper. Jazz!

I was a perennial sophomore, having transferred from Whitewater to my hometown college, and then on to UW-Madison as an English and History double major. Before I transferred, I got involved in the student newspaper and started taking my writing aspirations more seriously, wrote articles and dabbled in poetry. I met people who believed work could be the answer to a life calling, who saw news unfold and thought about issues of the day and reported on them. I still hung out with Nia, who was working as a baker at the Piggly Wiggly grocery store, but those student journalists also became my close friends. No matter who I was with, I passed as part of the group. Slang here, grammar there.

A group of us transferred to UW-Madison *en masse*: Catherine, Tony, John, and me. We were bright, talented, callous, and scrappy. We wanted to go to a "real" university where we could escape what we perceived as the depredations of Racine and Kenosha. My disdain for Racine's working class, even though I was one of them, was full-on. It took me a long time to appreciate the dignity behind the work my people did, especially my dad, and the pride he took in a job well done, no matter what it was. I was insufferable in my provincial superiority.

With my new friends I was going to "pubs," not bars, in Milwaukee and Chicago. I threw darts instead of dice; drank imported beer instead of PBR. But with Nia, I trolled the bar time underbelly of Racine and Kenosha. Places where nobody was carded, fights over the pinball machine or pool table were routine, and people slid off barstools, too drunk to stay seated. I flirted with dodgy guys who bought us drinks and got us high. After someone's girlfriend threatened to cut me up with a broken beer bottle I wasn't any more careful. I was outraged that a "sister" would come after me. It was obvious I had no interest in her loser boyfriend. No matter who I was with, I acted oblivious and above it all. I radiated an aura of sweetness and superiority. I was a dumbass kid and a wounded young woman.

I began to wear short black skirts, tall leather boots, and jaunty hats. I became a serial dater and so-called heartbreaker. No guy was going to hold me close or hold me down. Together with my new friends, I bolstered my ambitions to be where the action was—the state capitol—not at a school straddling the county-line road.

The year before I moved to Madison, Sean had gone to Ireland. His plan was to escape his large and clannish rural Wisconsin family to discover his Irish roots, only to learn, like everyone who does that, that he was more American than he realized. He had lived illegally in Ireland as a bartender for a year before being booted out of the country. He was in sorry shape when he got back, a young man confounded by his cultural identity, in debt, and lonely. Right before we met, Sean worked at the Swiss Colony in Monroe, Wisconsin, a business that ships Ye Olde (fake) Wisconsin Cheddars nationwide. He needed to make money so he could finish his education. He would do anything—detassel corn, shovel shit in barns, sort garbage, wash dishes, stock groceries in cold coolers, you name it—if he needed to pay for something. A dude with a work ethic.

We were both all of twenty-two years old when we met and already felt world-weary, working hard trying to change our circumstances. I recognized Sean as kindred spirit right away.

I always sat by Sean in class and made a point of striking up a conversation. It seemed my instincts about him were right. He was clever and wholesome, if you didn't count smoking pot and being a political hell-raiser. Sean smelled like a prairie and warm skin, and I pushed my coat and book bag close to his things when I sat down next to him. When I started to sleep with him, I found out that he used Yardley's Lavender soap, which seemed so European and radical. A man who didn't mind smelling like an herbal flower garden? I was inexorably drawn to him.

As my crush deepened, I start telling other people about him. I questioned my roommate Catherine endlessly after she met him in the student union the day we all had coffee together. "Do you think he likes me?"

"I dunno. It's hard to tell," she said. It *was* hard to tell. The two of them seemed to be more compatible as they talked about world events, the Irish Republican Army, Central American politics. I could see I had to start becoming better informed.

For weeks I worked on getting up the nerve to ask Sean to study with me. It was after a discussion section with Chris that Sean asked me first to go out with him to an improv show. He'd heard the Ark improv group had a really hilarious guy—Chris Farley—and would I like to go with him to see the show?

The night of our date I met Sean at the Rathskeller for pretzels and beer. I wore leggings, an oversized striped sweater, and a black beret on my head. I was certain I looked very French and chic. I was writing poetry (which went with the outfit), having recently been deeply moved by the Romantic poet William Blake and his artwork, and had begun to go to live jazz shows (which also went with the outfit) in a basement bar on State Street with my roommate. She used to play jazz clarinet in a band and knew all the tunes. Chris, the TA, made history and jazz seem like the height of smart-people cool to me, and Catherine and I were rocking. My downcast hometown and that first year in Whitewater were in the rearview mirror as far as I was concerned. Living in Madison was a gateway to new wave dance music, vintage clothes, and gorgeous, talented people. In Madison I could assimilate the vivacious Rita-type I'd aspired to be.

Sean was dressed per usual in flannel and jeans, his wool hat looked dashing. We stood in line together to order a pitcher and a fistful of pretzels. We were on an official date, and I was thrilled. We were both the same height, and I liked the feeling of being at eye level with him. Standing before the altar of beer and German-Wisconsin pride with him at the student union felt like a new order of life was taking shape. In the night sky above us, I believe the stars reframed my destiny.

"What kind of beer do you like?" Sean asked. "Lighter, darker? American, German?"

We both picked a beer made locally in Madison, one of the front-runners in the burgeoning microbrewery trend. I grabbed a napkin and pulled pretzels out of the display on the bar.

We chose an open table in the middle of the Rath that had been scored many times over by years of graffiti-carving students. Josie Loves Richard. Fuck. Buzz. Knock knock who's there? I had an urge to make a pencil relief of all the words and gouges in the wood. What would Sean think of the hollows and grooves in my soul, the gashes that I kept reopening with binge drinking and sucky boyfriends? I believed that he would find that behavior disgusting and weak. I did. It wasn't just him, or even men in particular. It was what I reasoned all people would think.

"So tell me what you like to read," Sean said. I couldn't believe my luck.

My last serious boyfriend (after Griffin) was from my hometown, and he liked to fix cars and hang out drinking in dive bars. We'd often meet late at night after I was done studying. He built a beautiful oak bookshelf for me because he knew I liked books, but he wasn't a reader or a thinker, just a talker, and I grew increasingly bored with his inability to care about anything but motors. Night after night I'd sit next to his handsome, juiced self and doubted he could say anything that interested me. Then during one of our late night make out sessions, he told me that there was this guy he knew in Milwaukee, "who liked to suck his dick."

"The guy could really suck," he reiterated. I didn't know if he told me because he wanted me to do likewise, if he just liked the memory, or if he was trying to tell me he preferred men. Still don't. When I broke up with him, he thought it was a ploy to get him to marry me. He insisted we weren't "done." He came to visit me once in Madison to convince me to get back together with him, but I knew it wasn't me he was pining for.

"I got this great book not too long ago," I told Sean. "A collection of Blake's poems and illustrations. He was really into mysticism and symbolism." Blake aligned himself with feminist writers and believed in equality and love. "He believed women should be fulfilled at a time when pretty much nobody did."

Who on earth says stuff like this in date conversation? I felt like I was talking out of my ass. Sean didn't flinch.

He smiled. "Blake, huh. Have you read Yeats?" Five minutes and two poets; I determined Sean was "the one." I devoured more pretzels, savored the salt, and drank the tangy beer.

I ran my fingers over the gouged graffiti on the table, feeling disturbed and ardent. The one I was waiting for had come.

BALADI WOMEN IN Egypt are not just characters in a dance story. The baladi people who currently live in Cairo migrated there with their families from northern and southern Egypt, many from the Nile Delta region in the 1930s and '40s. They were originally rural people (baladi means "country") who became blue collar workers and shopkeepers in Cairo. The baladi moved into certain quarters of the city where they lived cheaply, packing their families into small, multistory apartments, some with no running water or electricity. Two generations hence, contemporary baladi are still protective of their rural origins and fierce defenders of baladi traditions. *Balad* is defined as community, town, or country, and *baladi* means local or indigenous, nostalgically, like down-home, earth-bound folk. To urban baladi today it also means fulfilling a whole host of expectations regarding family and everyday life.

The baladi consider themselves to be the "have-nots," and believe outsiders, or "afrangi," (the middle to upper classes) are superficial social climbers. I considered similar messages from my own upbringing.

Baladi have a love-hate relationship with afrangi. Baladi aspire to be afrangi, but dismiss them at the same time. And afrangi think of baladi much in the same way as East Coasters in the U.S. consider the Midwest to be flyover country where people lead quaint, rustic lives.

Not everyone who is baladi is poor, but the ethos of poverty is central to baladi identity. A baladi woman is said to be able to play with an egg and a stone, and not break the egg. This means that a baladi woman is resourceful, a good bargainer, who will get her family through lean times (the barren stone) and remain prudent when chances are better (the fertile egg). To flaunt good fortune is to invite the evil eye.

I did not know any of this while I was in Nesma's class. But studying baladi the dance resonated long after the class, and I sought to learn more. Once I learned about the baladi people, I perceived certain similarities in my own family's history: my father's rural past as part of a sharecropping family, their eventual migration to the city, and the attendant challenges of that.

Although I will never be "country strong," or baladi in any sense of the word, I liked knowing that Egyptian baladi had words for these class and cultural stresses. I intended to lead a different life from the one I'd been raised for, and the world that I was starting to inhabit—taking dance classes, working on creative projects, devoting time to serious learning—was definitely afrangi. My mother had been raised in a large family as if she were hired help—babysitting, cooking, laundry, dishes—rather than being nurtured as a beloved daughter. Housework was all she knew how to do, and all she believed she could do. I had a love-hate relationship regarding my working-class culture, our struggles, the way I was taught to be a woman, as well as the ways I sought to get by, or in my case, pass in both the working-class and middle-class worlds. I had serious doubts that I had what it took to be part of either one. Love meant loyalty for my parents and me, and it was divided.

EVEN BEFORE I met Sean, the division between who I was and where I came from and what I wanted to be was crystal clear when I transferred to UW-Madison as an English major. One of my required classes was a Chaucer class. I found the auld middle English difficult. I would read Chaucer's *Canterbury Tales* in what felt like a fog of incomprehensibility. They were about characters on a pilgrimage, that much I knew, but it was hard to decipher what they were doing and what they were saying. I lost patience with the unfamiliar words and the glossary with footnotes, and I bought a book of Chaucer "translations" of the *Canterbury Tales* into contemporary English that I discovered at one of the local bookstores. I was desperate to get a sense of what I was missing. Soon enough, I read them like they were CliffsNotes, and my understanding of Chaucer and the richness of his storytelling never deepened.

The paper I had written about the "Wyves Tale of Bathe" caused the class's professor to call me into her office. She was a relatively young professor, someone with just a few strands of gray in her hair, a cute bob haircut, and one published academic book to her name. Other people in Chaucer class, not me, spent a lot of time reading aloud and dissecting the text. She was enthusiastic about their participation, moving about the room in what I perceived was scholarly ecstasy. It was astonishing to me that people found so much meaning in it. A semester before I had taken a class on the Romantic poets—Shelley, Keats, Blake—and luxuriated in it. I couldn't fathom I'd struggle so much with Chaucer.

In the professor's office, she got right down to business. "Tell me about what you know about the Wife of Bath."

"She was a lusty woman looking for a man?" I struggled to recollect it. The Wife of Bath seemed like one of my aunties who had had numerous husbands, but it was hard to get a grip on her character, written the way it was. I couldn't prove their stories might be connected. Plus I had been out dancing the night before at the Cardinal Club with my roommate Catherine until bar time. I felt tired and under the microscope of this professor's attention. I never went to any of my teachers' office hours and rarely ever talked with my professors. I didn't know how.

The professor's forehead wrinkled in response to my answer. "I called you in to meet with me because I don't know how to grade your paper."

I'm sure I looked at her with askance. "Really?" My Racine twang probably sounded like "rilly" to her.

The professor fidgeted in her chair and moved some books and papers around on her desk. I wished I had had something in my arms to hold, like a book, to protect myself against what was coming next. The Penguin Paperback Classic version of Chaucer was sitting on the coffee table back in the small apartment I shared with Catherine. The cover was a pilgrim in a black tunic. I felt out of time and place in the medieval world of her office, which had a poster of an exhibit of the Lady and the Unicorn tapestries on the wall. I was wearing black and red cowboy boots, a short skirt, and a jacket with a rabbit fur collar. My modern garb was tacky and flippant, compared to the Lady's sleek tunic.

"There's an issue I want to discuss with you."

I held my breath.

"It's your writing. It needs a lot of work. If you are ever to succeed as a professional you need to have better communication skills. I believe you are a smart young woman who is trying to convey important ideas, but your current skill level in writing means you are not prepared for the rigorous academic environment of this English Department."

I was not expecting that kind of office visit at all. My own major that I loved so much, English, and the other classes I had succeeded in, was all called into question.

"Where did you go to high school?"

"Park High, Racine." I think she tried hard to keep her features neutral.

"It's a problem when universities admit students from sub-par schools and then expect them to succeed in scholarly pursuits they are not prepared for," she said.

I felt devastated and humiliated. A rube. Everything she said was a hundred percent true and it was hard to take. I wasn't academically prepared. My term paper made no sense. I lacked intellectual sophistication and any substantial study habits. I had made it as far as I had in school in part because nobody took me seriously enough to level with me.

"I don't want to have to flunk you. If you agree to take Composition 101 next semester, I won't," she said. Her tone was firm, lacking warmth or friendliness. This business of bringing kids up to speed was tiresome.

I did everything I could to say "I will" with dignity before I flew out of her office and pummeled the stairs down five stories of the Helen C. White building. I was breathing hard, pushing my lips together so I wouldn't cry. I got to the landing outside the Union Terrace next door and let go at the edge of Lake Mendota, holding on to a pillar on the pier.

My idea of myself, and who I should be, was so wrong. I cried epic tears. Catherine was outraged on my behalf and threatened to report my Chaucer teacher. For what? The truth giftwrapped with a dose of elitist insensitivity? The professor's words ricocheted in my consciousness. I was a smart young woman. Ill prepared. I didn't think so at the time, but it took real guts for her to address all that. She was offering me a chance to save my GPA. But more than that, a shot at the future I really wanted. I pulled off my cowboy boots and shucked my pride.

I signed up for Comp 101.

NOT LONG AFTER Sean and I became a couple, we walked his dog Madra in the arboretum. She loved running free of the leash, and Sean liked to give her the opportunity. The sign at the head of the trail that stated something about dogs on leashes and disturbing plants and wildlife went unheeded. Madra was gushing down the trail in front of us, her paws were lapping the earth, and she was snuffling wet leaves with her nose. She charged through the trees and brush, flushing out birds and squirrels. You'd think there was a yeti in the woods, with all the slashing and scuttling. Her abandon was so complete that we ended up calling and calling for her when it was time to leave.

"Madra!" Sean whistled. Nothing.

We walked the tamped-down trails, hand in hand. Picnic Point by the university was for lovers, but the arboretum was for observers. But Sean and I had been so absorbed in each other that we'd forgotten about the dog.

Once we figured out that Madra had disappeared, we scanned the terrain.

I felt warm with the scarf around my neck. "Maybe we should stop," I told Sean. We found a fallen log and sat on it and waited for the dog. Soon it would be dusk. Sean whistled again. "Madra!"

We waited for the dog, knowing she would come back. This is what I thought of as love. Sitting on a log, waiting. It's the way a lot of women think about love, raised on Cinderella and male impetus. Female agency in love relationships isn't part of the lore. It's not considered as romantic as a man and his big gestures—think John Cusack with his boom box in *High Fidelity*. As much as I claimed to want otherwise, I had not learned to change that dynamic. I let men buy me dinners and drinks, didn't question their authority on matters of the heart. With Sean, I knew it could be different, but how?

Sean and I didn't intend to make love the first time we did. Sean had been at my house hanging out with me and my roommates. I lived on the far west side of town, and I invited him to stay because it was getting late and I didn't want him out on the dark streets on his bike. After spending the evening together in conversation with my friends, we were bonded by the sudden quietness of my bedroom. Our clothes came off. After some sweet kisses, he slipped inside me, as if we'd known each other half our lives. As much as I liked Sean, I was unsure sex was anything I'd ever really want.

When I'd awakened next to Sean in my room the morning after we'd first made love, I'd expected to have that day-after feeling, where someone's tipped me upside down and all the coins I have stuffed in my pockets fall out and I am scrambling around to pick them up. Like a beggar. Instead, he'd held me as if he'd always been sleeping with me, his hand warming my bare stomach. We had fit just fine in my single bed.

The arboretum was clotted with trees and bushes. No echo. Just a hum. The world outside the arboretum vibrated with traffic, homework, sex, meals. Here was a submersion into a green muted era. I pushed my boot against Sean's ankle and he looked at me, and therein was ancient driftless land.

I felt like I was with Madra as she leaped through time and branches, off the path into the tangled mass of love and uncertainty, my heart was fanning out, siphoning the light.

WHEN SEAN ASKED me to move in with him the following year in 1987, I told him yes, on one condition.

He wanted to know: would I make him do dishes for the rest of my life?

No. Now that I had a decent guy, I had to fulfill another certain singular love. I needed a cat.

Sean accompanied me to the Dane County Humane Society to fulfill his promise. When we got there, the whole assortment of livestock had been picked over because of the holiday gift-giving season. We had a few options. A pregnant feline about to give birth. A PTSD cat who hissed nonstop. One with battered ears and missing an eye. Another one had a bad habit of peeing in its former owner's bed (thank god that was disclosed). I fancied them all. Sean grabbed my shoulders and turned me away from them to look at him, willing me to be sensible. "Patty, you want an animal that will love you back."

"They just need a chance."

"Those cats could give two shits about you." That was the bottom line truth. None of them could make eye contact, two were actively hostile. The pisser seemed sweet, though.

Someone from the Humane Society stepped in before our argument became full-blown.

"We just got a couple of adolescent cats. Nine months."

We were led to a holding pen with two beautiful grey cats—one solid and one tabby. The tabby purred and put his whiskers against the front of the cage. Very friendly. His grey brother sulked and glowered from the back of the cage. They were litter mates. They had been surrendered because the family that had them said they had "kept them too long." I assumed this meant that the family's mean mother

ditched her kids' kitties as soon as they went back to school after
Christmas vacation.

"Ooo, I want that one," I said pointing the moody kitty. That one
had a poet's soul and smoldering good looks.

The stripe-y one continued to flirt with Sean. "Patty. See?"

He turned to the Humane Society attendant with a knowing
smile—as if I had a head injury or was afflicted with dementia. "We
would like to meet the tabby."

We brought Katze, the tabby, home in a cardboard box provided
by the shelter, and he popped right out if it as soon as we set it on the
floor. Katze seemed to feel immediately at home, intimidating Madra
first and then finding food and launching pads. In a matter of weeks
he dug up all our plants, tore down precious U2 posters from the
walls, licked butter from the butter dish, pushed books off shelves,
scratched the furniture, hogged the bed, acted like King Shit to the
dog, and ate my best friend's headphones.

I was Cat Queen, no ifs, ands, or buts. We were inseparable.
He always found my lap and could purr restfully in it for hours,
belying his destructive nature. My love for Katze was as I'd wanted it,
immediate, unconditional.

My love for Sean was much more complex. He wanted to live
in partnership with me, but I didn't know how to do that. Sean was
genuine in his desire to please me, but I didn't know how to tell him
what I would like from him or our relationship. What I wanted most
from a man was equality and respect, but how I was behaving to
achieve it was through righteous indignation. What I really needed
was compassion and language for the things that confounded me. For
myself, for my parents, for the man who was beside himself in love
with me. I was an amalgamated, blurred young woman. I couldn't see
myself clearly.

Just as Katze settled in our place with his kitty hurricane, Sean was
a bundle of man energy.

He'd come up behind me and kiss my neck and put his hands
around my waist. Told me how pretty I was, how sexy, how fun.
He exhaled his love into my ears. He walked around the apartment
singing lyrics about two cats in the yard, how life used to be so hard,
and that everything is easy cuz of yoooou. He told me again and again
moving in with me was the best thing that had ever happened to

him. His hands were always busy, with making food, holding books, reaching for me. When I found a grey hair and plucked it out of my head, he wrote a story about it, tucking the grey hair and his missive into an envelope for me as a keepsake.

The attentiveness went on like that. His hands rubbing my shoulders. Again. I was getting increasingly annoyed by his fondness, his horniness.

It also bothered me that my parents disapproved of me living with Sean.

After I moved out of Racine to go to school in Madison, my parents moved out of state. The manufacturing jobs that had sustained many Racine families from the previous generation had been slowly drying up in the 1970s. That trickle turned into a torrent in the 1980s when corporations realized they could set up shop in low-tax states and developing countries and hire non-union workers for a fraction of the cost. Dad's company made him an offer he couldn't refuse—relocate to North Carolina or no longer have a job.

Down south, my parents missed the fellowship of their old Lutheran church and found themselves drawn to a Pentecostal congregation. My high-strung and private father began speaking in tongues, singing, and playing tambourine in the church band. He led a bus ministry. Our sporadic phone calls took on spiritual urgency for my parents.

"The spirit of the lord is alive in this congregation, Patty," Dad said. "You wouldn't believe the joy." He told me about testifying. How he felt set free. The spirit authentically moved both my parents, and they were embraced by their new community of believers. But the things they told me about their new church made me think my parents were involved in a cult. They were pledging disproportionate amounts of their income to missionaries, rejecting friendship with nonbelievers, constantly proselytizing. My youngest sister Elizabeth, the last one living at home, was enrolled as a Missionette to learn how to devote her life to Jesus. In short order, I learned from my parents that my afrangi aspirations were also leading me to hell. The space between us grew geographically and emotionally.

I know my parents loved me wholeheartedly. It was their lack of confidence about their own abilities, and powerlessness to make their dreams manifest, that led me to question mine. It's one thing that compelled my confusion and silence after being assaulted. I had to tough it out in the ways they did, and my definition of resilience was like theirs: brash denial.

I'd announced I was moving in with Sean at Christmas dinner at my grandparents' house when my parents were back visiting my hometown. I know. How classically dumb. This guilty admission was greeted first by the sound of forks scraping dinner plates until Ma said, "You'll need to give us your new address." Afterward she sent me a three-page letter explaining that only women of questionable morals give themselves to a man outside of marriage. My parents didn't know the half of it. Plus, it seemed Ma had forgotten how I was conceived.

She sent me another letter later telling me that my life rightfully belonged to Jesus (not her and Dad), and to her credit, she was sorry about the earlier letter. Sean was a nice guy, and she hoped that she'd learn someday that he would be her son-in-law. This prompted a discussion with Sean about marriage that went like this. Sean: Do you want to get married? Me: Hell no. Sean: Keep me posted if you change your mind. That suited me. We still had to finish college. I avoided any talk of marriage, money, and children, with some long-range consequences, my mother's judgments notwithstanding.

Early on in our co-habitation, I was sitting at the desk in our bedroom trying to write. I shrugged my shoulders to push Sean away. He worked harder to please me, to distract me.

"Sean. Quit it. I need space." He held his hands as if I had slapped them. My righteousness burned. There were things I didn't know how to say to him, or any man, or to say tactfully. I was tired of being his college-boy joy.

"Space? What do you mean space? You have the whole apartment!" He spread his arms wide at the room. Besides the gender-neutral sheets we chose together, virtually everything we had in our place was mine. Everything he owned fit in one suitcase and a few milk crates. Unlike my bare move to the dorms, I came with a mountain of clothes, dishes, a penchant for rugs and curtains, too many books, and a desk. I was outfitted for a domesticity I felt ambivalent about. I needed everything. Especially the desk. And to be alone.

"You know what I mean."

"No, Patty, I don't." He didn't. He craved attention and excitement—he liked parties, live bands, lots of loving. His vibrancy, smarts, and zest for life were so very attractive, but I craved quietude and privacy, time to write and read. Most of all to put bad juju in the rearview mirror.

MOVING IN WITH Sean wasn't as shattering as breaking the law or getting attacked, but trying to understand myself with him was slow going. I would get it together, I told myself, after the epiphany that would naturally occur from getting it together. Then I would share with Sean my newfound insights. That was my logic then. Meanwhile I had to be vigilant. Everything had to be equal—laundry, dishes, you name it. There was an invisible line down the middle of everything, but Sean didn't see it.

Sean asked me what I liked and what I wanted. In and out of bed. I didn't know.

To feel free. To feel as if I'd never been violated. A very tall order and not at all specific. Ok, for example, how do you manifest sexual freedom? And what is it? Is love always conveyed through sex? Or is that how guys express it? There was no way I was going to say out loud anything as nasty as "go down on me" to him.

Could he ever understand me?

I sat at my desk, my back to him and yelled, *Don't tell me, don't tell me anything!* I was in a new world, surrounded by the things that should be in it, and the ideas I had about men and women were worn-out. Sometimes the world I saw was not wide open Madison, waiting for me to step into it and blossom. No. It was a place where dogs were neglected and choked on short chains, some men did grubby business, and every dream had a shadow.

A post-rape sex life is a complicated thing. Emotional reactions like the ones I had were not about disliking sex. I liked sex. I felt guilty about how much I liked it. The word dirty was very real to me then, and a constant subtext in our sex life. It was my upbringing. It was the shame of rape. Sean couldn't fathom why a young beautiful woman like myself would be so attached to restraint and routine. It was hard for me to talk about anything that made me uncomfortable, and by extension, wrong. During a time when I should have been reveling in physical love with a great guy like Sean, I was completely freaked out about a sexual timetable. Spontaneity wasn't an option.

Oh, all my years before recovery were such a waste of love! It didn't allow either of us the pleasure we might have had. I know that I needed that time, as long as it took, to prepare myself to deal with the trauma and let it go. But part of rape's insidious impact is that it robbed me of natural sexual joy for many years.

Thanksgiving. We were alone. We cooked a small turkey, drank wine. After dinner I felt drowsy and satiated. I wanted a piece of pie and a luxuriant conversation or an absorbing book.

Sean and I sat down on the couch and he began rubbing my shoulders. He moved the back of my hair up, exposing my neck. Massaging, and then kissing it. His kisses were insistent.

"How many holidays do we get to stay home and screw around?" he whispered into my ear and rubbed my arms, trying to be encouraging. He took my hand and placed it on his crotch. Hard. He moved his hands down to my knee.

I tensed. Dessert, not sex! I jumped off the couch to be away from him.

My head filled with reasons and judgments and my chest rose and fell. I was so angry about this unplanned proposal to get laid. I could not say, "Hey, honey, let's have dessert" or "How 'bout we talk a little first?" No.

I threw off my clothes and screamed at him, enraged, pointing at my shaking and naked body. "Is this what you want? Is *this* what you want?"

I never wanted to be pinned down ever again. I wanted to blink Sean away, wipe his fingerprints from the glass of the window, fly out toward the road and run. Instead, I stayed put, fuming, unable to move or speak another word.

COULD I BECOME undaunted by passion or devotion? I wanted love, peace, and soul. Baladi dance uses a series of alluring gestures, where your hips roll sweetly in their sockets as you walk or dance. Your arms reach, seduce. It seems to me to combine flirtation with affected modesty. Of course. Dancing baladi style, a woman knows she's all that. Unafraid of love or desire.

In dance class I was eager to be submerged, to become a baladi woman. Full of feminine power.

Nesma explained that a woman doing Baladi dance would never wear a sparkly two piece costume. The correct attire is a long sleeved ankle-length dress called a *galabeya*, and you tie a narrow scarf at your waist to accent your movements. You get a sense of a woman's curves and graceful movements in this attire, yet it covers most of her body.

Baladi is not a choreography. It is more a state of mind.

Nesma put on some music and asked us to practice.

I moved my shoulders back and forth to keep time, to play, to do nothing more than to dance, to elongate a gaunt spirit.

"Be fun! I cannot watch no stressy American dancers," Nesma said. "No Barbie. *Baladi*."

To set myself toward pleasure, I had to abandon fear. Be nice to my newly extracted self.

I exhaled and began again. I raised my chin upright. I opened my palms and danced with them up, relaxed my fingers, my face, and moved my hips one-two-three to the right, one-two-three to the left. Slowly, bit by bit. Full of feeling for the music.

I found a silver parenthesis, and while I was inside of it, I was neither baladi nor afrangi.

9

A NEW KIND of energy emerged in my body. I could feel the sensation of full connection in a simple undulation, when physical intention caused my spine to unroll from the top of my head to my pelvis. I stood up straight and strong. I felt the difference. I started to think that my mind and body were not separate beings who lived in the same neighborhood on different streets. My body connected to my mind for the first time.

Concurrent with this new physical awareness, my therapist Betsy helped me practice releasing what she called obstructive thought. She gave me the recorded tapes that encouraged mental images of floating. By allowing myself to "float" rather than resist, I could experience my feelings instead of withdrawing from them. I discovered within the cosmos of an undulation, I could unite body and emotion. This was the beginning of compassion for self, and its companion, courage.

These things started to work their way from the inside out, and it compelled in me a curiosity about performance. I believed performing belly dance in public, especially when you are not shaped in the manner of ideal womanhood, was the height of bravery. I still think so. I wanted to know how people found the nerve to do it, and equally compelling, not to make it seem effortless, relaxed.

When I started taking belly dance classes, I met a range of dancers, some with professional aspirations, and others seeking, like me, to emerge from their own fears and vulnerability. Most simply wanted to have fun.

Belly dance has a sexy and mysterious allure for a lot of people. When you tell them you are a belly dancer, people always say "ooooh" and depending on the person, this ooooh might be accompanied by a little shake of the hips or shoulders. The orientalist belly dance fantasy of sexual abandon and servitude of beautiful women in harems has been stoked in popular culture for a long time, from the seventeenth-century European explorers who considered the courts of the Ottoman Empire to be salacious and degenerate, on to the 1960s TV show *I Dream of Jeannie* (although I would love to have Jeannie's superpowers—to nod my head and blink away problems) culminating in the Bratz Genie Magic dolls. I'm sure there are many more.

The impression is kept alive today by "Sultan" dances where a tipped-off "unsuspecting" man is dragged onstage to be teased into submission by a belly dancer.

The true mystery and allure of belly dance is found not only in dimly lit clubs featuring sinuous dancers or campy orientalist scenarios, but in the hearts of determined amateur performers and their enthusiastic loved ones.

The Lake Harriet Dance Center still hosts a once-a-month *hafla*, a dance party of belly dance performances and social dancing in Minneapolis. By day, this particular dance studio teaches legions of children ballet, tap, and jazz, and the wear and tear in the lobby is apparent, from the top of the dingy ceiling tiles to the patched carpet underfoot. Hanging on the wall by one of the couches is a bulletin board crowded with kids' drawings and ballet shoe orders. Framed, soft-focus pictures of ballerinas in pink tutus decorate the walls. It seems the last place you would find belly dancers.

A *hafla* or *khafla* in Arabic is the word for party, and is traditionally about getting together socially, and these gatherings might include a dancer, drummers and food. Of all the culturally important parties featuring dancing, weddings are number one.

When Sean and I got married in 1996, I had just started taking belly dance classes and we hired a band that played a mix of folk and international music. Our friends Catherine and Ergun showed off their Turkish folk dance steps and my brother's Jewish father-in-law played klezmer clarinet for the Hora. I swiveled my hips and had a blast.

THE FOCUS OF the *hafla* at the Lake Harriet Dance Center is on showcasing student dancing. Family and friends arrive in packs, greeting the dancers and taking seats in the studio. That night, audience members sat in a mood of restless anticipation on the two-dozen metal folding chairs and mats placed on the floor scuffed by tap shoes and ballet shoe toe chalk. Sean and I were too late for seats, so we had to sit on gym mats on the floor. There was a sense of anticipation in the audience.

Sean has accompanied me to a lot of these kinds of shows. Sean loves good music and enthusiastic performances. He likes meeting the women who dance, and loves the music. He also has a sophisticated appreciation for the nuances of dance due to all that he's learned about it. He would never take part in a sultan act, and I'm relieved that holds zero appeal. But sometimes the dancers are not prepared enough, or are too self-absorbed, and they frown and make awkward movements, or strange facial expressions while they're dancing. For my sake, Sean takes the good with the bad. I had immersed myself in Minneapolis' belly dance culture—going to as many shows as I could, learning about all the dance traditions—and he'd been a willing partner. I'm sure it's not the role he envisioned for himself, but he'd become a belly dance husband. Good belly dance husbands are supportive at shows and above all, patient with pre-show jitters and liberal with post-performance praise.

At the *hafla*, the sound of swishing parkas got louder as the room filled up with about fifty people who took off their coats and got situated in chairs or on the floor. Chairs scraped. Gum was chewed eagerly in a few jaws. Multiple languages and laughter circulated the room. Two kids climbed over me and Sean for a better view, changed their minds, and went back over us and sat on the floor. That audience was comfortable, informal, a tableau of marriage and children. A woman in a floral headscarf next to me fiddled with a videocam, passed it to her husband, who patiently adjusted it and handed it back to her.

OUR GREATEST THRILL when we could finally afford a house was that we had more room to spare. In the early 1990s we were constantly bringing new people into our lives and welcoming old friends into our home. Sean and I used to host almost every weekend. We would have dinners, and people spent the night all the time.

It didn't hurt that we liked to cook and Sean was a home brewer. Our kitchen was steamy and warm during our lengthy Minnesota winters with boiling hops and soaking grains. Our beer cellar was always fully stocked. Artist friends created beer labels for Sean's original recipes, and we would spend our Saturdays labeling the bottles, cleaning and cooking, getting ready for another party. This wasn't work; it was love and recreation.

Last-minute hosting was our lifestyle, and in those years many people made their way to our hard, but amicable guest beds. We had a closet full of towels and bed linens. The way we looked at it, we had a washing machine and extra futon mattresses. The food co-op was just a few blocks away.

We lavished all comers with all that we had, and in turn they filled our lives with spontaneity and excitement. Guests showed us pictures from their trips abroad, gave us weird foodstuffs and ethnic crafts as gifts. Neighbors dropped by with freshly baked bread or homemade salsa to share with us for a sit down and a few beers. We were considered a good couple, and we believed we were too. We led an urban, neo-hippie, throwback life. We embodied the "think global, buy local" standard of living.

Then, one year, during the peak of Minnesota's visiting season, also known as summer in our parts, we were on the road. We went to six weddings in eight weeks. As a result of all those weddings, our guests stopped globe-trotting and started putting down roots. We all got work that turned into demanding careers. Some people had kids by design or accident. We started trying to get pregnant, too. Our casual, moment's-notice life was over.

THE *HAFLA* EVENING'S MC was a woman in a big blue cover up with a yellow flower in her dyed red hair. She'd been hosting the *hafla* for years. The flower in her hair trembled as she spoke.

The first dancer of the *hafla* was a woman named Ariana. Ariana, whose real name was Kate, was a plump brunette. She filled in a one-piece body-hugging *beledi* dress with gold and red beads. She wore a gold coin hip scarf on her hips and there were strategic cut-outs up the thigh of her dance dress. The two-piece costumes, the kind that reside in the imaginations of most people when they imagine belly dancers, tend to be worn by women blessed by thinness, youthful good looks, or the fierceness to wear them. Ariana was in the stomach-covered medium-glitz category.

I considered what the women of the old feminist newspaper collective I was once part of would debate regarding belly dance, and the *hafla*. Are belly dancing women demonstrating the power and control they have of their bodies, or capitulating to male fantasy and orientalist stereotypes? Aren't performers dancing for the male gaze? Would a *hafla* hosted by non-Arabs be cultural appropriation even if Arabs are there? What about the two-piece costumes and the shimmies? Is that titillating by choice or effect?

The feminist scholar Andrea Deagon wrote that "Belly dance exists at the point of conflict between women's expressions of fundamental truths, and patriarchal interpretations of this expression. It is not an easy place to be . . . the view of the general public has not kept pace with the feminist bent of dancers' images of their art." What I had been yearning for half my life, was starting to open up to me in the momentum of dance. The things I was learning to do physically and emotionally had been liberating. I also knew that the way people perceive belly dance is based on ideas of sexual appropriation of female bodies. I recollected at a different belly dance performance I attended, the event MC instructed all the men to keep their hands to themselves for the "lap dance." Good grief. Who would want to take the stage after that?

It's also one of the realities of being a female entertainer—no matter what your genre.

Events like the Lake Harriet hafla are an attempt to give dancers a space to form their dance identities, as well as an opportunity to show people that belly dance comes from complex, multi-layered traditions. The women of the *hafla* were doing their best to demonstrate respect for the dance and themselves.

Was it a perfect feminist expression? Of course not. Understanding the convolutions of belly dance and synthesizing its contradictions make it challenging to everyone, most especially to those who take the dance form seriously. It is why I love it so. All my great loves have never been straightforward or easy.

I conjectured that Ariana spent an hour multi-tasking before she got to the dance center. The kids and the hubby got frozen tater tots and microwaveable mac-n-cheese for dinner. A plate of cooling tots were on her dresser, but she couldn't eat them. She sucked in her breath and shimmied into her costume and then shimmied some more in the mirror, watching the beads sparkle and bounce around her hips. Not bad. The kids complained for no good reason about dinner while she glued on false eyelashes. A silent *shut up* went through her head as she simultaneously hoped the false eyelashes would go on right and stay put. Her hands shook when she put the rhinestone earrings in her ears. She saved the lipstick for last and gave her husband a big kiss on the cheek. He responded by grabbing her ass.

SEAN AND I had started saying no when people asked to stay or wanted to drop by. We needed down time as a couple and alone time for ourselves. "I'll do it when I have time," became a mantra in our conversations with each other.

Sean quit brewing beer, and the parties we hosted dwindled to none. I donated all the unused blankets and sheets. Got rid of duplicate serving dishes. Slimmed down the pantry.

Sean and I started to have bitter fights about who did what around the house. Coats and shoes and unopened mail piled up in the foyer. Unclean dishes were always in the kitchen sink. Weeds took over the garden. We had our new oven for months before it had anything of consequence baked in it; whereas the old one had been crusted over and on its last legs from overuse.

All those things were symptomatic of bigger issues: we agonized over unanswered questions about parenthood. Why couldn't I get pregnant? Was parenthood even the right thing to do?

We used to talk for hours in bed about books and ideas. Now that those ideas had been put into action we were scheduled all the way through to the hours before we fell asleep. We even put lovemaking on the calendar, which was an improvement over fighting about it.

Feeling hurt and disagreeable, we started couples therapy and learned new relationship concepts. Each of us should put "currency" into our partner's "love bank" through compassionate acts. Our therapist encouraged us to listen to each other and ask questions, instead of sniping at each other about our gripes. For people who make a living as professional communicators, we found this surprisingly awkward and difficult to do with each other.

We didn't want to have any fights during our precious alone time. So what did we do? We ran shopping errands to Target and other department stores. Had disappointing dates at overpriced, underwhelming restaurants where we gossiped about other people and felt smug. We talked about how we wished we had time to have people over, like we used to.

Our busyness had a monolithic quality that kept us from addressing the challenges of our relationship. Sean was accompanying me to the *hafla* to make a deposit in my love bank. But Sean and I were consciously seeking fulfillment in other areas too. This meant I devoted myself to a writing practice and subjected our shaky finances to my unreliable freelance income. Sean became the manager of the neighborhood food co-op, a growing multimillion dollar business, and took on a level of professional and community accountability that had been crushing at times.

It made me wonder about all the visitors and parties of old. Were we doing all that to avoid those angst-y questions about progeny and legacies? Was letting other people come and go at will through our days exactly the thing we needed to be doing to be happy? Did we actually ruin a good thing by actively pursuing our dreams? Was it overreach? We had to learn what I assume a lot of couples already knew; life is a bundle of contradictions. As much as we longed for children, they scared us because we'd become accustomed to a life without them. We established the careers we did because we believed in them, but the soul-work required was daunting. We ached for naturalness and romance, but the choices we'd made had made that difficult. I was seeking renewal and congruence by roaming the realms of beaded costume fringe and the padded flesh of my own hips.

BEFORE THE MUSIC started, Ariana took her place on the "stage" in a classic belly dance pose—chest elevated, one hand behind her head and the other at her hip. She was smiling a nervous smile at the wide open area of the studio's dance floor before her. Anne was having trouble getting the recorded music started on the sound system, so Ariana had to hold her pose. The audience tittered; I was nervous for her. Ariana was saying a little prayer to the dance goddess for all the things dancers hope for during a performance: that the performance will look crisp, the music won't skip, that there won't be any costume malfunctions.

Finally the music started, a mid-tempo song with a staccato 4/4 beat. Ariana started her dance but kept to the back of the room and clung to the sides of the stage. I imagined that's exactly what I would do up there. Was it garden-variety stage fright, or something else?

I remembered Grandma. Her kitchen table. "Look here," she said, when she made biscuits. Ma's luxurious white legs. The way the sun through the window made grandma look up and smile. The lump in my throat was a choking boulder then.

Arianna had to pull through.

Arianna held her mouth in a forced smile as she moved tentatively toward the audience. The audience sat on creaking folding chairs, immersed. People clapped encouragement in time to the music. Their engagement provided a breakthrough; her face relaxed. Her movements became more fluid, and she transitioned from a vibrational hip shimmy to a flowing undulation. Her dancing was not about bringing a technically proficient, memorized piece to the stage, but sharing her body's interpretation of the music. Hooting and wild clapping commenced.

Ariana's shoulders loosened and she was beaming when she finally took her place in the center of the stage.

My restlessness settled as I watched Arianna. Watching a belly dancer was better than prayer to an unknown god. I interpreted my obsession to absorb so many different performances as following the roadmap to dance in public myself someday. I could see a part of my own spirit in how she held her body. My torso relaxed over my hip sockets.

I was at the *hafla* to summon courage. It wasn't something that could be conferred just because I went in search of it. I had to produce it.

10

IN THE LOUNGE of the Reproductive Medicine Center, the furniture was exactly like the kind they have at the airport—flat black vinyl seats secured one to the other, each seat sharing a stainless steel armrest. People wait in there like they are waiting for the flight that will take them to a stressful family reunion. You are part of a clan, love it or leave it, but are still hopeful, maybe unrealistically so, that bad luck will finally be dispensed with, a history of slights forgotten. I imagined the tens of hundreds of couples who have warmed their asses there, hopes massaged for the umpteenth time. I remember that place reeked of heartbreak, and it was smothering me. I could smell its salty-sweet musk seeping from the closed doors behind the reception area.

Sean and I were there to get results from my HSG test, and I was afraid of what I didn't know about my body, and why it seemed to betray my wishes month after month. We had been trying for four years by the time I was thirty-six, geriatric in reproductive years. I was forced to admit to myself that conceiving a child the regular penis-vagina way was the worst way to go about it.

I picked up *People* magazine, the Catherine Zeta Jones-Michael Douglas wedding issue. Ms. Jones had the nerve to say of her two million dollar fete, that she just wanted something simple. God. Every bride says that shit. Not one means it. I hated her opulent gown, a V-neck. Catherine was quoted as saying that on their first date, Michael told her he wanted to be the father of her children. That would have been my *last* date with him. The article also claimed she was back down to a size six four months after her baby was born. Bullshit. She was spilling out of her wedding gown a little too much. It was the flagrant display of her nursing bosoms that got to me. Mine just seemed flat, appended to my chest, without feeling, except for a pesky itching.

I tossed the magazine on the stack of others—*Vogue, Glamour, Elle*. I was curious how many women have successfully conceived using sexy lingerie and come-hither looks. Was that how Catherine Zeta-Jones got her baby? I also know, based on the number of people that passed through that waiting room, many of us had not conceived after months and years of trying with the different sticks and wands and shots and drugs, screwing at the weirdest times without a drop of energy for it. Or, sat through the misguided directives from the well-meaning. Get your man to wear boxers. Stand on your head after intercourse. Put four pillows under your bottom. Don't move for a half hour after. Don't make love every day. Make love every day. Make love every other day.

It was hard to say what was worse, the silly boxer shorts thing, or the advice from those influenced by New Age. Tie four ribbons to a tree branch, and after a week count how many are left. That's how many children you'll have. I did it. All four stuck. Four kids? Right.

Or maybe I was being punished. When I played with Julie and Nia in Pierce Woods, we all vied for the "Mommy Dearest" type role, someone powerful and scary. Nice and nurturing meant being a spineless person. I snubbed my mother's attempts to domesticate me. I was *never* going to have kids. How I grew up is how women ended up pregnant too young, out-of-wedlock, and totally broke. I'd successfully avoided that fate, but had long feared motherhood as a life sentence.

My idea of family had matured since the defiant anti-housecleaning days. Now I'd like to have a daughter who would be free to ruin her doll's hair, or a son who wanted to play with them. I could be a good mom. And Sean. He'd be a terrific dad. He loves kids, is always able to connect with them. Sometimes, when we come home from long trips, we're glad to be home, but that's when we feel "it" most. The sense that something's missing—the neatness and calm of a childless house—makes the lack more palpable, brings home the fact that our home is empty. I learned that one and one does not always add together and make another.

I was also sure that if I did get pregnant, belly dancing would prepare me for childbirth. All that ab rolling would culminate in a beautiful, easy labor. As I sat in the waiting room, I tried not to let a sense of entitlement take hold. I was starting to learn how to live in my body, but truthfully it seemed too late. I scanned the room for something besides fashion and celebrities to read about.

There was not a single parenting-oriented magazine there. At the regular OB, that's all you'd get, along with the pamphlets on vaccinations and potty training. The clientele at the reproductive center were women like myself. Still youngish, hip. Disdainful of *Woman's Day*. Former doll neglecters. Infertile. Mostly white, middle class or better.

In the confusing panoply of emotions that coursed through me then, there was one thing I could not admit to. I still felt ambivalent about motherhood. Could I really do it? It scared the crap out of me. It was also enlivening, like cliff-diving. When we were called into the doctor's office, I had determined to let fate decide.

Dr. Campbell explained to Sean and I that the HSG showed two visual polyps—one growing at the opening to my right ovarian tube. A risk of ectopic pregnancy. But polyps may or may not have been the cause of our problem. I was listening to Dr. Campbell's polite assertions about our as yet unexplained infertility. Age contributes to irregular cycles, harder eggs, fewer opportunities for conception, less than optimum conditions. No one really knows the answer. "Science can figure out a lot, it can help, but nobody really knows sometimes," he said. My problem was thankfully not cancer, not even disease; it could just be a case of waiting too long to bear children. He recommended getting the polyps out as a first step.

THE BAND WAS playing red-hot swing in a bar that used to be a drunk old men's hangout, but has been reclaimed as an urban treasure. Live bands now play music those old guys grew up listening to, but the youthful crowds pushed them away to quieter dives. As I listened to the moderately loud bass, I decided, I'm still young. Young enough to have fun, young enough to have a baby, young enough to think I could be going out and parenting too. I dropped my belly dance classes so Sean and I could take swing dance in order to dance together as a couple. I loved swing dance, but tried not to be resentful of it because I was missing belly dance.

People at least a decade younger were crowding the dance floor, doing the swing with a professional flair, turning, jiving, dipping their partners. It's a rare dance floor that fills up on the first song, when everyone is still relatively sober. One young man had his hair slicked back, black, falling over one eye. He was wearing a delivery driver's shirt of some kind. The sort of shirt most of the men I knew as a child wore. Was this guy's purchased at a trendy shop, or actually worn once by someone he knew? I hoped he was not merely a fashion victim.

He was swinging his partner, a woman with matching jet-black hair, bangs trimmed way high on her forehead, ponytail bobbing with every turn and dip. Her pedal pusher pants hugged her hips, and her cropped top revealed a pierced belly button. She looked like she stepped out from an old-time calendar, her curves were part nostalgia, part naughty babe. Since I was dressed in a nearly identical outfit, down to the ponytail in my hair, I felt embarrassed. Sean looked his age, with salt and pepper hair, hipster glasses. I was thankful the barroom lighting was dim, erasing tiny wrinkles around my eyes, making a thirty-something me look twenty-something. I knew I was more pathetic in my attempts to be with it.

The dancers out that night were especially good. They seemed to be channeling ghosts from bygone eras.

I wanted to dance.

I grabbed Sean and took him out to the dance floor even though I know he hates it when I don't wait for him to get ready—whatever that means. The criteria changes all the time, depending on the number of other dancers out on the floor, how good they are, the particular song, how much alcohol he's had, if we're out with friends or alone. Sometimes we don't go out there at all, sometimes I go out and dance by myself, and sometimes we dance every song. Mostly he tries. I know some guys won't budge, won't dance if their life depended on it.

Sean was half-hearted in his rock step, arms limp as noodles. The foxy couple I noticed earlier banged into us on a turn and gave us a dirty look as if we were in their way on purpose. I pulled Sean into the center of the dance floor, which usually gets him to relax because we're not on the outside being watched. We got the rhythm going, and I was happy to be dancing, warm in the crush of other people dancing too. He twirled me into the cuddle step, but then stepped on my toes. He can be such a klutz, he doesn't seem to hear the beat of the music when he dances, he can't keep from looking down at his feet.

On the way home we argued. What was supposed to be fun turned out to be too much pressure. Sean pounded his hands on the steering wheel at the first stoplight we encountered.

"Everyone else was too good. We sucked," he said. I told him he shouldn't worry about it. He said, "I'm not a great dancer, I know that."

I shrugged. That got him even more pissed, because I didn't say, "you're great honey" or some such platitudinal crap. I was irrationally annoyed, envisioning other couples dancing effortlessly, not having stupid fights. I knew I shouldn't be so mean. I recounted in my head all the ways dancing in public made him intimidated—new steps, unfamiliar music, beautiful young people—and I was not gracious about it.

We were arguing about dancing because we couldn't argue about childbearing. We were keeping our fears to ourselves—if we said them we would jinx it. What would happen if we did have kids, and what would happen if we didn't? I imagined being bloated and sore from breastfeeding, Sean bugging me for sex, not keeping the bathroom clean, leaving the poopy diapers. Or what if we ended up battling a stillness in our house too wintery to understand, nitpicking each other because the recycling got left out on the wrong night (idiot!) or the dish sponge was left gooey and wet in the sink? Condemnation was on the tip of our tongues. Our insecurities came out on the dance floor.

SOMETHING KEPT ME from torching *Women's Bodies, Women's Wisdom* by Christiane Northrup. That I hated her book was a good sign. My friend was also egging me on. We'd had long discussions over tea in my kitchen throughout the course of our friendship about the state of our uteri, the state of our place in the world as women. Carol is bracing and funny—a real wise-cracker. We deplore the literature of our time that makes women out to be head cases, especially the chicly-earthy woo woo feminists who are actually trying hard not to, but still essentially blame women for what ails them. We were making fun of "women's wisdom."

"Hey listen to this," I told her. "Your uterus is your second chakra, got that? So if you're having problems, it could be related to, um, money, sex, and control issues with other people."

Carol said, "Do you know anybody who doesn't have any of those problems?"

We laughed like hags.

Carol grabbed the book out of my hands and read it for herself.

"It's also related to creativity issues—the second chakra," she said, wagging her finger in jest.

I didn't laugh about that. What if Christiane was right about it? What if the reason I couldn't conceive was because I wasn't opening myself up as a vessel of creation? I was essentially too selfish to share my uterus. It was a reminder, like the Bible, of a certain moral point of view. Christiane tapped into my guilt about being caught up in other interests. The demands writing my first book made on my personal and financial life. That I loved the belly dance classes so much I practiced every day around the house. Maybe there wasn't room enough in my uterus for my development and a child's.

Plus, Christiane's book had sold a ton of copies. Maybe she was on to something.

I told Carol, "This woman she cured had a cyst, like the size of a grapefruit. Her patient got some spiritual and emotional clarity and it just shrugged itself right out of her uterus and she went on with her life. All her problems with her mother were over. Could someone really birth a grapefruit cyst and repair her relationship with her ma?"

"Oh, Pat," Carol said, tossing the book on the table. "Do you think that woman with the cyst had ever considered that *maybe*, just maybe, her problem was physical?"

I SHOULD'VE STUCK to beer, the usual, but my mother-in-law Isabelle told me to live a little. We were in a supper club after all, where you didn't just have to have beer. Plus Hank, her boyfriend, was paying.

I watched the Elmo Supper Club bartender, wearing a loose-fitting Green Bay Packer's jersey load another glass with ice for me. He filled it halfway with vodka, added the spicy tomato juice swill, and threw in a wilted celery stick—which I ate before taking a sip.

A recent round of fertility treatments left me feeling crazy and messed up. I'd been trying to become pregnant, but right then I felt like I didn't deserve to be. I knew what kind of woman orders a third badly-made cocktail within an hour.

Sean and I had lived with blithe indecision about when to have kids. I didn't even hear the biological clock tick until the alarm went off. We felt estranged from our life's purpose, and in a peculiar relationship twilight. What would we be working toward in life as a couple if we didn't have a family? Sitting on the barstool at the Elmo,

I felt the weight of consequence. The Bloody Marys left an acidic ache in my chest that even drunkenness couldn't erase.

In that corner of Wisconsin, thirty miles east of Dubuque, Iowa and the Mississippi River, everyone knows everyone. The patrons at the Elmo all knew me, even though we'd never met and I don't live in the area. I was sure they knew about my failure to conceive, too. There's nothing to do in a small town but gossip and bar hop.

A few years ago Isabelle was thrilled to be elected Irish Rose by the Lafayette County Shamrock Club, the oldster version of homecoming queen. Sean and I had gone to her "coronation," where she wore a green vest over a white pantsuit, her puffy white hair topped with a large, green hat.

At the Elmo, I fought the urge to retreat to the bathroom when a round of Isabelle's friends came by to chat, widows who had cradled scores of children, and saw me as a child too. Isabelle's friends were sweet, fawning over my figure, my "good catch," aka my husband. Sean was hiding out from the onslaught by talking about the weather with Hank, Isabelle's latest boyfriend, a retired farmer. The women were working overtime to make me feel welcome, so I smiled. What they thought was my glamorous city life in Minneapolis was just a home with a dog and two cats.

The herd of women eventually dispersed to Formica tables that surrounded the supper club dance floor.

When she was my age, Isabelle said, the Catholic Church and society kept women in their place. Wife and mother was your only option. After birthing nine kids, her body was tired and worn out. Sean, the youngest, almost died in childbirth. A sympathetic doctor gave her birth control pills "to regulate her menstrual cycle" not prevent pregnancy. Otherwise the church wouldn't have approved.

As she talked, I felt my own sense of unease. That patriarchal past was not so long ago. My parents had raised me in religion too. But I was seeking, and expected, a different rite of passage through love and motherhood, one based on mutual consideration and equality, that was thwarted by my own uncertainty.

Isabelle's emancipation began the day she became a cook on a tugboat that went up and down the Mississippi River. When she found out she got the job, Sean's father told her if she took it, he'd divorce her. "I said, well then, my prayers have been answered twice in one day."

As she told me about that first year on the river, her voice became conspiratorial. For all her bravado, I'd never heard her talk about how she got through it. I am still stirred by her ability to remain emotionally buoyant after enduring so many years of putdowns and abuse.

"I would sit in my room on that boat sometimes, it had a window above the dresser, and I would just watch the Mississippi. It seemed I was always looking back that first year on the boat."

She told me she felt overwhelmed by feelings and memories. "I'd throw a little of what my life had been till then out in the water and watch it float away. There goes all those bad years." Isabelle motioned with her hand over her head. "I did that over and over."

The chaos of her life on land gradually took on the peaceful rhythms of the river.

Isabelle held her hands in the air; palms open before me and said, "Patty, these are what got me through." With those hands she catered weddings, sewed, ran a beauty shop, and kept going. I realized that she was trying to give me advice. Pretty and childfree Patty, adrift and pitiful? Nuh uh. She wasn't buying it. She said when the lawyer who filed her divorce papers asked her what she planned to do for money; she said she held up her hands.

THE POLYPS WERE removed, and I wished I could say the emotional turmoil went with them. Sean and I watched the video of the removal operation, comfortably ensconced in a leather club chair in the doctor's office, with a fascinated horror and artistic curiosity. I deliberated: I could do a polyp performance art installation. Make something out of this. It could be on multiple screens, I could add sound effects, or it could be like a silent movie. Placards could be made informing the audience of the plot. Patient sedated. Tipped uterus caused problems. Skilled specialist performed. Go doctor go.

Dr. Campbell then proceeded to create an outline of possible scenarios for future procedures. Dr. Campbell drew a uterus on a piece of paper, and added a circle representing the egg coming down the fallopian tube. A mass of washed and cleaned sperm, drawn like a pointillist cloud, were inseminated into the hypothetical me. If that didn't work, there was an increase in clomid dosage or HCG shots to enhance ovarian production. Finally, we got to a discussion of in-vitro, the last and most aggressive procedure. The doctor drew an ovary filled with dots and an arrow pointing outward. That was the egg retrieval. At the bottom of the page his pen finessed a petri dish where eggs and sperm meet. An arrow from the dish pointed to my hypothetical uterus.

We were at a crossroads. What to do with our lives, how to define what it meant to have and be a family seemed to be shrouded behind the doctor's lined legal pad.

Sean and I had become people accustomed to setting goals and reaching them. Infertility was something that made us feel so fallible, mortal. No amount of rationalization could change the tenor of our lives—we wanted a baby of our own, and it seemed out of our control. We had to face that we might never pass on to another human being our own flesh and blood. We hoped there was some purpose, something that would live past ourselves into a next life or generation. To know that's not possible—

I had regrets that we didn't start sooner, that I didn't heed the warning signals of declining fertility, whatever they might have been. We could have tried years earlier when I quit that crazy job I had. Practically nobody can afford children, but people have them anyway. Remodeling with a toddler underfoot—we would have managed. I could have paid more attention to my body's aches and pains. I shouldn't have listened to the HMO doctor who told me to drink more water and come back in six months if better hydration didn't help conception.

In the surgical video, what looked like a set of fancy tweezers went into my uterine cavity and pulled out the polyps. First the little one. Next, the big one was taken apart in pieces, the doctor explaining he was careful to keep the fallopian tube opening from getting damaged. Sean and I went "ugh" in unison. It was the size of a three-month-old fetus—the size of a kumquat. So little really. It looked like the kind of homemade super ball I used to make from layers of rubber cement when I was a kid. I'd put a dab of rubber cement on my thumb and rub it into a ball on my forefinger, then add another daub. I imagined a nugget of bone or strand of hair was coiled in the center of the polyp, and tissue grew and grew around it. Maybe in that "thing" I'd generated in my uterus, was something trying to be a person.

11

ROSINA-FAWZIA AL-RAWI wrote in her memoir *Grandmother's Secrets*, that dancing makes it possible for people to set out on unorthodox searches for themselves, to experience sexual and social issues in their own bodies. I felt that Al-Rawi, raised in another generation, who lived half a world away in Baghdad, was uncommonly wise. I found myself notching pages, underlining passages, savoring her voice as I read. "The story of one's life as it is written into the body can be retold and understood in the intense moment of dancing . . . Thus belly dancing becomes a source of inspiration, a means of collecting and strengthening oneself, and a clear and dynamic way of discovering one's wishes and understanding oneself, no matter how insecure and doubtful the future may be."

One's wishes.

According to Al-Rawi, desire for understanding stems from a midpoint on your belly. Failing to conceive, my belly felt soft and vacant. I wished for strength and affinity.

I needed a belly dance jump start, and it was on the Iron Range, in Virginia, Minnesota of all places, that I went to take a dance workshop led by Bellydance Superstar Ansuya. Ansuya is one of the gorgeous and impressively talented belly dancers who participate in a media empire of shows, workshops, videos and music cd's for mainstream consumption of Middle Eastern dance. About a hundred and fifty women gathered in the extreme northland of Minnesota, also known as the middle of nowhere, to learn from Ansuya how to put together a "scintillating" (her word) drum solo.

That morning, I was feeling a little sleep-deprived and bleary. The hotel recommended for out-of-towners was right on the rail line that went through town, and all through the night trains loaded with iron ore passed by on their way to processing plants in other cities and towns. We were handed earplugs and a weary explanation of the situation when we checked in. The train was regular and rumbly, and the earth hummed beneath the hotel before it arrived, and the rough dealings of open pit mining afterward. In nearby Hibbing, I'd gone to the Rust Mahoning mine, the largest open pit mine in the world, which can be visited as a tourist attraction. The giant dump trucks that moved between levels the size of the Grand Canyon looked like tiny toys in it, performing a stark choreography of extraction and commerce.

One of the neighborhoods where I grew up in Racine abutted railroad tracks. Our trains usually went by in the daytime, and when they came through we had to forgo hearing what was being said on TV. We yelled at each other over the din to be heard. In another neighborhood, we lived near Racine Boiler and Tank, and were serenaded night after night by the third shift's molten steel flume and the sound of constant knocking as workers fabricated parts, pipes, troughs, rings and rollers. The idea of belly dance taking root in a place like Virginia, Minnesota, or even Racine, seemed implausible, but as an antidote to the thumping subjugation of mineral resources, belly dance should have a unique place in any industrial heart.

At the workshop venue in Virginia, the first ones to show up were those who had been saving their money for up to a year to buy a Madame Abla costume or some such confection imported from Egypt. The vendor who sold them was a respected dancer who decided to retire and trade in on her reputation. Now she makes a living selling dance wares to women eager to project their dance desires through her product line. Some of the women who buy such frothy costumes have very little practical use for them—never having much opportunity to perform in them—but I know having one gets you closer to feeling like the jewel you want to be.

I watched women who looked like soccer moms and farm wives paw through the costumes, running their hands over the beadwork, flipping the skirts up to see if the material floated, hugging the costumes against their bodies. Many of those outfits came with a base price tag of eight hundred dollars. The women exclaimed over each one. "Look at this one. Oh, look at *this* one!" Some of them were really stunning—colorful bead work that cascaded over the stomach catching the light just right so vibrations are beautifully accented, or hip belts with lovely floral or geometric designs that showed off the dancer's good taste and technique. Then there were the truly horrid ones. Ones with beads or appliqué sprouting out of the bra where your nipples would be. Hip belts with v's so deep everything points down to you-know-where. The vendor had also brought costumes based on snake or reptilian themes with tight skirts that flared at the bottom. Women loved those too.

The *bedlah* that I have is not belly dance couture, but it's nicely made. I pair it with a classic green chiffon circle skirt. It's as much bling as I can handle, but the pre-made costumes from abroad were beautifully tempting. I ran my hands over the hard bras and spiky appliques, put my fingers into a handful of beads and decided what I'd look best in, and considered it. Burgundy with blue and gold accents. Did the vendor have a layaway plan? In the end, I knew that buying one wouldn't magically turn me into a better dancer, so I saved my money for more classes.

I thought about those costumes tucked into someone's farmhouse closet waiting for its owner to put it on some winter night, cranking up the music. That woman might feel her cold nipples warm up underneath that five pound beaded bra, her arms and bare stomach exposed to the bracing air and feel hot, hot, hot.

There were other vendors in too. People who sold ethnic goods from Afghanistan, Morocco, Egypt, Tunisia, places like that. They were there for the contingency of belly dancers who opt for wearing coins and embroidered things for their costumes. They were the women in the crowd who wore funky cover ups or pashmina in some earthy color or design, the ones who seemed to have embraced their inner nomad by waking up late and stuffing their unkempt hair in a clip. They approached the tables laden with chunky silver jewelry and blatant beads, embroidered clothing, and house wares with a cool demeanor. They had been around a souk or two and knew you can't act too excited if you want to strike a deal.

I loved it all—the sparkly stuff and the folkloric stuff, the ways we all justified our purchases—just because we couldn't leave without wearing one more bright and noisy accessory. Women love to shop, and vendors of all kinds have stepped in, providing more completely impractical and pretty items. Investing in dance attire, whether you wear it or not makes you feel radical, a little racy.

Some women in the Virginia crowd had graduated to trying on the costumes. They would take them into the bathroom to disrobe, and then come out to waiting friends wearing the costume, pushing out their chests and holding in their stomachs and then letting the fat flop over the beaded belts. Ask any woman what she thinks of her belly and you'll get a raft of negative opinions. How she wishes it wasn't so big, soft and pliable, but held in and up. Never hanging. Flat. We make brutal demands on our stomachs and pelvis, inside and out. A cabaret belly dance costume is really like wearing incredibly gaudy and heavy underwear in public. So women suck it in, smile, stand up straight, and hope. As soon as I feel the nap of heavy beading digging into my skin when I move, my performance smile gets bigger. Why do we dancers want to wear them? Lust over them? If I knew the answer to the many contemporary paradoxes embodied in the study of Middle Eastern dance, maybe I'd be making money selling costumes too.

ANSUYA APPEARED TO step down from the clouds into the crowd of women waiting for her. We ended up forming a circle around her, waiting impatiently for her to impart her superstar wisdom. Ansuya spoke. She was from Miami, she told us, and she seemed to exude some sort of Miami heat from the core of her beautifully postured size two body. Her hair fell to her butt, and as she talked she swept it up from behind her head and tied it in an artful knot at the back of her neck. Her makeup looked like it had been done by a makeup artist. Every line around her eyes was crisp, her eyebrows flawlessly proportioned. Lovely red lips. She looked airbrushed and serene. She was toned and tanned. Belly dance perfection. A model. A superstar.

I was wearing a burgundy tank top and black yoga pants. I had an orange fringed hip scarf on my hips that I tried to adjust for maximum coverage. My hair was unkempt in a clip, and I could stand to lose a few pounds. My pooch swelled from the beer, burger, and fries I'd had the night before for dinner.

Ansuya began to teach us a drum solo choreography. This is a dance wherein a solo dancer moves to a series of drum rhythms. Often the music is demanding, be it fast, slow, staccato, requiring crisp movements and strong reflexes. It is my absolute favorite thing to watch. A good drum solo is thrilling and exhilarating, and watching dancers interpret the fast-paced rhythms and deliver a physical performance of hip hits, shimmies, and pops and locks always leaves me in awe. *How did she do that?*

The drum solo Ansuya was teaching us was on one of her DVDs. She located the video and played her recorded drum solo for us in its entirety. It was an amazing piece, one where she was playing finger cymbals, doing all kinds of backbends, shimmies, and vibrations, beautiful turns, and floor work wherein she was using her hair to sensuously brush the floor.

Seriously?

I was way over my head.

Ansuya began her drum solo with doing traveling shimmies, turning left and then right and rolling up. We were supposed to follow suit. And then there was the finger cymbal section with a *ciftitelli* rhythm that had an accompanying complicated step. She explained how to follow along with a running patter that went something like this, "shimmy, shimmy, right foot forward and back, left arm up, right arm down, third phase Arabic, pause, undulate, and roll up." She was expert at calling out moves as she danced, but that didn't mean that I had the skill to follow all that. That was an accelerated dance being taught in a compressed amount of time. Normally, it takes me weeks, if not months, to master a new choreography. Not hours. Almost immediately, I was breathing hard and felt dizzy from trying to keep up with the superstar. Ansuya didn't appear to break a sweat. Throughout the day some participants complained the workshop was too hard, and one dancer threw off her hip scarf in a fit of pique.

All eyes scanned the room of dancers—who was keeping up with the Bellydance Superstar? Could anyone shimmy for something like forever and then gracefully lock her pelvis and hold it for the finale?

The youthful, sinewy, and confident ones, they could. They were what you'd call the whole package. They were the ones invited to audition for increasingly rare nightclub gigs. To the average person, they are the only visible facet of Middle Eastern dance. They are the ones other dancers secretly want to be, or kill.

A woman said to me, "You see her, over there; *she* bought that costume that looks . . ." A gold-and-black beaded costume seemed to escort one of those especially pretty, tiny women through the gym to a spot on the periphery where she gently put it out on the floor. "She'll look like a bumble bee in it," she concluded. Without the tension of a body inside, it looked mummified. Its stinger breasts pointed toward the ceiling.

Al-Rawi wrote in her book that patriarchal societies have forced women into stereotyped roles, and that feminine images (be it saints or witches) are controlled through female appearance, attitudes, gestures, and movements because of a fear of social chaos should the strength of female sexuality be acknowledged. Even though we weren't men, we consciously and subconsciously controlled each other with our jealous desires to be like the superstar. Al-Rawi cautioned that a woman evaluate these roles and images and decide for herself where she wanted to stand in the world. "She has to be very careful not to be misunderstood," she said. And I would add, not to judge. But that was harder to do.

POST-BREAK WE did some more shimmy marathons with Ansuya. I was working up a sweat and felt my knees turn rubbery with the exertion of keeping a steady 4/4 beat in my hips. Then Ansuya made us break into groups to practice the choreography she'd just taught us. When my group's turn came to demonstrate what we learned, remorse hit me in the chest when the music started. I couldn't remember the choreography or why I ever loved belly dance. I felt like the choreography *was* too hard, and that it served to remind me of the continued difficulty of mastering this dance form.

After each group had gone through its paces, Ansuya made all of us get together in a big circle again. We were told to sit down. Butts wrapped in various hip scarves hit the floor. Ansuya sat down too. She took a number of CDs and DVDs out of a bag she'd brought with her into the circle. She put them on the floor in front her with a definitive hard plastic slap. Women shushed. Humbled.

She grabbed one CD and held it up. "The music to today's choreography is on this one. If you buy it from me today it's two dollars off." She picked up one of the Bellydance Superstar DVDs. "This is a video from our latest tour. I only have limited quantities left. I can autograph anything you want, and if you want to take pictures with me, we can do that when we're done here." A few women got up to leave the sales pitch. Ansuya seemed unperturbed by the defection. Ansuya's polished persona radiated practiced sales technique. After teaching and dancing for four hours straight she didn't seem winded at all.

"We have a few minutes now so if you would like to hear about the Bellydance Superstars tour you can stay. I'll tell you about what it was like."

She explained how we might think touring as a belly dance superstar was glamorous, but it wasn't. They were twelve women trapped on tour bus, she said, often having to put their stage makeup on as they were driving down the road. They usually had no more than fifteen minutes to prepare to dance on a stage they'd never seen before. All the healthy types freaked out on the takeout and fast food. Tensions ran high, she said, but the women loved each other. Like sisters.

Her telling sounded rehearsed, and rather than demystifying belly dance superstardom, it seemed calculated to reinforce the image of a rarified company of incomparably gorgeous, unattached women road-tripping for belly dance. Ansuya probably sold more stuff that way.

I remembered a conversation I'd had with a friend about the roots of belly dance, and her skepticism about a time in the world's history where women danced together to prepare the body for childbirth, to cheer on a laboring mother, to worship the goddess. "If it sounds like a fairy tale, then it is a fairy tale," she said.

What might have been Ansuya's real narrative about being on the Iron Range? Nothing but carbs for miles. Sweet people, but no peace and quiet. A mining moonscape for scenery. Had Ansuya's sleep the night before her workshop been disrupted by the trains? How did that trip to the Iron Range fit into Ansuya's own artistic dreams as an internationally respected dancer? Where was the glamor to being a belly dance superstar outside of the realm of expertly lit shows and high-production value DVDs? I considered the hours upon hours in the studio she'd probably spent, pushing the limits of her spine, pummeling her calloused feet. Her show that night was incredible. It seemed she could do nearly everything flawlessly, from the luxurious floor work, to playing complicated rhythms on finger cymbals, all while dancing in magnificent form.

Yet her perfect delivery had left me feeling ambivalent. I reflected on the train cars loaded with iron ore, and the similarly repetitive DVDs and things for sale quarried from faraway places and traditions. Were we the gullible, sentimental audience the Bellydance Superstar media empire hoped would open their wallets? I felt like I was getting the contemporary version of the Enjoli woman.

Al-Rawi wrote that if you wish to become more awake, more aware, pay attention to the silence between the beats. In this scenario where were the women who thought like Al-Rawi? I was still sorting out how I felt about Ansuya, and the whole superstar idea, when she stood up for autographs and pictures. I stood up too. I decided to leave the gym, get water, stretch, and recover what was left of my shimmy. The kinship I sought was in the scrum of women improvising an imperfect creative life in unlikely places. Ansuya was surrounded by fans snapping photos. I could never see the two of us together, laid-back and framed.

12

SEAN AND I struggled to get through our first morning in London—starting with finding standup coffee to drink in a tea drinking world. Starbucks. Natch. We sat outside the café at a table in the cool of the morning while the caffeine and London's people passing by on the sidewalk pulsed through our veins. Our arrival was close upon the heels of the three tube stations that had just got blown up in July 2007, and our place was near the British Museum where the bus got hit. Neither of us were too worried. I read the tabloid that had been left on our table. I turned the cover page open to a full page photo of a topless starlet.

This was our first trip with our new self-identity. A couple who would never have children. This was going to be a geographic cure. But with most geographic cures, it seemed everywhere I looked reflected back feelings of disappointment and barrenness.

The most essential thing you need on a trip, said Rick Steves, the European travel guru, is a sense of humor. I really hate Rick Steves, his nasal voice and Boy Scout self, but Sean and I agreed, overnight before sleeping, that keeping a sense of humor, adapting to circumstance, refraining from judgments, was really the best course.

I had been grasping for good advice, such as how to proceed when life plans are altered, and that seemed as good as any. I had thought that having a child with Sean would be the starting line to a new kind of life. I never got pregnant, and after half-heartedly considering adoption, Sean and I quietly let the idea of parenthood go. We were seeking another kind of start to childless couple-hood. In London, Rick Steves' advice replayed in my head.

We'd arrived at Heathrow the night before and rejected the aggressive taxi drivers as we ran through the long hallways of the airport to the subway, our luggage pulling our arms out of our sockets as we rushed to get the last outgoing train to the city (with two minutes to spare!). As we sat on the tube, our bright windbreakers and matching backpacks announced to all in our car we were American tourists. We spent the next hour *en route* to the transfer station being glared at by the guy across from us.

We switched stations at Liverpool Street, then carried our luggage up narrow stairs at Goodge in Bloomsbury, where we finally arrived about one a.m. I still felt ok when I said to Sean, "We should've taken a taxi," as we got lost on the dark and eerie streets in Virginia Woolf's old stomping grounds. At long last, we were buzzed into our hotel and directed to a room with no bathroom and a sagging mattress covered by a threadbare and pilling quilt. I could hear everything—a TV, someone coughing, a toilet flushing—even with earplugs in. I tamped down my disillusionment and Sean's what-the-heck-is-this-place energy as I lay in bed. I'd spent hours prior to our trip searching the Internet for a place that was centrally located and affordable. I'd found this one, owned by an Italian family who also ran a restaurant adjacent to the hotel. I realized the photos on the website showing the place were some really good fakery.

We'd come to London because I'd wanted to recover some of the excitement and sense of discovery from early on in my relationship with Sean. Without a language barrier I figured we could do some hipster travel—not just checking out tourist sights, but finding those quirky bookstores, the boho ghettos, places where the broke and artistic hang out. That was the kind of travel we both did when we were young and unattached and ate nothing but bread and yogurt stuffed in our backpacks. Our backpacks had gone upscale—artisan cheeses, sparkling water, fresh fruit, farmstead meats. We observed regular mealtimes and took rest breaks. But we were sure London will be a great place to find the cool stuff, trigger creative serendipity and revelations, like the kind we had before we bought a home and tried to have kids, before getting away and relaxation became a necessity.

We'd also be seeing a belly dancer later, a woman named Amira who had a regular gig as the featured dancer at a restaurant called Mizmouna. Her dancing was described as "mesmerizing," the belly dance adjective usually used by the uninitiated, but that time so described by a fellow belly dancer. I looked forward to meeting her, hearing about what the dance scene was like in London. I wanted to further my belly dance connections, but I also fantasized about being part of an international dance scene. I could go to any country in the world and find a like-minded belly dancer friend, part of a sisterhood.

I was looking forward to being entertained, maybe seeing some new moves. I was sure it would be a highlight of the trip.

But in the light of day, we finally understood that our international B&B was really a flophouse. We had found funky, that's for sure, and didn't like it. As we ate our continental breakfast of toast, just toasted white bread, no butter, I tried to be cheerful to the other "guests" who, as it turned out, were mostly people with angry auras: the coughing woman and an old man close with discontent. The breakfast room walls were filled with greasy and crooked pictures of what I presumed was the host's family when they were all still kids. In the "back then" of another generation people seemed to have too many children they couldn't take care of and took for granted.

A TV mounted on the wall was tuned to a soccer match, or football, as the announcer called it. It turned out the Italian family had sold both the hotel and restaurant to a guy who seemed to love soccer more than hospitality.

We ate the toast as our host had an argument in the kitchen with a woman who was threatening to quit. Sean lifted an eyebrow. I felt my throat tighten. This was not an auspicious beginning. At all.

We politely informed our proprietor that we ordered a room with a bathroom and a shower—reminded him that we were paying a higher rate for that. He opened a ledger on the reception desk kept under the TV in the breakfast room, and he ran his fingers up and down the empty page with our sole reservation written on it. A question on his fingertips: How was he going to get out of this?

He told us that switching rooms was "no problem." No problem. He gave us the key to a new room and told us it would be ready when we returned.

At the café, I tried to put all that out of my mind while flipping pages of the tabloid. Kate Moss busted for a crack addiction and outed for having sex with women at parties. Jude Law shagging his nanny. One of London's subway bombers was pictured a full page tall, his backpack apparently packed and loaded. A security camera caught him browsing at a Boot's Pharmacy near the tube stop he blew up ten minutes later. The article noted he didn't buy anything, just sort of skulked around killing time. Who hasn't done likewise before an appointment with destiny?

I put aside the paper and noticed my husband furtively watching all the gorgeous young things that inhabit London as they go about their day. Despite the cool vaporous air, they were dressed for a party we weren't invited to: open jackets, low rise jeans, and thick leather belts emphasized their sensuous hips and bare bellies. Many wore high heels, never mind the condition of the sidewalks. Their gait was more like a saunter. All the rest held mysterious allure just by being different. I felt my Rick Steves good humor evaporate. Who was I kidding with my hipster traveler act? My age was showing in my hair, at my waistline, around my eyes, my feet ensconced in sensible tennis shoes, my coat zipped up to my neck. I was not aging gracefully, at least not by London standards. And Sean? He looked sort of like a chunky George Clooney.

I mulled over my belly dance costume hanging in my closet at home—how it had a thickly beaded belt that sits low on my hips, that when I wear it my stomach is bare, that we often used a saunter we called the sassy girl walk in our choreography. As I sat there in London, my belly dance life in Minnesota seemed silly and quaint. Underneath a lot of the dance costumes of my cohorts are knee and ankle braces, breast uplift pads and body stockings to hold in the flab around our middles. But wasn't it because of belly dance that I'd learned acceptance?

I remembered a power ballad I'd heard on the radio back in Minneapolis, "This One's for the Girls." The singer had a message to her older listeners in that song, something about tossing pennies in the fountain of youth, but I'd dismissed it then. It might have helped in London. I stood up from my seat at the café and shook my shoulders to slough off my fretfulness. It was the street life, the tabloid's in-your-face sexuality.

"Hey, babe, I think it's time to get moving," I said.

Sean finally looked away from the people walking by. He stood up with me, and we began to walk toward the Thames. A couple blocks later he drained the last of his coffee and looked around for a trash can. We couldn't find one, so he stuffed the empty cup in our backpack.

The simmering resentments and stresses of our lives we attempted to put on hold: We were on vacation. We'd been pulled apart by the challenges of infertility treatments and found ourselves on a trip suddenly in need of definition.

As more and more insufficiently dressed women passed us on the street, though, I said, "I wonder where they work, dressed like that?"

My husband shrugged. He seemed lost; his facial expression was soft. He'd been hypnotized. London was a Roberto Cavalli dream, with umbrellas. My husband's normal curiosity and interest in his surroundings I'd interpreted as a personal slight. Watching what I judged was my husband's lust for other women, I felt like I was trying to hold onto something I was not entitled to anymore. I didn't stand a chance next to the historical or biological attractions. The sights of London inspired dread. Every colossal building I looked at felt heavy on my shoulders. The Thames looked murky and bacterial.

He was enjoying himself. He was on vacation. From me.

I took his hand in mine.

Even though my water repellent windbreaker was bright red, I was invisible to my husband and the masses on the sidewalks that bumped into me with annoying frequency. My hood covered my head and kept my hair dry, but my tennis shoes and the bottom of my jeans were soaked. My face was encircled by my hood like a wimple. I rationalized, I'm a spiritual being seeking a higher truth, worshiping at the altars of Anglophile art and architecture, neutered, sexless, stoic, and against my wishes, touristic. It wasn't enough to feel my husband's warm hand in mine. I sought reassurance. To feel sexy.

This was the story I was telling myself, but it wasn't true. The dangerous travel virus of misery and disappointment had infected me, but I wasn't yet symptomatic. I was still smiling for the camera. Look! There I was soaked on the Millennium Bridge, soaked on the Tower Bridge, soaked in front of St. Paul's cathedral, working it hard, trying to enjoy the indifferent buildings and people around me. At that moment, sitting on the steps of St. Paul's smiling up at my husband, I'd held onto the hope that London would still reveal a delicious cross-cultural treasure, that the belly dancer we would see later at dinner would be wonderful. Joyful, sensual, playful. All the things I desired for my relationship with Sean.

I allowed myself the fantasy of belonging to this huge and fast-paced city. Since we couldn't have children, we'd be the traveling couple crossing the continents, making all our tied down friends jealous. We could have romance, art, and intellectual discussions without interruption. We'd be part of that breed of benevolently patient people who are tolerant of slow service at restaurants, we'd play the worldly, eccentric aunt and uncle to awestruck nieces and nephews. I ticked off all the continents in my mind I've been to: The Americas, Europe, Central Asia, Africa.

But before we left the U.S. we took our nephew to the zoo only to have him howl the whole time as he struggled to get out of his stroller. Out of the stroller he tested our agility time and again as he continually toddled toward danger. He was a little monster who liked to hit people and throw things. He ate gum off the sidewalk and threw up. We lasted about a half an hour. Would it be different if he were ours? How would we deal with a crying kid with a poopy diaper in a foreign country? Would our gratefulness to be parents override any arguments I know we'd have about whose turn it was to change the child's pants? Would we even travel if we had kids?

Yet even without the kids we didn't have romance and hipness.

We got to the tower bridge and walked across it to the South Bank side of the Thames.

"Now you can say you've seen the definitive London spot," Sean said as we reached the midpoint on the bridge.

We stood side by side in the rain, looking down into the brown river water. I kept my peace. I'd thought Big Ben was the definitive London sight.

As the day wore on, my husband's looking became longing. I clenched my jaw and my hands curled into fists from cold frustration. There's nothing in any travel guidebook I've encountered that explains how to handle things when you are faced with the provincial person you are in real life, and what to do when it doesn't compare with the image you have of yourself as a sophisticated and adaptable person. The trip designed to forge our new identity as a couple wasn't going well at all.

Sean and I tried drying off by browsing a bookstore on the South Bank. A woman started a commotion at the cash register. While she vociferously complained about the treatment she was getting, the staff got more and more agitated, demanding she leave. Meanwhile, the man who had been browsing the table of books next to mine started loading the front of his coat with books. Sean looked at me and I looked at him. I'd remembered a night years ago when we were working at the food co-op together and he'd stopped a man who had stuffed two whole fryers in each underarm of his coat. Sean stood in the doorway and demanded he hand over the chickens. The guy smiled and unzipped his jacket. The guy pulled the chickens out of his coat as if it was all a big joke and left. I was so relieved he didn't have a gun I cried.

Thereafter, we were a crime-busting team, catching and prosecuting shoplifters with regularity before we moved on to other, less dangerous jobs.

We had none of the old fight left in us. Sean and I kept a complicit silence as we watched the man in the bulging green coat slip outside and get away.

WE TURNED THE key in the lock of our new, improved room and opened the door to a jumble of furniture, two single beds tipped on their sides, and a dresser angled away from the wall. I felt the two sides of my heart split with a whoosh of recognition in my chest. Here it was before us, the state of our relationship summed up in a rough hotel room denigrated by deferred maintenance and an atmosphere of accumulated disappointments.

Our host assured us it would be "no problem" to make things right. Give him an hour.

When we returned an hour later, we saw the two single beds had been thrown out on the street in front of the hotel. Back in the room, we saw they had been replaced with a double. The bedding was ok. An unusually large bathroom held a toilet, bidet, and tub. Unlike the communal bathroom, there were no visible footprints on the floor tile. The effort it must have taken to make the room passable should have made me feel more grateful.

The rain had finally stopped, and Sean opened the window near the bed to watch dusk settle over the row houses nearby. It wasn't late, but after the day we had, it felt like the middle of the night. A cool, damp wind blew in and settled everything. If there was ever any question, we were staying. We didn't have the energy to change hotels.

"Hey let's fill the tub, like we did that time in San Francisco," Sean said.

We'd stayed at a fading hotel in Union Square that had a huge old tub and scalding hot water. That time we'd bathed together after sightseeing, made love afterward, and fell asleep for a satisfying nap before going out for the evening.

Sean needed reassuring as much as I did. Sure, he liked looking at the beauties on the street, but they never gave him a second look. I understood why a man's middle aged crisis could include a red sports car. He felt invisible too. I told him no. I was tired. I required a nap. I dropped down on the bed, intentionally skipping the bath. I was sore. Jaded. Every muscle had been extended to its limit. My head felt twice its size, swollen.

The very thing I claimed to want, joy and play with my husband, I didn't do. I didn't care if I was missing an opportunity for catharsis. My eyes burned and watered into my pillow.

I watched my husband look out the window at the row houses below. A few people had dilapidated little patios with plants in pots, chairs for sitting, but mostly the ones nearby were bare—which seemed better.

Sean's back was curved as he looked down at the inner workings of London situated around our hotel room. He crossed his arms and held his shoulders with his hands. I recognized the posture. He wasn't cold; he was apprehensive. I weighed other trips, other rotten accommodations: the reek of pigeon in Casablanca, the seven locks on the door in Washington, DC, New York's amazing shower stall mold, the broken toilet in Paris. We were used to roughing it, taking our chances, feeling a sense of bravado that we could take a little shit in the heart of a world-class city to get closer to its real essence. You wouldn't catch us recharging our batteries at an all-inclusive resort. Bad hotel rooms and middle of the night arrivals didn't seem so terrible. That was before I thought about myself as the barren castoff among London's attractions.

Sean wanted to know what was the matter.

"Dehydration and jet lag." That's what I told him. It was true, but it was really an excuse.

I considered one of those made in Minnesota believe-it-or-not stories, the one where a surprised badger or other wild animal comes down the fireplace into someone's living room after getting smoked out. Sean had a defensive, panicked badger with him and he knew it. He didn't want to get attacked, so he kept a vigil near the window instead.

I GOT DRESSED up in jeans and a semi-sheer button up lace top with rabbit fur at the neckline. I wore an "extreme" cleavage bra, did my hair, wore chandelier earrings, put on lipstick. I wore the kitten heel shoes I'd splurged on during the hour we waited for our room to be made up. A low heel for sure, but a heel at any rate. After all, I needed the same thing as my husband. A little romance and sensual pleasure. A night out in the big city. After twenty-plus years together we had to admit there's not too much we can do that is new anymore. Sean didn't say anything about my outfit.

Nonetheless, my sense of humor was somewhat restored after a nap. Our dinner reservation at the Moroccan restaurant was for much later in the evening so we could watch the belly dancer's set. We decided to walk in Notting Hill to take in more sights. Living rooms glowed from within in the dark. We peeked into places to see people who exhibited great taste in furniture and art. This was the London I came to see, relaxed and elegant. I longed to be invited in and conversed with. A funny and erudite conversation would be just the ticket.

I started up such a conversation with my husband. What did he think of all the things we saw? What were his impressions of this monolithic town? If he could describe it in one word what would it be?

"Divergent," he said. The word coated my tongue with a metallic flavor. Divergent. I couldn't agree more.

WE GOT OFF at the restaurant's tube stop an hour early, long before our dinner reservation, but judging by the number of empty tables when we got there, that didn't seem to be a problem. I'd made the reservation on the advice of the belly dancer back in the U.S. who had been there. She claimed the place would be packed. I was ready to kick off my pinching shoes, have a big fat drink, and be entertained.

As I looked around the place, I fell in love. The walls were exposed brick, and the sections that were plastered were painted in popular Moroccan colors—blue and bright orange—colors that look good in bright sunlight or dim candlelight. A Moroccan flag hung in one corner and the floor was covered with Zemour carpets woven with geometric designs. Hand pressed metal lanterns hung from the ceiling, casting an overhead glow into the dining room. Lamps made with goatskin and designs painted on them with henna were scattered strategically along the floor. Moroccan couches lined the entire perimeter of the restaurant, piled with pillows. Tables were pulled up close to the banquets and a few free standing chairs were available. The restaurant was quiet, a few scattered diners here and there, their meals held in beautifully painted tagines or on colorful plates. It was warm and romantic. I squeezed Sean's hand. We weren't in dreary, mean London anymore.

Our host took us to a secluded table in an alcove. I spoke up. We were there to see the belly dancer—where was the best seat for seeing her dance?

The host's handsome smile caved in. "Oh, she's not dancing."

The "why" that came out of me sounded spoiled and pathetic.

"She broke her leg coming out of the subway car in the tube. The belly dancer has a broken leg."

The belly dancer has a broken leg. My husband and I stared rudely at the waiter. We willed a belly dancer to appear. He had no idea how important this was. She was to be the bringer of wonder and delight.

I felt like I was digesting my stomach lining.

I was back in cold damp London again, and worse than that, reflexively thinking about the subway terrorist. I couldn't help but feel like our fates were inextricably linked.

At Sean's request, the waiter moved us to a table closer to the bar. Sean squeezed himself between our table and the couch, throwing seat pillows toward the empty table next to us. His jaw was clenched. "I am never, ever, going to make plans with you to see another belly dancer again."

We'd come all the way to London to have Sean finally reach his belly dance threshold.

I knew he'd seen too much of the less glamorous side: my attempts to master difficult movements that look so awkward in the learning stage, the loud and irregular finger cymbal drills, hearing the same song over and over again while I perfected and adjusted the choreography. Sean had supported me by sitting through countless shows ranging from professional to amateur. He understood belly dance for all its complexities, how it had helped me physically and spiritually, but the slate was wiped clean. He couldn't take anymore. He had seen his share of belly dancers and was over it.

I threw the pillows he'd tossed away back at him. My friend Carol once told me she had a row with her husband in a hotel room in Portland that ended in a pillow fight. My husband's insistence that he was done with belly dance made me feel as if he was capable of suffocating me with one of those scratchy wool pillows.

I looked away from him after I gave him my meanest stare, looking instead at the rugs scattered on the floor which now looked crumpled, dirty, and disheveled.

Sean read my mind. "It's amazing that dancer hadn't broken her leg sooner." He nodded toward the floor. I felt guilty in that moment. I really had not given *her* plight much thought. I wanted her to fix a universe of things I thought were wrong, but to her, dancing for us was just another day on the job. One that ended badly.

I imagined the train had left the station just as the dancer was stepping out on the platform, the door catching her pant leg, the train pulling her along. With the help of a bystander and one wrenching pull, she was free. I understood the truth of her situation to be like mine, complicated.

I had known plenty of dancers, all graceful, who had fallen and broken some bone, arm or leg. I knew this because the body has its own timetable. It was easy to misjudge, maybe wait too long, or move too suddenly. For instance, if Sean and I had started sooner would we have conceived?

The belly dancer's leg was broken and my husband and I were in a slump.

I looked into the menu to hold back morbid loneliness. I was confronted with so many seemingly inconsequential choices: red wine or white? By the glass or the bottle? A meat tagine or vegetable couscous? Appetizers or not?

Sean liked belly dancing, sure, but he wouldn't plan trip activities around it. Not at all. I should have admitted that in planning to go to London I really wasn't fully devoted to our relationship even though that was the trip's stated purpose.

We decided on a bottle of red, a meat tagine, bstilla for an appetizer. It was a stylish purgatory.

A couple of Moroccan guys wearing jellabiya took their seats on some stools near our table. One had a drum, the other a pair of cymbals. They were warming up their hands, getting ready to play some music.

The waiter leaned over me and lit the candle between us. It illuminated the artfully fractured inlaid tile on our table.

AFTER DINNER, MY shoes pinched my feet, and the clip clop
sound I made on the sidewalk was maddening. Sean was in a funk. As
I continued to clop down the street, Sean got hit with a big wet glob
that got his hair, glasses, coat. In the light of a streetlamp, it was thick
and sticky, a sickly beige, as if someone had flung a serving spoon full
of hummus at him. Bird shit. We had nothing with us to clean it up
because we'd left our backpack at the hotel. That's when Sean lost it.
He was sick of wet shoes, jet lag, high prices for everything, and most
of all, our lodgings. Sean informed me, right there on the street, that
these things were my fault. I didn't literally shit on him, but I had in
every other way.

"I mean, god, Pat, if I had booked that hotel, you'd kill me. If
you hadn't wanted to come to London in the first place, we'd be
somewhere warm and sunny, like Spain."

When he finished his tirade his face was puffy and his eyes were
tearing up. I was afraid he was going to cry. People passed us on the
sidewalk as they had all day, unaware of our suffering. I couldn't look
at him without wanting to laugh, but not in the Rick Steves I-have-
my-sense-of-humor way.

I noticed a Boots Pharmacy up the road. I touched Sean firmly,
as I would a child in an emergency, in a way that would engender
trust, not panic. I said calmly, "Hey, I see a store up there. You'll be
fine." I led him up the road, careful not to spread any of the pigeon
mess around.

As I crossed the threshold of the store I imagined the subway
terrorist pictured in the tabloid, loaded with bombs, killing time.
Had he gone into that pharmacy with second thoughts, hoping that
his outrage would be tempered by tidy and benign retail, to be given
a sign that life was worth saving? I was starting to understand. I took
my time. Gentle oat and aloe cleansing wipes? Unscented? I decided
on mercy.

13

AFTER WE GOT back from London, one night in Sean's arms I cried like I'd not cried in years. We were in bed, the sheets crisp and clean, his touch a comfort. I was frightened, my body held in suspension. I was sobbing, but no tears. I was keening.

Sean clued in. It was these kinds of questions:

"So are you bored with our lovemaking? Is there anything you'd like me to do different?"

He asked at the right time. We were not fighting about sex, dishes, time together, money. I told him no, not really. I didn't know how to explain to him the void I felt. I wanted to be aroused, the vibrant part of my personality drawn out. I desired so many things, most of all to feel undivided and unconstrained.

A magazine survey I read in *Ladies Home Journal* (now there's an authority) claimed that people—like me—who have secret thoughts are a bad marriage risk. And I'd like to know who doesn't?

I don't even know if I believed that how I felt was as high-toned as personal freedom. I'd been guilty of thinking my husband's smart, solid working-Joe self was not good enough. Were we good enough for each other? I considered the holding pattern—what do we do now?

Before that period of marital division in London, my life had started to feel like a step forward out of the shadows. And it was. But all those Disney movies I watched as a kid came back to me, along with adult sense and feminist shame about being a woman on a pedestal. Validation as a woman in almost any culture means to be looked at and positively appraised. Had I always wanted someone to look at me the way the prince looks at Cinderella/Sleeping Beauty/ Snow White, etc.? But I couldn't think of anyone who had ever gazed at me that way.

Sean's a man in motion, gratified by active efficiency. He would never do just one thing at a time. His curiosity is direct and serious.

He loves with intense loyalty. Being the center of his attention is one of the best things in my life. The flip side is that it can be tiring to be his partner. He rarely sits still. He has a tendency to overdo things, and when he's tired he's brusque and off-putting. Sean hates to wait. For anything.

Sean's attention to me was exacting, honest, wholehearted—but not worshipful. Deep down, maybe adoration was what I had always been holding out for. It's what I hoped for long ago in my dorm room. As a little girl, I accepted that's what love must be like.

I dreamed about the perfect man: sensitive, artistic, and good-looking. Kind about my mistakes, encouraging, patient. Would that be better?

I was under the influence of some intimate pressure. I imagined myself in new scenarios outside my current life, each one more removed from present reality than the other. I automatically believed Sean wouldn't understand. Facing the truth was too painful. I was driven to distraction with the force of my own suppressed sexuality and creativity. Dance had been a catalyst for all of the things I was starting to understand. But the desire to live fully as a woman and artist still weighted the rest of my life. In my mind's eye I was again and again goaded by a lust to be perfect, brighter than before.

WHEN I WAS a girl, I kept a locked diary. In it I made declarations: I was never going to be any man's slave. I was going to leave Racine. I was going to get a cat who didn't run away.

In those days I was inspired by John Boy from *The Waltons*, the TV character who stayed up late to write, to whom the whole family warbled "Goodnight, John Boy" at the end of the show. I needed the emotional acceptance John Boy got and wanted to feel the physical grandeur inherent in making grand pronouncements. I'd also diligently read the Bible and was impressed by the larger-than-life characters in it. I wished for my life to follow a momentous and powerful path, like Moses, one marked by serendipity and conviction. Hence the diary declarations.

I was determined to construct an escape hatch, but I didn't know how to do that. I held on to the idea that, like John Boy, I would write my way out. A few decades later I'd finally comprehend that my pre-adolescent ego had been right all along.

My diary got broken into because I made a big deal about writing in it. Was it my sister or one of my brother's sneaky friends? It's hard to say what was worse, the betrayal, or the fact that the things I wrote were ridiculed by kids in the neighborhood. The neighbor boy who liked to light ants on fire for fun, and liked me more than I knew, said to our kick-the-can crowd: "Who cares what Patty thinks of our raggedy town? Who cares that she doesn't want to be bossed by a man? Cats come and go. That's how they live." Where were the clandestine loves? Undisclosed crushes? The top-secret secrets? I had a dumbass diary.

Even though those diaries were sold in volume in a bin at the Kresge's store I didn't know anyone who actually wrote in one. The skinny lines in the damn things made it nearly impossible. Anne Frank had her diary named Kitty. Anne believed that keeping a diary was key to understanding the world. You could write things in it that you wouldn't dare say out loud.

It didn't occur to me in my outrage and superiority that anyone else had a similar inner life, that my sister, or the neighbor boy, for instance, felt the same din of uncertainty. That lighting ants on fire and exposing my soft spots were about banishing fear. I got it back, finger-printed and dirty.

I consider that my initiation into the writing life. Even though it took me a long time to take myself seriously, I understood early on that when you care about something as fearsome as personal expression, you risk getting hurt when it goes public. It wasn't until I published my first novel that I'd experienced the miserable condition that no amount of love, friendship, or hard work seemed to help.

When my first book was published, I felt crushed by certain reviews. I exposed my work to the kind of scrutiny I felt was mortifying. I spent days afterward in stunned slow motion. I felt the weight of rejection accumulate in my lungs. Every moment of the day was scourged by powerful dismissal. I forgot about the people who were impacted by its message or loved it. Wracked with insomnia at night, all the faith and perseverance that got me so far leaked right out of me. I was a mess.

My dance instructor encouraged me to stand up straight and open the back of my heart. Her simple observation about my stance made me think my insecurity and lack of emotional preparation was all too apparent. I summoned Nesma's question: what does a woman expect of the life?

My mother always told me that when you need to sort yourself out, you need to sort something out. When I was a kid, Ma would go on occasional housecleaning junkets: starching curtains, washing walls, day-long ironing marathons. It's how she dealt with the emotional and financial pressures of our family's life.

It turned out my filthy microwave oven made me see, literally, that I was wallowing in debauched self-pity. As I was wiping the built up grease off of the microwave and kitchen cabinets around it, I broke down and soaked the front of my shirt with tears that wouldn't stop. I don't believe easy epiphanies necessarily have a place in well-written literature, but I was sure as hell having one in real life. My chest was sore afterward from the physical effort it took to finally let it all go.

I required determination to continue my writing career, certainly, but more than that, I had to be honest. All that I'd put into my writing, the very stuff I understood as my reality, was called into question by a bad review. *So what?* I hadn't done anything worse than write a little save-the-world novel.

Recognizing my propensity to want to believe in a happy ending over redemption made me get real. My heart's tiny back door slid open. I felt its little scratch inch through my spine as I stood up straighter and let its secrets out.

SEAN AND I decided we really did need to do something different. We tried sexy undies, wine, new positions, but nothing changed. Every time we made love, the bed squeaked. Just like in the movies, cued to know something's happening in the next room. The voyeur in a person gets aroused. Whenever I got on top of Sean it started, like some dog toy. At first it was amusing.

But it was indicative of something out of repair, the habit too resolute to change. I was doing what I was always doing, getting on top of him, his hands on my hips, my breath in his ear. He was not transported by ecstasy, nor was I. That noise was not sexy. It was Pavlovian: The bed was squeaking; he was ready to come. The bed was squeaking, he was distracted and so was I. The bed was squeaking, squeaking, squeaking. Finally it stopped.

HERE'S A QUESTION that was posted to the site learn-to-belly-dance.com.

> Will belly dance improve my sex life?—Y.K.

> Dear Y.K.,
> Yes. How could it not?—*Delilah, belly dancer on duty*

ONE SATURDAY AFTER dance class, I came home and found our bed was in pieces. The whole thing had been dismantled, and like the scarecrow in the *Wizard of Oz*, our bed was all over the room. The bedding was in a pile. The mattress smothered the bed pillows. The frame was here and there, against the wall and zig zagged across the floor. It looked like the work of some psycho.

Sean appeared in the middle of it all, vacuum nozzle in hand. He looked like a domestic at a cheap hotel, dressed in sweatpants, no shirt. His prominent chest hairs curled over the line of good taste.

He pushed up his glasses, and I saw the sheen of sweat on his forehead. His eyes were bulging. It looked like he'd been crying. He pulled his hand across his eye to catch a tear.

"While you were gone I've been tightening the bolts on the frame. All of them. I'm sure they were causing our squeaking problem." That's how Sean tackles problems. By throwing himself into fixing things.

"You wouldn't believe what a mess was under there," he said, and pushed his glasses up the bridge of his nose again. "At least ten pounds of cat hair."

My heart beat through my throat. Here Sean was trying to demonstrate his support, by literally strengthening the substructure of what we slept and fucked on.

Sean began to blur before my eyes.

I was a fool.

"Here," Sean said. He handed me a flattened penny from the Shedd Aquarium he'd found under the bed. "You need this."

I HELD A yard sale with a friend. Among the items I had out were loose-fitting sundresses, blasé shirts, and a one-piece swimsuit with a skirt. All the ways I camouflaged my body.

Cindy picked up the swimsuit and laughed at it. At me. "I can't believe you ever wore this!"

I couldn't either. That suit was a symbol of the canker devouring me; the thing I couldn't see for a long time. Being raped didn't *make* me feel like I wasn't good enough, it was *evidence* of what I'd already suspected about myself. I had been disentangling this marred viewpoint for years. All those sessions with Betsy, all my attempts to master undulations and shimmies. Long-held attitudes about my body and its value went out with the granny swimsuit. In the warmth of that late August day, laughing with my friend about the cruddy swimsuit, I felt buoyant.

Around the same time, I had my first class show performance. I'd put a lot into preparing for it. I'd rehearsed the choreography countless times in my bedroom in the weeks before the show, trying to move my arms gracefully over my head, snapping my hips, undulating left and then right, working hard to perfect the circle-and-a-half that always seemed to elude me in class. Before I fell asleep at night I'd run through the dance in my head.

All the emotions I'd tamped down went into designing a costume, hand sewing a hundred coins onto a bra, trimming a sequined fuchsia vest with black-and-gold braid. Acquiring scarves and coins and sequins for a hip belt fired my imagination. During those increasingly warm days that spring, I sat outside, hunched over my improbable bra with a thimble on one finger, sewing, in the worst possible posture, my hopeful heart egging me on.

I was certainly a striking and rather overdressed figure when I appeared with my class in the community center gym for our debut performance. The other women had kept it simple, leotards, hip scarves, circle skirts. I'd wished I had. My whole ensemble was uncomfortable as hell, the vest tight in the shoulders and under my breasts. The belt was held together with fabric stiffened by glue and safety pins that dug into the skin around my hips.

Our music, a song called "Bedouin Wedding," began with a series of recorded call-and-response and random drumbeats before settling into a distinct four-four rhythm. Every muscle group in my body trembled as I stepped out onto the gym floor: shoulders, hands, knees.

I walked in, hands on my hips, making sure to keep my head on an even plane and not bounce like a typical beginner. I was gliding, serpent-like, but I'm sure I bounced before I got to my place on the left side of the "stage" where we were to arrange ourselves out on the floor. I nearly died from nerves, trying to convey the wonderment and mystique of a celebratory gathering on what was really a basketball court ringed with people sitting on folding chairs.

My face felt taut from the smile I forced myself to make. I glanced at the other dancers and noticed forehead sweat and a look of deep concentration—fear. I worried my knees would give out, but my face relaxed when I saw people in the audience smiling back at us. The music cued the dance choreography and my heart skipped because I actually remembered it. A different kind of body memory took over. Hip hits, circle-and-a-half, a little bit of shimmy, all that energy flowed from my body to the audience. I was a natural! I could perform! At the end of the dance I threw my arms up over my head and bowed and let relief and triumph surge through my being as people clapped. Honestly, I felt great, like a real belly dancer.

After the show, a little girl came up to me and patted my breasts and ran her hands over the coins that draped over my chest like fish scales.

FOR YEARS I had been searching for how to be authentically sexual without being cookie-cutter sexy. I knew sensuous movement had sexual power, and it was that aspect of belly dance I was unsure how to integrate into my sexual relationship with Sean.

I had hoarded a huge store of confusion about my earliest sexual experiences and it was overwhelming. How to sort them out? I felt silenced because I didn't know how to say it or codify the bewilderment, and packing it down and away left a dull coolness in my heart. When I had gone away to college I was making a very adult decision, but I was an emotionally unprepared teenager. After I had been assaulted, it was much, much easier to be in denial about what had happened. I didn't have the means to come to terms with it. I didn't have emotional maturity. I understood unfairness, but not systems of subjugation or how to fight them. The scaffolding holding me up was rickety. I wasn't able to speak in my own defense and I don't think I could have survived the inquiry. My life would have been a shambles. I knew I was in trouble and that was enough. I bent to accept the self-judgement instead.

I was starting to understand the difference between physical expression that you did for yourself, like dance, and the various physical sexual personae that limited me—good girl (no cleavage), bad girl (too flirty), victim (drunken dumbass).

I couldn't help but consider how many selves women press out or manufacture in their lifetimes, and that the one I wanted most— to be unconstrained—was the one that always seemed out of reach. There seemed to be no template for that one. I needed that to come before all those other usual female identities: mother, sister, wife. I remembered the historical romances of the 1970s that I snuck away from a neighbor's bookshelf, novels wherein a woman is forcibly seduced by the handsome lord and then falls in love with him before he rides away to fight another war. It was something women I knew read to escape drudgery, and this was the sexual drama handed to us. We were not the creators of our own destiny—especially if we wanted to be lovable.

Dance had brought me to a new threshold of awareness that other things were possible, but there were times when I believed I was asking too much of the universe. I rationalized my life in terms of a common dilemma—lack of time or commitment. The truth was that I wanted to be magically carried away.

I DIDN'T WANT to go it alone. I needed to be held tightly. I wanted to get away. The force of both desires were equal.

It started with a simple suggestion. Betsy proposed Sean and I greet each other at the end of the day by wrapping our arms around each other, and that we hold each other until we start to feel our breathing and bodies relax. "However long it takes," she said. Ever the overachiever—or surely it was the point of the whole exercise—I enjoyed the sensory niceties. How Sean smelled like lavender, how warm his body was, the feel of his shoulders. How much better we both felt when our bodies finally parted.

She also encouraged us to think about sexuality in terms of pleasure and play, not give and take.

"I know how much you two love each other," Betsy said. "And you both seem to be reasonable people."

We nodded. With one caveat: Most of the time.

"There's a gift that you can give each other, and that is the power to grant wishes."

We both looked intently at her.

"Say yes to each other's requests as often as you reasonably can," Betsy said.

Say yes? Really? I'd always thought power was my right to say no. It is what I and legions of women had fought for. "No" was the byword. I was still indignant that a senseless act of sexual aggression had so much impact on my self-worth. "No" was how I stood up for myself. I had a deeply held belief that I had a duty to defend myself, and by extension woman-kind.

Despite my professed duty to be done with patriarchy, I was not in the vanguard of self-appreciation or self-respect either. I struggled with chronic insecurity, especially when it came to sexual desire. For almost my entire life I equated desire with being dirty and getting pregnant a life sentence.

I would argue part of the issue is thus: abhorring our bodies is the first thing women do in the morning and the last before we fall asleep. I used to think: Could I ever look at myself in the mirror and not feel like I am doing something wrong? *You are ill-prepared. You are too dehydrated. You are asking for too much.* To address this required even more than moving muscles in new ways. It had to be scraped away at the bone.

In the e.e. cummings poem "love is a place," *yes is a world/ & in this world of/ yes live/ (skillfully curled)/ all worlds.* A world where I imagined people weren't bodiless or wordless.

Sean and I were partners, and our disagreements didn't always have to be man versus woman, nor did the past have to define the present. We both had the power to help each other by being amenable and compassionate. I had to allow myself to be both true and vulnerable in our relationship, and do what appeared unthinkable.

My "no," which so often was couched as an endless list of preconditions, was more about protecting my vulnerability than it was about meeting my needs or sharing sexual enjoyment. It caused me to snub meaningful sexual connection. I had the power to be the rejecter, the one to say *don't.* I believed it made up for a time when I didn't have it.

IN BED I was lying on my side, two pillows pummeled into a deep divot for my head. Sean's one pillow was slept flat. He wore nothing; I wore a full set of pajamas. Sean slipped his hand under my top and rested it on my bare stomach.

Which one of us needed and wanted the other more? I listened to Sean's breath, felt the hairs on his arms rise as he caressed me. My skin was alongside his hand and there it was, that old dorm-room feeling: I should prepare myself for a roof collapse or an interruption that won't happen.

Instead of giving my body over to that stale old predicament (so similar to Grandpa's hoary beer can heap), at the very least, I could experience the pleasure of having a better relationship with my breasts and hips in every way.

When my friend Julia was at her mother's deathbed, she said that her mom's last words were: *What is the answer to the question? Yes. It's yes.*

I turned toward Sean with the first of many reasonable requests.

III

Walks and Traveling Steps

14

WHEN I HAD been taking belly dance classes for about seven years, I encountered a new belly dance style that was proliferating faster than the Bellytwins' dance fitness empire. I'd gone to visit my brother and his wife in Chicago and Sean and I went with them to Kan Zeman, a well-known Lebanese restaurant. They were indulging my interest in belly dance and Kan Zeman staged numerous shows on weekends. But the dancing I saw was nothing like what I'd been exposed to in restaurants in the Twin Cities and abroad. Instead of a soloist in a shiny beaded costume, out came a group of six women of various shapes and sizes dressed in big black skirts, coin bras, and belts made with giant colorful tassels. Their heads were wrapped in unusual scarves decorated with flowers and jewelry. They danced in a line around the restaurant together in what seemed like perfect symmetry. They yelled and whooped as they danced, and played finger cymbals the entire time they were performing.

Occasionally they would stop their line, and two women would dance together in serpentine sync, doing undulations, rotating their torsos in simultaneous backbends with graceful snake arms. The other dancers adopted a different and singular movement to accompany the duet, and they seemed to be supportive bystanders as well as dancers. Here it was, the thing I didn't know I'd been waiting for: a sisterhood of dancers crowding a restaurant, making noise, sharing the pleasure and excitement of dance with themselves and the audience. It was an exuberant and absorbing performance. A revelation.

After their show I made a beeline to speak to the dancers. They were called Read My Hips. I asked how they managed to have such tight choreography and they gave each other knowing looks and burst out laughing. Stephanie, the leader said, "It's all improvisational. We don't know what we're going to do until we get out there. But we practice a lot and learn to read each other pretty well." What I'd just seen was known as tribal style belly dance.

WHILE I HAD my tribal belly dance epiphany in Chicago, one of my dance instructors had one too. At Rakkasah West, the Middle Eastern dance festival held annually in southern California, she had seen FatChanceBellyDance perform. They had also recently put out a video that explained the basics of tribal belly dance. It was from this video that my teacher taught us the beginning moves for tribal belly dance. Kora was a former cabaret restaurant dancer who had retired, but still taught classes. Most restaurant dancers "retire" in their late thirties or forties because restaurant owners like to hire lithe young women to lure new customers. This isn't true of every restaurant venue, but it is a prevailing trend. Entertainment equals attractive young women. Kora was searching for a way to continue challenging herself in ways that went beyond that sexist reality.

"Remember when you learned hand signals for turning left or right?" Kora's voice sounded like it came from the east wind, breathy and timorous. Kora stopped talking and observed us taking in her question. Kora was one of the most introverted instructors I've ever had in any subject. Often it seemed like she was gathering the energy to speak, as she pulled in her breath to collect it, and she measured out her words as if following a complicated recipe. I couldn't imagine her in the role of a gregarious restaurant dancer, but I saw the evidence of her success in performance photos. She looked fresh and self-possessed. This was an aspect of Kora I didn't expect, but do we ever suspect demure women of wanting visibility or possessing sensual energy?

Kora extended a multi-braceleted arm in the signal for a left turn. She held her arm in silence. We all nodded.

Kora's hips were round and broad, and she favored a blue fringed hip scarf that she made herself. The most remarkable thing about her dancing was not her hips, but her arms. She could hold them up longer than anyone I knew, and extended them with a graceful curve in the elbows and a beautifully turned out wrist. Kora looked elegant and dignified. Her upper body was so nicely drawn out in her movements.

"That's the concept for tribal style dancing. We give each other signals about what to do. That's how improvisational choreographies are created." Could it be that easy? The Read My Hips group looked so polished and their transitions so effortless. Just give a signal, and boom, everyone is in sync?

Kora turned her back to us and began a Ghawazee shimmy with both arms relaxed and extended out to her sides. The Ghawazee is an exaggerated three-quarter shimmy with a pendulous side to side movement of the hips. The Ghawazee dancers were Egyptian street performers in the eighteenth and nineteenth centuries, and the women were known as flamboyant entertainers, hence the name for their shimmy. I like doing the Ghawazee shimmy because you can let everything go and the fat on your ass and the back of your thighs jiggles with abandon. It feels good to do it, like flying.

"Ok, everyone, do this," Kora said, and we began our own Ghawazee shimmies in place with arms out. Then she lowered her right arm down toward her right hip and stepped back on her right foot, and then forward and back. "That's a cue to follow me. I want you to do a half turn to the left when you finish that forward and back sequence, and then turn again to the front."

We all tried it. It was really a compelling way to dance, to pay attention to what Anne would signal, and do it on cue. It required good reflexes and mental acuity. You have to tune in to the leader and the other dancers in order to do it well. Kora showed us more basic moves and signals that would allow the group to move in space and switch leaders and followers. Most of the cues involved some kind of arm position. For example, arms raised straight over your head was the signal for doing a Basic Egyptian hip hit. Lowering them down to just over shoulder height meant that dancers were supposed to do a half turn. When the group of dancers turned to face the front, if the leader had not turned and was facing toward the dancers, it was a signal that she wanted to pass on the lead. The next person in the formation could step forward to do that, or we could dance in a circle until someone decided they wanted to take the lead. This kind of dancing involved group connection that channeled individual energy and multiplied it.

I'D ONCE KNOWN someone who inspired in me a similar ripple-effect. Mary Martin was a well-known campus radical when I was enrolled at UW-Madison, someone who had organized protest rallies and gave fiery speeches. She was energetic and opinionated. Unlike a lot of university politicos, Mary got along with everybody. Mary grew up in a smallish city in Illinois, a place not unlike Racine, and her way of being was unequivocally egalitarian. Her social circle included the homeless as well as the governor's daughter. Invitations to parties at her place were coveted. Her attitude was upbeat and spirited, charismatic. Whatever her cause, people wanted in on it because they liked her. Like everyone else, I admired her.

One day on my way across campus to meet my boss at his office, I happened to run into Mary on the Library Mall. She asked me how it was going.

"Shitty," I said. I was still working at the Program to Prevent Woman Abuse a year after I'd graduated. I had a double major in English and History. I was restless to leave the domestic abuse business, and begin an illustrious career as a writer and editor. "I've applied for every job I possibly can. The PhDs are getting hired for everything."

This was the problem with living in Madison post-graduation. It is a very livable city, chock with bike lanes and pedestrian paths around all of the picturesque urban lakes. At the time, I was living across the street from B.B. Clarke Beach Park on Lake Monona in a tiny under-maintained apartment with Sean (the bulging kitchen ceiling that threatened to drop on us had collapsed after we moved out). We loved our lake access and during the summer we'd go out for late-night dips with Madra to cool off during the heat of the summer. I biked to my job along the lake path. From our bedroom's picture window we watched the lake in all its blue-grey moods. We both liked nothing better than reading in bed together on an overcast day, periodically stopping to watch the water trundle in and wobble over the nearby shore. The fact that the lake's waves didn't fluctuate that much made life there seem continuous and permanent.

"I hear you," Mary said. "I had to take a job with American Girl." American Girl is the doll company that formed in 1986 and had their headquarters in Middleton, outside of Madison. At the time, American Girl was launching its line of dolls and books featuring strong, fictional female characters, its mission to teach history and inspire girls. Now it's a multi-million dollar doll company owned by Mattel, with sales second only to Barbie.

She was writing press releases for American Girl. We both considered this tragic. Little did we realize that Mary's leadership ability and popularity made her a perfect publicity flack. She didn't want to be hawking dolls. She wanted to run an issues-based nonprofit and fight the good fight. Mary wanted to change the world. I wanted to find my place in it.

While I was a student, I had the opportunity to be exposed to academic feminism and meet women involved. For the first time, I could take classes in women's history and study women's literature in depth. I immersed myself in ideas of female liberation, and my wonderment was naive, voracious.

I read everything I could get my hands on by women I'd previously never heard of: Louise Erdrich, Toni Morrison, Doris Lessing, Margaret Atwood. I took classes from the renowned women's studies professor Linda Gordon who was particularly intriguing to me. She was calm, well-spoken, radical. Her book *Heroes of Their Own Lives* described an un-presumed agency of women in domestic violence, and her approach to thinking about familial power dynamics was exciting and new. (I also liked how she always wore the same classic silver hoop earrings every day, a style I adopted.)

It seemed to me like I had lived in a time warp and needed to catch up. Those authors gave me a context for better understanding the female experience, and feminist theory provoked me, and spurred my thinking.

Yet I struggled then to manifest my own ambitions. I wished to write, but whenever I sat down to do it, I felt like I had nothing to say. Nothing erudite and informed. Nothing earth shattering. Nothing that would provide answers to problems. Nothing.

I had no stunning revelations. I had no answers. I was stymied. I didn't think that my particular "female experience" meant anything to anyone. I was sure that in my case, writing about struggles for independence and self-determination was a waste of time.

"I feel like the job I want doesn't even exist," I complained.

"What's that?" Mary asked, ever engaged, curious.

"Editing. Ideally a women's publication," I said.

"That would be cool," Mary concurred. "You know, I've had the same idea. This town needs one. For women, by women. I'm so sick of Erwin and *The Progressive* magazine's old boys' network." Erwin Knoll was the magazine's outsized editor. He was an intimidating, irascible peace activist who had published an anti-abortion piece in the magazine, giving the group Feminists for Life a platform. It was an act for which he would never be forgiven by legions of women.

"Yeah," I replied. I pulled my backpack higher up my shoulder. *The Progressive* was definitely out of my league.

"If the patriarchy won't hire us to do what we want, I say we create our own jobs and fuck them." Mary said these things with verve and buoyancy. She had a knack for making radical change and swear words sound sensible and extraordinary.

Mary had a point. Feminist newspapers were springing up around the country with provocative names like *Sojourner, Off Our Backs,* and *Outwrite.* It seemed ridiculously obvious that Madison should support one too.

"We need to organize a meeting" Mary proclaimed. By "we" I understood Mary needed to organize a meeting. That's what she was good at.

"Ok," I said with conviction I didn't feel. Publications cost money, and I certainly didn't have any. I agreed to help because I was in Mary's orbit. I didn't want to seem cowardly.

IN MY EXPERIENCE with the feminist newspaper and dance, I found creating something of interest or beauty in the moment with a group (where no two perspectives or dance formations are alike) was energizing. I was really excited by this potential. I got to know not only the shape of the hips in front of me, but the contours of many necks and shoulders, and how we could use our back muscles and arms for nonverbal communication to dance together. That's why Kora and I, and others, had been so inspired when we first saw it.

The concept of tribal belly dance was first introduced in the 1970s by Jamila Salimpour in San Francisco. Jamila instigated this approach to belly dance by borrowing from many folkloric traditions around the Middle East, so that dancers could more readily perform in groups, especially at Renaissance Festivals.

Performing outdoors, sometimes in natural landscapes with or without stages, and subject to the vagaries of weather conditions, dancers needed a way to easily read each other and stay in sync. It was easiest to perform without the hindrance of a certain set choreography, which can render staging inflexible. Dancers also needed a way to perform well within a constant rotation, especially if a Ren Fest gig went on for multiple weekends. The early Ren Fest dancers also adopted what's become the typical costume for tribal dancing: full skirts, puffy harem pants, bras and belts layered with coins (not shiny bedlah beads), and fabric head wraps. Jamila believed ethnic jewelry combined with natural fabric costuming would look more authentic to Renaissance reenactments at such festivals.

Many others, including Carolena Nericcio of FatChanceBellyDance, also in San Francisco, established American Tribal Style in the 1990s, and have created and contributed to a tribal dance vocabulary that allows belly dancers to take cues from each others' bodies and movements to be fully improvisational. It gives dancers a method to create group choreographies in the moment during performances. Each group has a leader, and with a certain hip twist, floreo, or arm position, she can cue her fellow dancers, or "followers" to understand her steps and transitions so everyone in the group can dance in a coordinated way. It's quite ingenious.

Nowadays you can find multiple genres of tribal dancers, including fusion, steampunk, tribaret (cabaret and tribal), and goth. Tribal belly dance has a frontier feeling to it in that respect—it has inspired a new generation of dancers.

Kora had paired us up and put Post-It notes on the floor between us. That was to represent the center space of the dance, and whether we were dancing as a big group or in a duet, we needed to be aware of and move around a center. In a matter of hours, I could see right away how tribal dancing could result in exuberant flying skirts. This new dance vocabulary emphasized the relationship and bond we shared with each other's bodies as we twirled, turned and undulated *en masse*.

THE FIRST MEETING of the feminist newspaper drew an assortment of women. This was a time before email, and organizing occurred through leaflets, word of mouth, and phone calls. Turnout was impressive. We sat in a circle, of course, and discussed what we should name our publication. I don't remember that we ever talked about whether we should put out a women's newspaper. It seemed like a forgone conclusion. Mary Martin was a ball of energy, and she offered to take minutes and facilitate the meeting. I don't think those minutes ever got distributed.

While I struggled with what to say, one woman piped up. "I think we need to think of a way to incorporate all of our voices, because we are feminists from many different traditions." We eventually agreed that we would call our newspaper *Feminist Voices,* with a woman's symbol part of the "o" in voices, and we would operate our monthly endeavor as a consensus collective.

The life of the body, and a woman's control over hers, is also a core focus of feminism. In our newspaper, this was identified, extrapolated, politicized, and discussed time and again in our articles about women's rights, issues of the day, examining systems of abuse, racism, poverty, and war that held women back. Each article asked the question: who has ultimate control of a woman's identity and her body? In addition to news, we published book reviews and creative works by women. I started writing profiles and edited the section on creative writing.

I was initially unaware of it, but I was starting to gain useful professional skills in producing a newspaper and shedding some of my timidity to argue a point. For example, during an editing style debate on the best way to spell woman, was it better to take out the "man" and spell it womyn? I successfully argued, even though my voice shook, that every woman should determine that for herself, and everyone agreed. Earth-shattering? No. Important to me? Yes. *Feminist Voices* helped create a place for feminist dialogue in and out of the press, getting more women engaged at the state capitol, talking about their concerns with childcare, employment, lack of access. It was powerful stuff, decision-making, and I felt as a group our ability to do so was exerting an influence on the world.

I also think tribal belly dance might be considered more democratic in that everyone ostensibly gets a chance to take the lead and contribute their signature moves to the troupe's performances. It's what initially attracted me to learning the style, and the way dancers relate to each other is often like being in a collective. There's lots of talk about how to do things together. I've often thought of it as being grounded in feminist practice.

You wouldn't think so, but being part of a feminist newspaper has some of the same shock value as being a belly dancer. There are times when sheer female physicality is overwhelming to people. It affects people to see women empowered and united; sometimes they are disturbed, and other times excited, even turned on. I think a woman fully embodied in her own skin, extending her energy outward, is what the poet Anne Carson says is to "take our flesh in our teeth."

ONE OF THE quintessential activities of recent feminist generations is Take Back the Night, where people demonstrate to end rape culture. I went to my first Take Back the Night rally during the year *Feminist Voices* was founded. In 1988, a number of us planned to cover the event for the paper. Sean accompanied me. The rally started on the Library Mall with a speak out, and marchers walked up State Street to the capitol for a candlelight vigil.

The TBTN rallies first started in the late '70s in countries all over the world as way to expose the prevalence of rape and remove the stigma of being a rape survivor. Even today, the rallies give women an opportunity to speak out against domestic and sexual violence, and raise awareness in their communities to work toward better solutions for women's safety.

When we arrived at the mall, "survivors" were offered a purple armband. I extended my hand for one, and the woman pointed me to a "woman-only safe space" to congregate there. I looked where she was pointing. I couldn't believe how many women there were! Not only young women like I expected, but women who could have been grandmothers. A hoard of them. Instead of joining the survivors in the safe space, I put the armband in my coat pocket and walked with Sean toward the stage of speakers.

"A woman is raped every two minutes in this country," said the woman at the podium. "One in four women has been sexually assaulted." The speaker held silent a beat, like a preacher, to let those statistics sink in. "And you know what? So many of these rapes go unreported. *Unreported.*"

"The *system*," she emphasized, "is not friendly to women. We have been silenced! *For far too long.*" This wasn't the first time I'd heard these statistics, but hearing them yelled out into the night sky made them seem heavier than ever. The crowd clapped and woo-hooed. The very air was redolent with outrage.

I held my armband tight in my hand, still in my pocket, the very portrayal of a silenced woman. I kept my eyes on the speaker while Sean looked at me with askance. The armband in my hand generated the heat of denial. I didn't need this. To revisit trauma. Especially not in public. The thought made my hands sweat, my heart pound, knees shake. I held a certain part, the heartbreaking part, of female identity right in my palm, and I was crushing it. Refusing it. I felt wretched, undeserving of anyone's sympathy or righteous indignation.

I rationalized. I was one of the lucky ones. I hadn't gotten pregnant. I didn't have visible scars. You couldn't tell by looking I had been raped. I didn't appreciate that these were often universal truths, true for men and women who have been assaulted or abused.

Nor was I being a good reporter. I took no notes. I was a pillar of salt.

Why? I was angry. At myself most of all. I was weak and made bad decisions. My need for atonement meant that I was to suffer the consequences. Alone.

I held on to rape and felt bad about it. My viewing platform was small, limited by a sense of separation from everyone else. I was afraid if I let go of my observant, judging "self" I would disappear entirely. I couldn't forgive the young scared me right before my eyes.

Even though the women I met in college all talked about "bodies," very few in my circle really understood theirs or used it as a means of articulation. When my roommate had recurring vaginal yeast and bladder infections, for instance, she had trouble making distinctions between the two, as if the gynecological and urinary systems were one itchy burning mashup inside of her. We would joke about "getting it" but we never wanted to admit to subpar sexual experiences or reveal our desire for each other's platonic affection.

When I got involved in dance a decade later, I started to think it could be a way for me to take feminist theory about owning my body to practicing it in real life.

During the march up State Street the voices of women around me poured out in chants:

"Claim our bodies, claim our lives, take a stand, take back the night."

"Whatever we wear and wherever we go, yes means yes, and no means no!"

I walked along, solemn, stoic. Not galvanized.

Sean and I left the Take Back the Night rally before the candlelight vigil got underway. I was antsy and handed off my unlit candle to someone in the crowd. I didn't want to stay for what was sure to be a powerful spectacle and formidable visual reminder of the prevalence of sexual assault. Instead of feeling the collective power of womanhood united, I felt confronted and disturbed.

WHEN YOU LOOK at someone's face for any length of time it can feel very strange, as if you're looking at them with a magnifying glass. Eyes speak. When you are *this close* you can tell if someone likes or respects you, and whether or not they are comfortable with you so near. Could I let someone get close?

When I met Sean, this was something I struggled with. I sought to be immaculate, untouched by the grubby fingers of human experience. We worked on trusting each other, first by giving space, and then moving closer. I didn't want him to know I farted, cried, or burped. I didn't want to howl in orgasm. If Sean, or anyone, heard me, they would know I was untidy and disordered, a terrible person.

Betsy said that the negative things we say to ourselves have a dedicated listener—our subconscious. "Your subconscious doesn't have a sense of humor," Betsy said as a warning to be mindful of what you are telling yourself (which I found very humorous). I knew she was right, though. If negativity is what the subconscious hears, that's what you project and circulate.

Learning to dance a duet in tribal belly dance is also to practice the art of intimacy, which is both a comfort and a dare. Depending on the moves, there may be inches between you. Duets are most arresting when the movements are slow and sensual, and this requires familiarity and trust. Two women dancing together in this way can express female solidarity, but it took practice for me to get comfortable with doing it.

Could I open my arms to beckon? How exposed would I feel if I aligned my chest with another woman's or circled my torso with hers? Could I undulate with her in unison? I knew it would be important for me to remain open so we could give each other freedom of movement. I had to be willing to accept that my dance partner sweated and smelled, made mistakes, and articulated quirks too.

One of the challenges of this is being able to look eye-to-eye with your partner when you dance. That might not sound that difficult until you try it. Most of us are not accustomed to dancing close to people we are not romantically involved with, nor do we readily communicate through close contact. In Maria Finn's memoir *Hold Me Tight and Tango Me Home*, she wrote about that, how she felt the utter strangeness of resting her chest on another's in the tango, feeling the pressure of different hands on her body. Belly dance duets are not like tango, we are not touching, but I think there is the same sense of a back-and-forth exchange of energy, and a process of sharing your body in close physical space with someone.

I thought about my parents and their Pentecostal religion and the phenomenon of speaking in tongues. It's a belief that the involuntary and erratic sounds coming out of your mouth happen when the Holy Spirit takes hold. By speaking in tongues, you are sharing a sacred language. Even though it is usually explained as a verbal sensation, according to my parents, it was also a physical spectacle. People speaking in tongues would keen and kneel, sway their bodies, or whirl around, drop to the floor, and sometimes people would shiver and shake. It was a pageant of spiritual gesticulation. What they described happening in their North Carolina church sounded a lot like some of the trance dances I'd seen on video from different places around the world.

The instantaneous possessions that occurred for my parents, and similarly the dancers on video, were generated in part by a strong human desire to have an embodied spiritual experience within a community of people. One where people bear witness to your mystical display and support its occurrence. The Whirling Dervishes saw it as a pathway to the divine. I think this is true of nearly any physical activity, or even group therapy. I'm not devout, but I think transcendent might be a good word for how it feels.

As I started to master important movements over the years, like layering a shimmy on a traveling step while playing finger cymbals at the same time—and smiling—I started to wonder what to "do" with the intensity of the experience and what I was learning. I remembered those nights at the Lake Harriet haflas, questioning if I'd ever get the nerve to perform. The answer to what to "do" with belly dance was what I'd aspired to do when I first saw Habib. Share enjoyment. Yet dancing for an audience with expectations was an exhilarating and frightening prospect, especially as a soloist. That's why I staked my burgeoning confidence on being part of establishing a tribal dance group blessed by a small band of musicians.

When I was performing with my tribal troupe, I particularly liked dancing duets with a woman named Jackie. She was a sweet person and a woman with a rock-and-roll soul. She wore her black hair piled high in a bed-head style and liked to wear velvet-trimmed costumes with lots of silver doodads. She had studied Persian dance, which emphasizes sweeping arm motions and storytelling movement (currently outlawed in Iran), and Jackie expertly channeled its elegance and grace when she moved.

Jackie's belly was particularly luminous. Soft flesh from her stomach pressed against her hip belt, and when she shimmied it rippled in a pleasing rise and fall.

I always sought out people to dance with who were genuinely enjoying themselves, like Jackie. When Jackie and I practiced together, her brown eyes shone with mischief. "Pat. How do we do this again?" She'd flamboyantly mangle a cue; and then she'd laugh.

Jackie's eyes, above all, extended her sense of humor, warmth, and openness.

As a group we were always experimenting with the tribal dance vocabulary, but whatever Jackie did had finesse. She was organic and unscripted, which I also thought was the point of tribal belly dance. I saw in her a creative renegade. I was starting to identify with that, and I had a desire to channel this vigor to my everyday mind, not just the distressed self that strived to let go of the past in the dance studio.

When I first started doing duets, my first impulse was to hold my breath. It was my way of handling what seemed like an identity crisis—how do you merge your dancing with another's on a progression of movement? Jackie the rule-breaker got me to try new things. Sometimes I felt nervous about doing that, but most of the time it was thrilling. I aspired to be more like Jackie: easy-going and original. Jackie's body expressed her mood; it was as simple as that.

I could feel myself relinquishing boundaries in our duets, and instead of holding myself in, I was softening, pushing my belly, my arms, and my distinctly female psyche outward with more composure and grace.

THE DISTURBED FEELING I'd held over from the Take Back the Night rally put an irreparable rip in my perfectionist covering.

After we had got home, Sean found me sitting up in bed, the pillows behind my head.

"Why did you take that purple armband? And then stuff it in your pocket?"

"I wasn't thinking," I told him. That was true. To a degree. I had a habit of speaking like that. Leaving things out to avoid talking about my real feelings or to avoid conflict.

"Patty." I looked at him. I could feel the corners of my mouth turn down uncontrollably. Sean had no expectations that a woman be "pure" or virginal, but confessing rape to a man, even one who was my current lover, elicited peculiar mixed feelings, nausea and lightheadedness. I expected to be judged as harshly as I judged myself.

"What are you thinking?" Sean was trying to get to the root of my haunted demeanor. He slid into bed next to me. Looked me in the eye.

"I was . . ." I swallowed. I couldn't say the word. Not yet. "My freshman year. I got drunk at a party and a guy followed me into my room. He pulled my pants off and . . . fucked me . . ." I swallowed some more.

Mercifully, Sean got to the point. "You were raped?" He addressed me and the wondering air in our bedroom.

I nodded.

"Patty, I'm so sorry," Sean said. He didn't lambaste my attacker. He didn't offer any platitudes about how not all men are bad. He didn't say "these things happen." He put his arms around me and held me close. His body transferred comfort to mine. I'd finally told him and he accepted it.

"Did you ever report it?" he asked carefully after a time. I shook my head.

Echoes of the rally seeped into my consciousness. *Unreported!* Only forty percent of all rapes are reported. That's because the reasons not to are higher than a stack of legal briefs.

I didn't report it because I was seventeen and didn't know any better.
I didn't want to be a narc.
I was drunk underage.
My whole dorm would have got in trouble.
I didn't trust anyone enough to talk about it.
There was nobody to talk to about it.
I didn't know how to define what had happened to me.
I deflected all inquiries regarding whether or not I was "Ok."
Nobody would believe it.

I couldn't pick my rapist out of a lineup.
I had no stomach for speaking to a cop, going to court, or seeing
a university tribunal.
I had no credibility.
I had no money.
I didn't want my stupidity and shame publicly exposed.
It was better to keep quiet.
Tough girls put up and shut up.

None of those reasons would ever make a catchy TBTN marching slogan.

"What about Peggy?" Sean asked. I didn't even tell my sister. Did it honor our relationship that he was the only soul to know? Or not, because it took so long for me to tell him?

No on all accounts. He seemed abashed. Telling Sean was cathartic, but it didn't result in greater insight. I appreciated his empathy, but I still felt like sexual assault was something no man could know.

The scrap of survivor fabric didn't inspire me to take a public stand. The TBTN chants were true, but not felt in my heart. Being surrounded by active, concerned feminists wasn't enough. Nor was the love of a sensitive man. I thought I'd feel better, but I didn't.

What I needed was a passageway. A crossing. I knew I had to turn away from my filthy beggar's faucet, and head toward a tributary with clean water. I didn't immediately recognize it, but when I started to put my body in motion, I'd finally found a route.

15

THE PRATT ICE Cream Social was typically chilly—the tips of my fingers felt numb from holding my veil in the cool breeze of the spring thaw—the first Friday in June. We were scheduled to dance at 6:30 p.m., so those with desk jobs rushed over, only to discover the costume elements they'd forgotten—jewelry, veil, dance sandals—when they packed up before work. We were a sisterhood of stiff, crabby, and cold belly dancers.

The event featured hot dogs and baked beans, ice cream, of course, and the community education department's dance classes provided the entertainment. It always drew a dedicated crowd no matter what the weather. The people who live in Prospect Park in Minneapolis tend to be educated, involved, liberal. A place where an ice cream social is embraced as wholesome *and* ironic.

The ice cream social and its cruddy weather was exactly the kind of thing that made me question my sanity. Feeling ordinary underneath the glittery costume I wore made me wonder why I do these things, how much of myself I really wanted to put out there. At forty years old, I was at the halfway point in my life. I was a middle aged Midwestern woman learning to live in her body, not the dance goddess I was pretending to be.

I'd met all but one of the dancers in one of the classrooms, and we'd quickly helped each other into our costumes, nervous fingers carrying out the ritual fastening, pinning, and straightening of our *bedlah*. I'd put my head through the halter strap and my arms through the shoulder straps of my bra, and Carrie fastened both hooks as I held my breath. When she was finished I let my breath out and felt the bra top dig into my chest. Perfect. Tight and uncomfortable. I looked in the mirror to make sure the bra fat caused by a too-tight costume wasn't that bad. You want your costume tight; you want to feel it digging into your skin. I put my hands under the beaded cups and pushed my breasts up and down to make sure they were firmly ensconced. I ran my fingers through the bead strands and felt the stragglers fall from my bra top down toward my upper abdomen. I lifted my arms over my head, jumped up and down and did a quick shoulder shimmy to make sure everything stayed in there where it should.

Janice, a statuesque blonde whose level of empowerment wearing *bedlah*, and on rehearsal days, various Victoria's Secret accoutrements, handed me a roll-on body glue of some sort and asked me to roll it on her shoulders and back where her costume's shoulder straps connected with her skin. Her fingers shivered as she rolled it on the edges of her bra and breasts and patted it all down. I ran the glue stick over her back, pressing her straps into the gluey area. It got on my hands, and I tried not to get my fingers stuck in her hair.

"Has anyone seen Vanessa?" I asked. We would have to adjust our lineup at the last minute if she didn't show. We were dancing a cabaret choreography, hence the beaded costumes.

More than anything, I knew Vanessa wanted to be one of the gals, but she was born male. Vanessa was pursuing belly dance for all the same reasons I was, and perhaps most of all as a passage to feminine expression.

After dance class we'd have a chance to talk, and Vanessa would always play at being upbeat. It was challenging to learn anything of depth about her. She said she worked as a nurse, but when I asked where, she said at a "local health care facility." When our instructor distributed a contact list of the students, Vanessa's name wasn't on it. I respected her need to protect herself, but it troubled me that I couldn't figure out how to be a better friend.

Once Vanessa told me she was going to have to miss a bunch of dance classes because she was going to have surgery on her foot. I sensed "foot surgery" might be code for having a different sort of operation. That would have explained things. When she returned to class, looking exactly the same in every way, tenderly nursing her right foot and still on crutches, I felt tentative and guilty.

In the 1800s in Cairo, there were belly dancers known as *khawals*, men who dressed like women, who had long hair and wore eye makeup. They were both common and stigmatized. Likewise, the Turkish were entertained by dancing boys called *kocek* who danced in drag. Sometimes they were so convincing, the foreigners thought they were watching girls, not boys.

Over the years I've seen men do belly dance. The first was a group of Jordanian men who would dance along to a local Twin Cities band, Electric Arab Orchestra. They were not the featured entertainment, but they did everything from traditional line dances to intense shimmy sessions.

Serkan Tutar from Turkey hypes himself as the "Male Belly Dancer," and his hips can fly. The Egyptian performer Tommy King presents himself with elements of female and male genders in moves and dance costuming. But these dancers are by and large masculine identified. As far as I know they are not seeking to live their lives as women.

Noor Talbi is an internationally-known transgender belly dancer from Morocco. As much as she has gained popular acceptance, in part due to her extraordinary beauty, the country's authorities will not change her gender on her ID card.

Belly dance has not been an exclusively female dance, but men doing it, with or without a female identity, are often seen as transgressive. But I also know from my own experience, women doing belly dance are also seen as transgressive.

After performances with Vanessa in my group, audience members would sometimes say something cryptic under their breath about "that guy" that danced with me. To them, Vanessa was a distraction. I admired Vanessa's continued pursuit of belly dance despite the odds against her, but I also knew certain audiences were bewildered. Whenever she danced in public it seemed to some people she made a "mockery" of what belly dance should be when you see it—female.

AS WE WERE getting changed into our costumes at the ice cream social, we discussed altering our lineup if she didn't show. Carrie and Janice would be in the front row. Me and Eva in back. We had none of the usual banter about costumes, hair, makeup, or jewelry. Nobody was in the mood. We were stressed and anxious because we were dressed in skimpy, sparkly *bedlah* outdoors on a gloomy and cold evening. We all wished we could back out.

As we stepped outside, we were trying to keep our skirts from blowing up in the blustery wind. Right away people from the audience asked to take pictures of us and the local cable access channel came to film our performance. The attention was very flattering and way overdone. Eva feared her corporate co-workers would see her on TV.

She put her veil all the way over her head as she walked through the crowd toward the stage.

A foreign man with a hand-held mini cam approached us and asked in a very polite and stylized English what cultural group we were from. Our dance instructor, who met us next to the stage, explained to him we were "American belly dancers." He looked at our made-up faces, the bright and shiny bras peeking out from under our cover ups and veils. He asked us what we were dressed up for. She pointed at the stage.

He filmed us in our cold huddle for a few seconds and then left to join the audience freezing in the amphitheater stands, presumably to record our act.

That's when Vanessa, who was MIA earlier, pushed her way into our circle. It looked like Vanessa had her hair done at a salon— probably why she was late. Usually she wore her hair in a simple page, but that day's hairdo was a French twist with not-so-wispy pin curls shellacked with hair spray framing her face. She had a blue rhinestone butterfly pinned jauntily in place on her head. Her royal blue *bedlah* was beaded with gold fringe that covered the chest beneath. Vanessa's sheer harem pants glittered underneath skirt panels of baby blue organza that swished in the wind.

THE FIVE OF us took off our veils and cover-ups and trooped on stage. As Vanessa moved into place next to me, murmurs went through the crowd. I clearly heard someone say, "What *is* that? A guy or girl?" A clan of teenage girls started to giggle uncontrollably. All eyes were riveted. On Vanessa, of course. As the strains to the upbeat "Hadouni, Hadouni" burped out of the sound system, my hips snapped with a vengeance as I held my mouth in a forced smile. People can be so mean. If whatever about you doesn't conform, people don't feel the need to be polite. I glanced at Vanessa dancing her heart out.

I figured if she could dance freely, so should I. I relaxed and focused. I nailed the down-up-down on first the right, and then the left hip, at exactly the right drumbeats. I did a leisurely hip circle, raised my arms, and began the 4/4 shimmy—the one that looks like your hips are vibrating of their own accord. What's really happening underneath that billowy circle skirt is your knees are pumping out the 4/4 beat. If you're positioned correctly, leaning slightly back on your heels, knees bent and body fully grounded, the fat on your hips and buttocks moves in synch with the beat. It's one of the first things you're taught when you take Middle Eastern dance, but it took me years to perfect it. Cassandra includes a fifteen-minute 4/4 shimmy marathon in her classes. She said that it conditions you for the short time you might actually do it in a performance. Even now, it's so hard to make it look effortless.

I held my arms over my head, and shimmied, smiling at the audience members who I felt dropped the attitude toward Vanessa and were generously clapping along. I was feeling pretty good about my little 4/4 when I saw Vanessa's hip belt drop off her hips and fall onto her feet. The heavy belt had forced the organza skirt panels to her ankles.

The crowd quit clapping and someone gasped. My throat went dry. Vanessa's pin curls and the butterfly in her hair trembled.

All of us dancers, including Vanessa, kept going. The happy, celebratory rhythm of "Hadouni, Hadouni" and our beautiful and sweeping moves were, for a moment, like a caricature of joy.

Then, in an uncommonly graceful movement, Vanessa stepped out of her dance belt and fallen panels, and kicked them away to the edge of the stage and kept dancing.

Martha Graham said that dance is the hidden language of the soul. Is that the soul she meant? The striving, fragile and imperfect one? Or did she mean the other soul, the one that moves fluidly through space with spirit and beauty?

The gold and blue bead pile at Vanessa's feet at the ice cream social surely revealed one plain truth. You can only dance with the body you have.

My own upbringing was sharp with righteousness about what was a proper female destiny. As a woman, how important it was to be pretty and demure. I'd rebelled against the religious structures that fueled it, only to find myself, ironically, attracted to a glittering female façade. Yet I'd found my way through the mainstream's surface fabrication of "sexy belly dancer" into something real and feminine that fueled my own reinvention.

A few years ago Vanessa contacted me to tell me she was transgender. She was seeking certain role models and our dance teacher Amina Beres was one of them. Amina is uncommonly vivacious, and a unique personality in the dance community. She isn't devoted to one dance style as the "true path" and her classes are dynamic and buoyant. She welcomed Vanessa and was patient with everyone. Amina's celebratory performance style can transform the energy of a whole room or theater. Vanessa and I were both moved by Amina's example. She is an unapologetically spirited person.

Vanessa had also confessed that she'd been abused by her family, ostracized and ridiculed for her desire to express herself as a woman. Vanessa's one of the many trans women subjected to the most hateful, deadly violence, peevish audience members notwithstanding. No wonder she kept quiet about her gender in class.

Vanessa and I were both shaped by outmoded conceptions of womanhood. To me that past floated like Habib's orange silk veil— dramatically twirled around and tossed away.

I recalled those nights when Griffin and I would go out on the road and he would drive in the lane of oncoming traffic, testing me, asking me if I wanted to die. The answer could have been yes and no in that car. I was waiting for something to appear in the windshield before the end, like a big, blue, quivering butterfly.

On stage, a cascade of beads was trembling over my own unfit stomach. Awareness traveled through me, past silent dark highways, and pushed aside everything in my heart but this. Vanessa and I had made our way off those back roads by wearing *bedlah* in the Minnesota cold.

16

SOMEONE CANCELLED, SO we cleared our calendars and went. We found a place on Lake One at the last minute in the Boundary Waters Canoe Area Wilderness of the Superior National Forest on the US-Canada border inside the arrowhead region of Minnesota. The cabin was accessible only by boat, and we couldn't believe our luck. A place with a double bed, kitchen, and indoor plumbing situated on its own little island in the wilderness awaited us. Our car was packed with fresh food, contraband bottles of wine, and a candle for romance.

We took turns boring through the middle roads of Minnesota in our VW until we got closer to the Boundary Waters. Sean drove the one lane roads that led to Lake One, constantly turning between lake and forest and moose crossing warnings. Sean loves driving that way, it reminds him of growing up in the driftless region of Wisconsin with its hills and views and switch-back turns. We were listening to a fusion of sitar and tabla with flamenco guitar and despite the un-India-like pine trees and non-Spain lake waters, the music went well with the scenery. A fusion of sensibilities. The same as my husband. Complex, fervent, a tad out of place wherever he is, an ardent seeker at heart.

I am outwardly calm, inwardly anxious, a ruminator.

When Sean and I met we were immediately inseparable. We believed we were soul mates, but we never talked about our goals or what we wanted out of life. We didn't have any plans beyond a nebulous sense that we should save the world. But before that, our approach as a couple went about as far into the future as the next week. We just assumed we would get along.

Now two decades later, we take turns being pensive and overworked, and despite our best efforts, keep giving each other unsolicited advice about being stretched too thin. We do not spare each other from the truth, because we prefer our disagreements bracing rather than smoothed over. When we first got together we fought with righteousness over the territory of our lives—who did what and for whom—until we realized that it was healthier to try harder to understand. To approach our differences with hope, not fear.

Our routines are precious to us, our daily walks to the Mississippi river, home cooked dinners. Sean started brewing beer again, and we were hosting friends for dinner on weekends. We were also planning to throw a pit barbeque party at the end of summer to celebrate the season's local bounty. Every day we attempt to wake each other to love.

On the road I was trying hard to overcome a tendency to think of the Boundary Waters as a habitation both porous and well-defined, but losing the battle. Some things are just too conspicuous, too apparently true. In college, my mother had predicted (in a moment of pique) the following for my future as if she were reading it from a fortune cookie: I would marry a poetry-spouting hippie with a VW van who would drive me away to hot springs and music festivals. She nailed it. Now my poetry-spouting hippie has cropped hair, says food co-op grocer things like "stocked endcaps," and is driving our new VW to deliver us to peace of mind in the Boundary Waters.

Ma's assessment had disappointed me at the time. A hippie? In a van? I hoped one of those college rich kids would become so besotted with me that I'd live a be-jeweled, mansion-ed, jet-setter life, something that elevated me from lonely alleys and ticky-tacky homes. I realize this was part of some disco fantasy, but how could I have thought that those things would ever make me happy? I was so unknown to myself then.

A week ago, I was driving alone through the belly of Wisconsin between my hometown and the Twin Cities to see family. I drove in a fever, the birch and pine trees of the Dells a green-and-white blur, grazing past trucks and cars, speeding away from the scenery. The road was a sinuous tablet of dotted lines empty of words, me gunning the car. I had outrun the past and was streaking into the immortal sun.

I'd stopped at the rest area at Portage, the fancy new one, the one my former brother-in-law complained cost too much in taxpayer dollars. I stopped to get a Snickers bar. New vending machines don't hum and don't allow the food to thunk to the bottom. The Portage vending machine whispered its request, A6, to an internal arm, and it airlifted the Snickers to a silent and seamless resting place so I could pluck it out of the machine. When I held it, it was cold, and when I ate it, the peanuts got stuck in my teeth.

In the bathroom a three-year-old boy was at the sink enticing the automatic soap dispenser to methodically drip more and more taxpayer dollars into his little tyke hands. "Whateryoudoing?" came a mom's singsong voice from the toilets. "Nothing" the boy said, a six-inch merangue of soap slicked the sink. He shifted his weight and continued with the soap dispenser. I got a reflexive ache in my chest. It happens when I see a child doing something I suppose a child of mine would do. I scooped a handful of that soap from the basin, and the boy's mouth opened into an astonished O. No sense in wasting it.

The Boundary Waters are a boreal forest of lake, rock and pine along two hundred miles of the Minnesota-Ontario border. We'd heard the tales from our friends who camped, portaged their gear and canoes over rugged terrain for miles, and sat for days in open water, fishing, being rained on. Finally someone said, hey, it's not all Euell Gibbons out there. Get a cabin.

I pointed out the moose warning signs to Sean. "I see 'em," he said and smirked. Someday a majestic moose will appear to us.

Twice we had come up north specifically to site moose. In Canada on Hecla Island all we found were clammy swamps and swarms of mosquitos. While we were hiking up and down the Superior trail on the north shore of Minnesota, a moose was proving to be a nuisance along highway 61. A classic male moose with a rack. All week he'd been stopping traffic unbeknown to us. He'd been tranquilized and carted away in the hours before we learned about it.

I told Sean about the Wisconsin rest area kid. "You woulda done something like that when you were a kid."

He nodded and rubbed one knee without comment. It's his ritual gesture of phantom pain when he's reminded he's not a father. I could see the little Sean, fascinated by automated systems, a loyal attendant waiting on his mother, a canny penitent if he was ever naughty. Sean survived his childhood by being both shrewd and charming and minding the sibling score-keeping.

"You'd find a way to waste taxpayer dollars," I told him. We both laughed at that.

I also told him I bought a Snickers. In regular life we never eat junk food, but on road trips we look forward to a couple favorites once the carrot sticks run out. The aforementioned candy bar. Doritos.

WE MET THE owner of the lake cabin in a gift shop café and walked to the boat landing where we needed to load and launch our canoe to get to our little island. Frank told us that he and his wife and toddler son lived on the other side of the lake. His family has owned cabins in the area since the 1950s when his dad bought them from the original owners. His voice was buoyant, optimistic. His face was open, conscientious, conveying his family was a respected part of the history of the Boundary Waters. He brought us into the boat house, which smelled musty from the cycles of wet, cold, and dry.

He handed us a bottle of greasy mosquito repellant. "Here, you'll need it. In fifteen minutes they'll be eating you alive."

I was certain the DEET would saturate my skin cells and cause strange dreams in the short term, cancer in the long term, but I did as I was told.

Frank assigned us a canoe, lifejackets, oars. We went out and looked at the canoe. It was clear it was going to take us more than one trip back and forth to get everything over to our island and it would be dark soon. Giant boulders with facial features overlooked the lake waters all around us. Trees and lichen sprouted out of the rocks. Everywhere we turned things looked menacing in the fading light.

Sean and I headed toward our assigned canoe, acted cool, like we knew what to do.

"You guys know how to do this, right?" Frank put his hand on top of one of the canoe paddles, and I took it from him as someone intent to make a vow.

"We practiced getting in and out of one on Lake Harriet last weekend," I told Frank. We always declare we're going to do more canoeing, take advantage of the Minneapolis lakes, but we never do. Sean looked at me like why'd you tell him that.

Frank had a look on his face I recognized. Worry.

We had all our groceries neatly packed in bags and coolers, our gear in backpacks. When we made the reservation we were warned that anyone renting the island cabin has to factor in canoe time. So plan your trip and your food accordingly. We thought we were packing light and smart, but truthfully the back of our car was full of yuppie paraphernalia. You couldn't see inside the bags, but there was an Italian espresso maker in there along with real half and half, bottles of imported oil and vinegar, organic salad greens, a dozen free range eggs, smoked fish, meat from grass-fed animals. You'd think we went up there to open an upscale deli.

Frank looked at our bags and took a deep breath, one that I noticed was remarkably devoid of reproach, merely fateful. Frank said, "Put your things in my boat."

On the lake we trailed behind Frank's row boat wake in the canoe, guilty and grateful. We didn't have to figure out how to get to the cabin on our own. We didn't have to make two trips.

Frank easily unloaded our stuff at the cabin's dock, lifting bags while standing in the boat without capsizing it. "You can take it from here. Have a good week. Bon voyage." In a cheerful twinkle Frank was gone. We picked up our bags and headed up the hill to the cabin.

On the screened porch is a chenille couch from the 1940s. The kitchen was a garage of lapsed appliances. A captain's chair appeared to be where people through the decades had sat down to take off their boots. A flush toilet and a daunting plastic stand up shower were in the bathroom. A double bed was all that fit in the paneled bedroom. It was almost exactly like one of the houses I lived in when I was a kid. I knew my sisters would turn tail if they had to stay at a place like that. To them vacations mean hot tubs and swimming pools, food deliveries, and leisure shopping. It seemed to me that my nostalgic feelings for bad decorating and depravation was a sign that I was paradoxically privileged. We had the place for a whole week.

THE MORNING CLOUDS were heavy in the sky, pewter. We glided easily as we paddled. There was enough resistance in the oars that we were not complacent. The ancient glaciers of the Boundary Waters left canyons of rock, strenuous shores, and hundreds of peaceful tiny beaches. There are over a thousand lakes bounded by fir and pine trees. It is one of the world's most striking landscapes; inhabiting it was never easy. The only way to travel place to place is by water. The forests are a jumble of tree roots and fallen leaves. Hiking off trail was impossible. The Ojibwa and Sioux tribes dwelled here in small numbers before the fur-trapping French Voyageurs came in the eighteenth and nineteenth centuries. Today Boundary Waters visitors try to recapture their wilderness experiences, perhaps romanticizing its charms.

I felt the elemental magnetism of the boulders squeeze my shoulders and smelled the mineral brew of stone, roots, and waters. As we floated through a rock canyon, there was too much sameness in the boulders and the trees on the shore. The landscape quickly took on magnitude I couldn't correspond to. I quickly lost my sense of where we were. Before we left town Dad suggested I learn to read a compass. I always get lost whenever I go somewhere for the first time, and sometimes many times after that, even with street signs and recognizable landmarks, like Dairy Queens and gas stations. Out there? I reviewed the compass-temperature gauge I impulsed on at REI. It was on a lanyard around my neck. I found true north, but had no idea what to do about it. It was 54 degrees and threatening rain. That I understood.

Even though I had breakfast, I was hungry before ten a.m. In a waterproof pouch we had bread and ham and cheese and a salted nut roll. If my hands had not been so stiff with cold I'd have got the salted nut roll out of the pouch. Sean was confident we were where he thought we were.

I was missing my dance class. Instead of sashaying around in a hip scarf, I was in a raincoat and rain pants on the search for walleye with Sean. I had to hold my arms up at the elbows to keep my oars at the right angle for dipping and sliding. I held my abdomen, to find my center of gravity. While the Boundary Waters provided a spectacular backdrop, the dance studio compelled me. Right that minute Jenny was back in Minneapolis saying to my dance cohorts, "Tip and roll your shoulders, let your torso release." As I did those things in dance class, I did them in the Boundary Waters.

I'd always thought dance was the thing I did to offset unease, reticence. Yet there I was in a canoe using dance moves to enhance my endurance. A beautiful shoulder shimmy probably wouldn't save me in a bear attack, but the ability had made all the difference in the rest of my life.

THAT FIRST NIGHT we had made love and we lay—he naked, me in pjs—in the little double bed, paging through a book about catching walleye. You never saw a guy want to catch a walleye so bad. His idea of relaxing is to work at something—a thought, a project, an idea. Sean's mind and hands work together, fixing or fidgeting. Walleye would be that week's obsession.

Dad had laughed at the fishing manual. "Who needs a book to catch fish?" Someone who was never taught how, that's who. Sean's dad didn't give him this essential tutorial to manhood. He was a burned-out couch potato by the time Sean came of age.

We learned walleye like deep water and rocky points in the summer, spawn near the shore in the spring. We debated. Is June considered spring or summer in the Boundary Waters? The book said something about jigs—white, chartreuse, neon pink, one-quarter or one-eighth ounce. It also suggested Rapala lures, because walleye like a "down deep husky jerk." They like minnows, they like "salted rubbers," they like bugs. They are aggressive in the morning and less so in the afternoons.

"Sounds like you, babe," I said. He slapped my arm with the book.

"There are two things you can do," the book advised. Go out fishing in a big boat with a "downrigger" or troll the shores in a small boat with a "big juicy night crawler" on the line.

Our grand plan was to eat them. Our cabin pantry was prepared. Cast iron pan. Butter and flour. Salt and pepper.

When we met, Sean seduced me with a whole roasted chicken and dinner with all the fixin's. I lured him with persistent sweetness, impractical wit, and a few good term-paper typing skills.

"What's a downrigger?" I asked.

SINCE MOTORIZED BOATS are prohibited in the Boundary Waters, we were *de facto* in a canoe trolling the shore with our big juicy night crawlers that were positively anemic on the line.

We were keeping up our spirits by sighting eagles, watching fish jump in the distance, inspecting all the spangled colors of moss and lichen on the prehistoric rocks and saturated logs licking the shores.

"Hey, Pat. Let's row over there," Sean said. We headed toward an inlet. "I hear they sometimes like to congregate in warmer waters."

Sure they do. We had been speculating on the nature of walleye since all of last night. The boulders were smaller at the inlet and the whole area felt much more cultivated. It took a while to paddle there, but when we arrived I was content. I liked the spot, it was less windy, more optimistic feeling. If I were a walleye, that was where I'd go.

The open water of Lake One unnerved me. Sean paddled forward with purpose. That is the difference between us.

I cast. I loved the feeling of holding the tab on the spinner, feeling the line fly out to the water. The plonk of the lure in the water, the way the bobber held the promise. My brother spent a summer trying to catch salmon in Lake Michigan. I remembered the chill of anticipation.

Sean's line took a hit right away. He yanked his fishing pole to snag the walleye and reel it in. A log surfaced near the canoe on the line. "Dang," he said. Dislodging the hook took some finesse. "Goddammit."

My bobber sank! I gave a yank on my pole to secure the hook in my fish's mouth to haul it in. I reeled in a whole lot of nothing. The sinkers dripped water into the boat. The worm was gone.

For the rest of the morning clever fishies ate our worms without a single one getting caught. They were under our canoe, taunting us. I was certain. From below the surface of the water, the fish were seeing how gullible we were, throwing snacks to them hither and yon.

We decided to leave the inlet and row around to the other side. It was windy and the misty rain that started had turned into drops. Our canoe banged into the side of the rock, and its metallic clang went right into my jaw. We both put our paddles out and pushed against the rock to get away. The waves were increasingly insistent requiring constant maneuvering with the paddles. Rainwater moistened my face, slicked my coat and pants. It sucked.

"Pat!" Sean yelled.

His bobber had decisively sunk and his fishing pole was totally bent as he pulled up. An actual fish was clearly on the line. Sean wrangled the fish and pole. I heard the rub of his arms against his windbreaker, the clack of the fishing pole against the canoe. We were rocking back and forth in the boat when I reached for the net. We had a camera and a tape measure locked up in the waterproof bag in case we caught something. To have proof.

The fish was big, over a foot, and thick. It was fighting against being caught and while Sean's fishing pole strained against its weight I attempted to net it. It kept flapping out of reach, and finally I got the thing in there, where it decisively tangled itself in the net.

"No," Sean said.

"Is there something wrong with it?" I asked.

"I think it's a small mouth." He meant a bass. Not great tasting.

"We need to throw it back."

"Looks like a walleye to me," I said. The fish was impressive, with its turbulent pissed off demeanor, prehistoric sage green gills, its glassy eyes. What we had been keeping a vigil for.

We were once again being pushed by the wind toward the boulder we ran into before. I retrieved my paddle and steered us away from it.

Sean and I both worked to free the fish from the net. Sean held the fish up from the hook and I used my fingers to try to untangle the net from its fins. It had tired of flopping and now we were worried that we were killing it with our ignorance and inexperience, taking too long to free it. My hands were freezing blocks and Sean's were not so steady. Norwegian TV Chef Andreas Veistad always says every good meal starts with a murder. I laughed when he said it, his arms wrapped lovingly around a beautiful sheep that would soon become dinner. I laughed because the sheep seemed so oblivious to this fact of its life. As we are to our own.

"Never mind, Pat." Sean reached into the tackle box for a knife. He cut the line, then sliced a hole in the net releasing the fish from our captivity. It sank, down and out of sight.

"Don't they float if they are dead?" I asked.

I didn't realize watching it go would feel like the end of an epoch. A small green mortal submarine. How quickly our enterprise went from amiable to apprehensive, from life to death. We'd ostensibly wanted a delicious pan-fried walleye, but what Sean and I also wanted was proof of immortality, to avoid the stingers of death and separation.

At the dance studio was an image of Oum Kalthoum, the legendary Egyptian singer, depicted in a caftan painted on silk, framed by lyrics written in Arabic with henna. The written Arabic surrounding her body looks like waves. One of her songs, *Seerat el Hob*, The Topic of Love, goes, "As for love, I give my soul to it. There is nothing in the world that could ever, ever be more wonderful than love." Her arms were raised up in an ecstatic gesture.

All we could really do was to tip and roll our shoulders and let them release to love and heartbreak. It had quit raining, and we were left with the slime of freshwater fish on our hands.

WE ROWED TO a spot where one of the rocks sloped to the water, as good a place as any to get out of the canoe.

Sean got out first to steady the boat and held my hand so I could wobble out. We both stretched and yawned. It was nice to be on solid rock. We walked up to the tallest point of our little rest area and looked again at the business of Lake One. It was midday and we saw other canoeists and campers on their sojourns.

We stood and watched, inhabiting the private landscape of this one big rock.

"Let's eat," I said and unwound the damp scarf from around my neck that doubled as our tablecloth. We ate our sandwiches. Never mind that our hands were filthy and our hearts scored by the thieving walleye and calamitous bass.

Sean touched my arm. I felt retrieved. Our bodies turned toward the west as our canoe bobbed nearby, its furious dance on a paddle's oath.

17

A DANCE BAG is what you carry when you have a dance life. I picked up my own big bag containing a hip scarf, finger cymbals, a practice veil, a skirt, water bottle, dance shoes, a clean t-shirt to change into, a notebook and pencil to write down choreography, and some spare change.

Dance bags vary considerably. Mine is an oversized pouch with a woven design on the outside. Some women carry gym bags, others stuff things into designer purses. My favorite idiosyncratic dance bag is the one Susan carries. It's a small trick or treat bag with a skull and crossbones on it that she took from her kid after Halloween one year. Before that, she used to carry her stuff in a plastic Target bag. See? That's how it happens. In stages. The longer you dance, the bigger and more elaborate your dance bag gets.

At the dance studio, we all take turns at first-floor door security, the last one in opens the door for the next, and so on. I was buzzed in and waved my thanks.

The first floor landing was worn from the thousands upon millions of steps that crossed here. Posters of upcoming classes and events—belly dance, karate, Pilates—are taped to the walls. I listened to the familiar scuff of my shoes on the grimy terrazzo stairs. In the summer, it was the slap of flip flops, and in winter, the grating abrasion of boots and residual sidewalk sand. I got to the top, a little out of breath, and waited. At the door is a woman dressed in a nondescript winter coat carrying a big dance bag. Judy. She was wearing yoga pants and tennis shoes, her hand was over her eyes, looking in, pressing the buzzer twice. Through that door and up these stairs came women from all over—the suburbs, the cities, even from the neighboring states. The women who take classes with me are accountants, scientists, artists, linguists, waitrons, radio announcers, medical technicians, and freelancers of all kinds.

The set of stairs leading up to the third floor studio was carpeted and threadbare, and I huffed my way up to the top. My heart was really beating. From stair-climbing and adrenaline. At the landing, I was greeted by the outsized image of Oum Kalthoum, the legendary Egyptian singer.

The door to the studio had a window covered with a brown paper bag and the hand written words *Dressing Room.* Open the door and behold. There was the beckoning Sunroom and women in various stages of undress. Adjusting their boobs into sports bras, sitting in their underpants rifling through their dance bags, taking off their socks to step into a variety of dance footwear.

"Hey, Pat," Rosemary said as she slipped her lean bod into a leotard.

Even now, as soon as I cross the threshold of a dance studio, my mind empties and my spirit feels lighter. I know the shape of at least a hundred hips by heart, fellow dancers and teachers who have taught me how to dance. I have been taking Monday morning class with the same women for years. I know their bodily quirks almost as well as I know my own. Broad shoulders, myriad butts, hammertoes, you name it, I know it.

The Sunroom was the big south-facing room on the third floor of the Birch Pharmacy building, which was also the top floor, and it had a row of windows on three sides of the room. On the fourth wall, mirrors faced the windows. It was almost always sunny and warm.

The Sunroom's hilltop view of the neighborhood was remarkable for its clear view of Minneapolis roads and buildings in all directions. Before class began, we congregated at the windows and watched the street life below. During class, the window ledges were where everyone stopped to catch their breath.

I have watched it snow and rain out those windows, felt the heat of the rising sun, heard the muttering trucks from the road and felt their reverberations in the shaking floorboards. The city that enclosed us in the Sunroom is a peeling wallpaper gathered from different epochs, tattered roofs, brilliant billboards, cafes, and vintage shops.

I gave Susan a punch in the arm. "Slug-a-bug," I said and nodded toward the red Volkswagen Beetle parked across the street.

"That's there all the time. It doesn't count," she said.

On the way to class, I heard something on the radio about a college woman who got excoriated in the press because she spoke out in support of no cost contraception coverage. A DJ had called her a slut and a prostitute. As I looked out the Sunroom windows it was on my mind. I considered the women in my class, our hardworking and earnest selves, and thought of that outrageous putdown. Dawn worked with troubled teens at a local hospital's psych ward. Jean worked as an emergency room nurse. Susan worked in finance. I'm pretty certain that DJ would feel the same way about us. That belly dance is what women do to get sexual attention. He would consider us especially pathetic because of our ordinary looks and natural female fat.

Judy asked me and Susan if we saw the obit of the belly dancer in yesterday's paper. Seemed apropos of the day.

"Her family wrote in it that she would be shimmying down the streets of heaven," she said.

"Cute," Susan said.

"Yeah, that's where we're headed," Judy said. "I mean, maybe not heaven, but you know, dead."

Susan and I laughed uproariously. That *is* where we are headed and we were summoned by dance to resist such mortal claims.

I don't believe in god or heaven, but it would be heartbreaking if all that dance life, ours and hers, is merely released only to the clouds. Once we are gone will there be someone to look out the windows on the eastern side of the Sunroom where the sun comes up? Will she survey the cityscape as diligently as we have? Luxuriate in the studio floors? Will new dancers experience what we have felt? To learn how it feels when your body learns to speak a new language?

All of us have made arrangements, with varying degrees of difficulty, to be there for two hours to devote ourselves to sweating it out in a high-intensity belly dance class.

We need energized, liberating certainty that we are resilient, dazzling.

OUR TEACHER JENNY was teaching us a drum solo choreography she created. It was only three minutes long, but it took me and the women in my class months of diligent practice to learn how to do it confidently. Most drum solos are all about the hips, with controlled, pretty movements that emphasize the feminine. Jenny's drum solo was full-bodied—we used our arms, shoulders, and torsos to turn and tip our bodies and maneuver around the floor. Included in the choreography was a long turning sequence, interspersed with precise undulations and dramatic use of our whole bodies, hands and faces. A dancer's dance. One that required dexterity and deep muscle engagement. Jenny's movements in the drum solo were warm, earthy, and zesty.

It challenged all of us. My frustration built during the times when I had to keep trying, and practicing, over and over the things that felt unnatural. Like tossing my head and my hair with what looked like abandon. Doing giant hip circles with distinct stops and starts on the beat. Turning my body in ways that conveyed a lack of inhibition. I felt so clumsy and stiff. All those turns sometimes made me nauseous. I couldn't believe that after almost two decades I would still find myself feeling like a beginner. There were times in the process I had wanted to leave class. The demands of grace and fluidity as a grounded and earth-bound dancer were too much. If I could do what she was asking us to do *I would be her*.

At one point in the choreography, we quickly turned to the right and left and dropped our pelvis on the beat. Jenny would call out to us, "Drop to the right! Drop to the left! Center. Tuck. Turn!" As she shouted out the moves I thought about the hip hop song, "Throw Ya Belly" by Toronto-based Turkish hip hop artist Evren, about throwing your belly to the left and right and all through the night.

The basic Turkish Romany dance move is *gobek atmak*, which means to "throw the belly." It's a very different move, danced to 9/8 rhythms, not an Egyptian drum solo or a hip hop beat. Yet I couldn't help but think about the idea of throwing your belly. I decided to think about mine as if were a big playful balloon. Instead of my belly being a source of embarrassment or shame, it could encompass the room with a warm, spirited air.

JENNY MOVED US back and forth over the length of the Sunroom floor. I was undulating my body from the top of my spine through my sacrum as I moved sideways down the dance floor. Step together step. Undulate. Undulate. My arms were gracefully curved overhead.

"Add a shimmy on it," Jenny yelled to us over the music.

Being able to shimmy while standing in place was one thing. To layer it on another move, say a hip circle or an undulation, and then move with it while finger cymbaling on the beat, was to achieve mastery of a whole new level. We powered through it and did it. The dynamic and strenuous drum solo had taught me to do the very thing I thought I couldn't.

Every hour we put into this we were gaining physical recall that deepened our love of the movements and the music. Over time, Judy developed a dancer's back. Susan's got a rockin' shimmy that started out shaky to begin with. We were working hard and loving it. With each step on the beat, each attempt to master new technique, we vacated the cells holding us back. Propelled by the momentum in the Sunroom we found in ourselves a hard-working, pumping heart.

We moved our hips in a sinuous undulation with a shimmy on it. All together my classmates' hip scarves shimmered with each tip and roll of the pelvis, glossy rainbow trout in a brook, making our way back and forth. Sun flashing from metal scales, we were smooth, understood, uncaught.

Patricia Cumbie writes about women's lives, dance, food and travel. She is also the author of a young adult novel, *Where People Like Us Live*, and the winner of the Carol Bly Award for Nonfiction. Patricia has been a member of a number of performing belly dance and folkloric troupes. To meet Patricia and find out more about her writing, visit www. patriciacumbie.com.

The Shape of a Hundred Hips

by Patricia Cumbie

Offering an insider's perspective into the world of belly dancing, this text goes beyond the glitz factor of the artform to challenge assumptions people may have about it as suggestive or exotic. *The Shape of a Hundred Hips* is a memoir that juxtaposes dance and sexual assault recovery that takes the reader into the living room, bedroom, and dance class. It promotes the idea that people can gain insight and take greater control of their lives through intentional movement and artistic connection.

From the author

Belly dance is how I gained confidence and compassion for my lost sense of self. Raised Christian in the 1970s, I was expected to be virginal before marriage, and demure forever after. When I'd heard about Women's Lib. I secretly wanted to be one of those so-called selfish women who were calling their own shots. When I took up belly dance to understand how to live in and accept my body, my grandma thought I was a stripper, and my feminist neighbor was convinced it was objectifying. I realized virtually everyone had a lot of misperceptions about what belly dancing was about and I wanted to change that.

Discussion Questions

1. How is a memoir different from journalism in which the author made her career? Patricia writes about ways that she felt restricted and constrained by her upbringing. How did her background set her up to potentially be victimized and make her feel ashamed? How did silence serve to suppress her physically and emotionally, in childhood and throughout her life?

2. When Patricia is followed to her dorm room and raped after a night of drinking, she has trouble processing what happened to her. She knew it was wrong, but didn't call it rape. Patricia felt guilty and at fault for what occurred. This was the early 1980s, when there was a burgeoning awareness of on-campus rape and violence against women. What has changed about how rape is addressed in our society and major institutions? What has not?

3. There are many themes in this memoir—sexual violence, class, female identity, family bonds, and overcoming timidity and self-doubt. Which themes resonated with you the most?

4. When Patricia falls in love and meets the person who would eventually become her life partner, she begins the relationship feeling emotionally guarded, afraid to share the truth of rape and her feelings of insecurity. How does she finally achieve greater physical and emotional intimacy? What were the situations that helped transform her relationship?

5. The Shape of a Hundred Hips offers an insider's perspective into the world of belly dancing that is perceived as outwardly fascinating, but rarely understood. This book goes beyond the glitz factor of belly dance to challenge assumptions people may have about it as suggestive or exotic. Have your thoughts or attitudes about belly dance changed? Why or why not?

6. Patricia also explores the questions of empowerment vs. exploitation in belly dance culture—the objectification of bodies, orientalist fantasies of female subservience, and appropriation of other cultures. How could people in Western or non-Arab cultures show respect for the art form? How could people address patriarchal and cultural norms that contribute to the misinterpretation belly dance?

7. How much of a person's life experience is determined by the physical encounters they have living day-to-day in their own bodies? What is your personal experience with inhabiting your body?

The full Reading Guide available at http://binkbooks.bedazzledink.com/ for-readers-and-book-clubs/